Some Words of Jane Austen

Some Words of
Jane Austen

Stuart M. Tave

THE UNIVERSITY OF CHICAGO PRESS
CHICAGO AND LONDON

THE UNIVERSITY OF CHICAGO PRESS, CHICAGO 60637
THE UNIVERSITY OF CHICAGO PRESS, LTD., LONDON

© 1973 by The University of Chicago
All rights reserved. Published 1973
Printed in the United States of America

INTERNATIONAL STANDARD BOOK NUMBER: 0-226-79016-9.
LIBRARY OF CONGRESS CATALOG CARD NUMBER: 73-78670

FOR *Douglas, and Niels, and Karen, and Janice, and about time too*

*T*HE most beautiful lives, in my opinion, are those which conform to the common and human model, with order, but without miracle and without extravagant behavior.

Montaigne, "Of Experience"

*I*F one wants uncommon experiences, a little renunciation, a little performance of duty, will give one far more unusual sensations than all the fine free passion in the universe.

The Autobiography of Bertrand Russell

Contents

Foreword

This book tries to say a few central things about Jane Austen and omits much. It assumes a reader familiar with the novels and their critics. It does not work through each novel and attempt to account for all important events and characters; so anyone reading a chapter for a comprehensive, self-contained analysis of a text will be disappointed. It tries to say a few central things but its way is eccentric. It takes a few of her words, and even then only some of them chosen from the list of those obviously important, and it tries to show something of the meaning and definition of her world. It is digressive on the word. Her world is so fully and integrally shaped, in a vision that sees the whole and the smallest part, that one can touch it anywhere and begin to trace the pattern. The same passages and words can be returned to, as they are, some of them several times, in this book, and each time they present more meaning as the angle of return varies. I have been dependent on the many scholars and critics of Jane Austen, and especially interested in those who have studied her words, C. S. Lewis, David Lodge, Mary Lascelles, Howard Babb, and others. The book assumes a reader familiar with the secondary literature, who will recognize the commonplaces and the controversies and where they are used or refused. It leaves itself clear for a directness of assertion, that as the limitation of her world requires no apologies neither does its simplicity. As the limitation is not a deficiency to explain away but a condition of greatness, the simplicity is not to be improved, as though it were not enough, by trying to convert it to the complexities of a modern sensibility. Jane Austen is not the worse for lacking our ironies, violences, or unresolved mysteries, and she is not made better if we insist on finding these in her. She is the more valuable and the more interesting as she is herself, and her simplicity is her difficult triumph.

For the grants of time and money to write I am grateful to the University of Chicago and to the American Council of Learned Societies, both of them generous. To Sheila Berg and Jeanne Templeton, so skilled and patient in the typing of illegible manuscript, my humble thanks. I have a long debt to the many students at the University who, in coming to learn more of Jane Austen, have taught me so much. I would say more of my colleagues if I thought this were a thing more worthy of, say, Wayne Booth or Sheldon Sacks. For my wife it is a small enough return for bearing with it in the doing.

Jane Austen's words are cited from the edition of R. W. Chapman, published by Oxford: *Novels,* 3d ed. (1932–34); *Minor Works* (1954); *Letters,* 2d ed., corrected reprint (1959). The usual abbreviations have been used:

NA	*Northanger Abbey*
SS	*Sense and Sensibility*
PP	*Pride and Prejudice*
MP	*Mansfield Park*
E	*Emma*
P	*Persuasion*
MW	*Minor Works*
L	*Letters*

Limitations and Definitions

Jane Austen was fond of dancing and excelled in it ("Biographical Notice," NA 5). She often writes about it in her letters. It is the sort of thing one might expect, that enjoyment and ability in moving with significant grace in good time in a restricted space. In the earliest letter of hers that survives, written when she was twenty, she says, "I danced twice with Warren last night, and once with Mr. Charles Watkins, and, to my inexpressible astonishment, I entirely escaped John Lyford. I was forced to fight hard for it, however" (L 2). There is a lot of action going on in that small space. Even more important, three years later we find that she did dance with John Lyford, on an evening when she had what she calls an odd set of partners. "I had a very pleasant evening, however," she tells her sister, "though you will probably find out that there was no particular reason for it; but I do not think it worth while to wait for enjoyment until there is some real opportunity for it" (L 56). She does not fight for escape but makes the best use of the conditions, and if that's not the whole of art at least that is where it begins and that is where it ends. We need not fret or labor to refute them who think her novels limited because their dimensions are limited. It was never a problem that bothered her. She knew better. Those lines, forever quoted—about the little bit of ivory two inches wide and the work with so fine a brush as produces little effect after much labor—are not a serious account of her own art; they are quite other, an ironic contrast of her chapters with those of her schoolboy nephew who, in her affectionate fun, writes "strong, manly, spirited Sketches, full of Variety and Glow" (468–69). She knew that she had made the choice not of weakness and the merely female, but the choice of difficulty, originality, and meaning. She had always known the absurdity of an art that thinks it is strong and full and large because it tries to run in a large world.

Before she was fifteen she wrote that economic and wicked parody entitled "Love and Freindship," where the heroine of the "novel" begins her account with this: "My Father was a native of Ireland and an inhabitant of Wales; my Mother was the natural Daughter of a Scotch Peer by an italian Opera-girl— I was born in Spain and received my Education at a Convent in France" (MW 77). That is nicely done. It spears with delight and efficiency the wordy pretensions of the romance to move us rapidly through wide kingdoms of life, and it suggests that the origin is not quite legitimate. In fact, in a romance the characters don't know where they are or when they are. They cannot handle space and time. "Our neighbourhood was small," the heroine tells her correspondent, "for it consisted only of your Mother." Well, that *is* small, though "small" doesn't seem to be quite the right word; but then what could be when "neighbourhood" has made the whole situation irretrievable? This one neighbor, however, seems to have been a valuable friend to expand the heroine's vision, because "Isabel had seen the World." That is, "She had passed 2 Years at one of the first Boarding-schools in London; had spent a fortnight in Bath and had supped one night in Southampton." Time and space seem to have evaporated in the course of that sounding sentence. We cannot have much faith in the wisdom Isabel can bring from these experiences, whether it be the first glorious generality—"Beware of the insipid Vanities and idle Dissipations of the Metropolis of England"; or the second and less grand admonition—"Beware of the unmeaning Luxuries of Bath"; or the concluding highly specific and personal memory—"and of the stinking fish of Southampton" (78–79). The heroine fears that there is no probability of her ever tasting these dissipations, luxuries, or fish, doomed as she is to waste her youth and beauty in a humble home in Wales, when there comes a violent knocking on the outward door of her rustic cot. This brings on a quick-fire dialogue, as the family discuss interminably the need for urgent action—" 'Shall we go now?' (said my Mother,) 'The sooner the better.' (answered he.) 'Oh! let no time be lost' (cried I.)" and so forth (79–80). It is the hero, who, as one might expect, has "lossed" his way. He has, in noble manliness, scorned his father and has mounted his horse to set forward to his aunt's house. His father's house is situated in Bedfordshire, he says, his aunt's in Middlesex, "and tho' I flatter myself with being a tolerable proficient in Geography, I know not how it happened, but I found myself entering this beautifull Vale which I find is in South Wales" (81). That young man needs one more lesson before he is tolerable.

The simple geography joke is a Jane Austen kind of joke. She uses it again in "Catharine" (MW 199–200) and it turns up much later in Harriet Smith's question, "Will Mr. Frank Churchill pass through Bath as well as Oxford?" Frank Churchill is on his way from Yorkshire to Surrey, but Harriet's mind is on Bath because that is where Mr. Elton is, Mr. Elton whom she loved in vain and who is now with his bride in Bath. Emma, who had been hoping that the coming of Frank Churchill would put an end to the talk of Mr. Elton, is disappointed. "But neither geography nor tranquillity could come all at once, and Emma was now in a humour to resolve that they should both come in time" (E 189). It is amusing when a weak-minded female like Harriet has difficulty locating herself and others (and she is not the only one of her kind in Jane Austen), but even in an instance like this there is evidently something more at work than an absence of elementary information. A correct knowledge of geography—to know where one is—and tranquillity of the right sort—to live satisfactorily where one is—seem to be related virtues; both, if they come, come as earned acquisitions, in time. Harriet is ignorant and because she is ignorant she wistfully inquires after a geography that will meet her desires. With varying degrees of foolishness and awareness there are many characters in Jane Austen who do the same thing, reshape the space and time they inhabit to make it a creation of their own wishes. In that same scene of Harriet's there is Mr. Weston, a good-hearted man but one who is always reinterpreting what happens so that "every thing has turned out exactly as we could wish" (188); Mr. Weston is making the days and hours of Frank's visit, and the distances, what will best meet his idea of the happiest combinations. At a later point in the novel he makes the difference between Frank at London and Frank at Richmond the whole difference between seeing him always and seeing him never. Richmond is only nine miles and what were nine miles to a young man?—an hour's ride (so he says), where London is sixteen miles—nay eighteen—it must be a full eighteen and that's a serious obstacle. Before he is finished London might as well be in Yorkshire but Richmond is the very distance for easy intercourse. Better than nearer (317–18).

There is less innocence in this mode when a fool like John Thorpe uses it to establish his command over others (NA 45–46). Thorpe insists that he has just driven his horse twenty-five miles in two and a half hours. Actually it has been twenty-three miles, by the authority of road-books, innkeepers, and milestones; but Thorpe disregards them all because he has "a surer test of distance." It is now half after one and the town clock had just struck eleven when he left and his horse cannot go less than ten miles an hour: that makes it exactly twenty-five miles. But in fact he has lost an hour; it was ten o'clock when he left. So his horse has really taken one hour more to go two miles less, which is much more reasonable, though he is never persuaded. We know already—though Catherine Morland does not—that Thorpe is a man of such vanity and stupidity that he is below the level of awareness that can enable him to know true from false. His more artful sister Isabella has similar problems with watches (it is always a sign of danger in Jane Austen). To Isabella it is inconceivable, incomprehensible, incredible, that the hour is not what she thinks it is "and she would neither believe her own watch, nor her brother's, nor the servant's; she would believe no assurance of it founded on reason or reality," till James Morland produces his watch, and to have doubted a moment longer *then* would have been equally inconceivable, incredible, and impossible (67). If she arrives for an appointment five minutes too early it is her friend who has been so late. "I have been waiting for you at least this age! . . . Oh! these ten ages at least. I am sure I have been here this half hour" (39). As Mary Crawford walks with Edmund Bertram in the wood at Sotherton she tries to make him give up his decision to become a clergyman; she is making an attack upon his integrity of mind. They have walked at least a mile in this wood, she says at one point. "Do not you think we have?" " 'Not half a mile,' was his sturdy answer; for he was not yet so much in love as to measure distance, or reckon time, with feminine lawlessness." He is still safe. They have looked down the whole vista, he points out, and saw it closed by iron gates: it could not have been more than a furlong in length. "Oh! I know nothing of your furlongs," she answers; it is a very long wood and they must have walked a mile. " 'We have been exactly a quarter of an hour here,' said Edmund, taking out his watch. 'Do you think we are walking four miles an hour?' 'Oh! do not attack me with your watch. A watch is always too fast or too slow. I cannot be dictated to by a watch'" (MP 94–95). That feminine lawlessness has in this instance its charm, and it is a dangerous charm. Mary is a manipulator. She tries to obliterate lines of distinction, or being more deeply corrupt, as we know by the end of the novel, she really doesn't know where they are. But they are there, those iron gates and those coordinates, and they are real.

Time and space in Jane Austen are not what a reader raised on twentieth-century literature is likely to assume they must be by nature. They are not problematic or oppressive. They are not puzzling mysteries and they are not impositions upon the human spirit to be rebelled against or transcended. On the contrary, they have coherence and help give shape to human life; they are there to be used or abused. If they seem to simplify life they do not make it easier, because they allow no cosmic excuses. They are limited and must be understood, but the limits set the conditions within which action must be taken, here and now or not at all, and it is the ability to act with rectitude and grace under these inescapable conditions that distinguishes among human beings. Mrs. Croft, as a naval officer's wife, has been a great traveler in many places of the world, east and west, but we hear little of that; what we hear and admire is how happy she could be, as long as she was with her husband, even in the "confined" space of a man-of-war: even in a frigate, any reasonable woman may be perfectly happy in one of them (P 70). Captain Harville has been in distant countries; but we see him with pleasure, through Anne's eyes, having gathered his wife and his family together in rooms so small as to astonish but with such ingenious contrivances and nice arrangements by him as "to turn the actual space to the best possible account." It is a picture of domestic happiness (98). To be unable to stay in one place, to be restless, is to have an unsettled mind. "To any thing like a permanence of abode, or limitation of society, Henry

Crawford had, unluckily, a great dislike." It is the first thing we hear of him and it is a moral judgment, because he will not settle at his country home, where he has duties to both his tenants and his sister which he neglects; his shallow kindness to his sister is that he will take her or fetch her anywhere she likes at a half-hour's notice (MP 41). After Emma has arranged for Harriet to marry Mr. Elton only to discover that Mr. Elton wants to marry not Harriet but herself, one of her difficulties is that they all must continue to live as close neighbors. "Their being fixed, so absolutely fixed, in the same place, was bad for each, for all three. Not one of them had the power of removal, or of effecting any material change of society. They must encounter each other, and make the best of it" (E 143). Mr. Elton has just announced that he is leaving Highbury for a few weeks in Bath and Emma is agreeably surprised and admires him for contriving it. But there is a littleness in Mr. Elton that makes him choose this way out—the Mrs. Elton he brings back from Bath is conclusive. Emma sees his meanness in the resentful manner of his announcement, and that she is prepared to admire the contrivance of escape is a sign of her own weakness at this point. Her own superiority is that, bad as she thinks it is to be absolutely fixed in the same place, she not only knows she has not the power of removal but she learns how to develop the superior power of encountering and making the best of it. Not many are able to do that.

To refuse, to try to break these conditions, is to refuse life, though it may seem to be freedom. In the extensive grounds at Sotherton Maria Bertram has a very smiling scene before her—it is the estate of the man she is about to marry. "But unluckily that iron gate, that ha-ha, give me a feeling of restraint and hardship. I cannot get out, as the starling said." Henry Crawford urges her to pass around the edge of the gate, unless she thinks she is prohibited. "Prohibited! nonsense! I certainly can get out that way, and I will" (MP 99). And so she does, as after her marriage she runs away with Henry Crawford. No sentimental starling, she has entered her cage voluntarily, but she refuses to accept the conditions of her choice. She has chosen that stupid man she marries because she is unable to endure the restraint imposed by her father and must escape from him and home as soon as possible (202). So she runs from the restraints of home to marriage, and finds that a restraint, so she runs from marriage to another man, and when that proves impossible she ends, fittingly and terribly, living with her aunt Norris in an establishment in another country—"remote and private . . . shut up together with little society," in mutual punishment (465). There is no condition that can satisfy Maria because she has never learned in time, has never been taught, to accept those limiting conditions which are unavoidable and to which she must shape herself; if she were able to look within herself she could find sufficient space for the largest action, for the finest restraint. The Miss Bertrams as children thought their cousin Fanny Price prodigiously stupid because "only think, my cousin cannot put the map of Europe together—or my cousin cannot tell the principal rivers of Russia—or she never heard of Asia Minor"; they themselves have long been able "to repeat the chronological order of the kings of England, with the dates of their accession . . . Yes . . . and of the Roman emperors as low as Severus . . ." But that early information of distant geography and chronology formed their minds only as it was used by Mrs. Norris to flatter them; they were left entirely deficient in the "acquirements of self-knowledge, generosity and humility" (18–19), the more intimate and essential knowledge of time and space.

In that limited space there is much to be done. Jane Austen's characters do not have the option of solving their problems by going some place else. It is Mr. Elton who contrives to go to Bath. Frank Churchill, accustomed to selfish success in the artful management of time and space, finds himself once thwarted, is sick of England, wants to go to Switzerland. The Maria Bertrams and the Lydia Bennets run away. But Anne Elliot is dependent on time alone: "no aid had been given in change of place." What she does is to submit and she bears it. There had been no novelty, no "enlargement of society," no one had come "within the Kellynch circle" who would bear a comparison with Captain Wentworth, no second attachment possible to "the nice tone of her mind, the fastidiousness of her taste, in the small limits of the society around them" (P 28). It is in those small limits, not only accepted but made even smaller by her own fineness of mind, that she becomes so great. Captain Wentworth is a man who can go off to sail the seas and win glory and make money fighting the French, but it is only at the end of those adventures, when he returns from that grand world to the small limits, that he is forced to face his real "enemy," as he calls it, "My own self" (247). Characters in Jane Austen do make important journeys but if it is a useful change of place it is not because limiting conditions have been relaxed but because they find themselves where they must understand a new set of definitions. Typically the journey does not take them to vistas, rocks and mountains—as Elizabeth Bennet in a moment of weakness wishes it would—but to another house with other dimensions in its rooms and with inhabitants who make new demands on them. Or if they are out of doors it is usually on someone's grounds, at Northanger or Pemberley or Sotherton or Donwell, where the impress of the owner defines the place. Give a weak head the delightful sensation of running and jumping on the Cobb at Lyme and it falls lifeless. Even at a picnic on Box Hill the essential question is whether Emma can comprehend and resist the pressures of a very strained situation. It is a powerfully ironic moment when "Emma could not resist" and said to Miss Bates, "Pardon me—but you will be limited . . ." (E 370).

In that limited space there is much to be done and it must

be done in the right time and in the right tempo. The essential chronology of her novels, the time in which the action occurs, is a year or less. In *Northanger Abbey,* the first, with the youngest and most naive heroine, the action requires little more than eleven weeks. In *Persuasion,* the last, with the oldest and most mature heroine, there is a much more important weight of time, of important events that occurred eight years before the beginning, and Anne Elliot has weightier problems to bear; but even there the action of the novel is concentrated in some months when all must be resolved. There is a pressure of time on Jane Austen's characters, but it is not because the young women have to get married. Twenty-seven seems to be a critical age (SS 38); Charlotte Lucas is twenty-seven and it is clearly now or never for her. But the more truly critical question is how the women use their time. Charlotte's advice to a woman who is interested in a man is that she should "make the most of every half hour in which she can command his attention. When she is secure of him, there will be leisure for falling in love as much as she chuses" (PP 22). It is advice on which she herself acts and deliberately marries a fool, securing him within three days of the time he has been rejected by her best friend. But her notion of making the most of every half hour is not a use of time but a collapse and destruction of its meaning, a surrender to its pressure. Anne Elliot is twenty-seven too and she must face the possibility, as she has for some years, that she may never marry; that would be sad, but it is not the worst thing that could happen. The time is critical for Jane Austen's heroines not because they must marry in the year or less of the novel's action, but because it is a time in which they face a series of problems and must make the decisions that will determine their moral characters. The heroine is usually in a year in which her character is indeterminate, in the sense that if she makes the wrong decisions, in this place, in these months, the girl who, for all her faults, seemed to have such potential at the start will be a

defective woman by the end. The dangers of her faults, often
the accompaniment of her strength, will have become real evils
that fix what she is henceforth. Even those heroines who are in
need of little development must prove themselves by facing the
tests of a year that requires either the proof or the end of all
their strength. The marriage is important not for itself—in Jane
Austen most people who are married are not to be especially
congratulated for that fact—but because the ability to be worthy
of or to make the right marriage is dependent on the growth
that the time of decision has required.

In romance the instant intimacies of new friends or lovers are
offered as proofs of a superior order of feeling. In "Love and
Freindship" when two girls meet "We flew into each others
arms and after having exchanged vows of mutual Freindship
for the rest of our Lives, instantly unfolded to each other the
most inward secrets of our Hearts" (MW 85). But such imme-
diacy is possible only to those who have nothing but a surface.
"The progress of the friendship between Catherine and Isabella
was quick as its beginning had been warm, and they passed so
rapidly through every gradation of increasing tenderness, that
there was shortly no fresh proof of it to be given to their friends
or themselves" (NA 36–37). But there are indeed gradations
and what moves so quickly over them comes to a quick end because it has no measured growth of knowledge and emotion.
Marianne Dashwood is a girl who is unable to bear the confinement of two days of rainy weather and who sets off into the animating gales of a high southwesterly wind; she finds it a delightful sensation and declares she will walk there at least two hours.
In twenty minutes she is surprised to find that southwest means
a driving rain full in the face. The one consolation that remains
is to run "with all possible speed" down the steep side of a
hill. A false step brings her suddenly to the ground (SS 41).
And there is Willoughby, the man with whom she will "speed-
ily" discover that they have everything in common, with whom

there is the immediate familiarity of a long-established acquaintance. "But how is your acquaintance to be long supported," Elinor asks, "under such extraordinary dispatch of every subject for discourse?" (47). It is a good question because this speed exhausts itself soon and exhaustion is certainly where Marianne's love of Willoughby takes her. The quick time of her animation is an illusion. Marianne does not move. Her opinions do not change. "Undoubtedly. At my time of life opinions are tolerably fixed. It is not likely I should now see or hear anything to change them" (93). She is seventeen.

To be fixed in the same place, as Emma saw herself and those with whom she had to live, makes a demand on the quality of life. To be fixed in opinion at her time of life, as Marianne sees herself, is to have stopped living and it makes her vulnerable. In that limited space one either grows or dies, in a limited time.

The chronology of Jane Austen's novels is usually worked out with a quiet but unfailing care. She doesn't force the dates and their movement on the reader's attention, but they are there and they can be and have been worked out; they are evidently part of the basic structure which simply must be there for her to tell a story as they are primary conditions of life. In *Pride and Prejudice,* for example, the date of the ball at Netherfield is not given to us, but it can be determined from other information to be Tuesday, November 26. Much later in the novel this is confirmed when Bingley meets Elizabeth and says, "It is above eight months. We have not met since the 26th of November, when we were all dancing together at Netherfield" (262 and 400). That exactness is important—"Elizabeth was pleased to find his memory so exact"—because it means that he remembers with feeling the last time he saw Jane. Whatever can happen happens in time, day by day, week by week, month by month. It is only in the romantic fancy of Catherine Morland that nine years is "a trifle of time" (NA 186). In Jane Austen's reality things happen in a shorter compass and with measured urgency.

What we are given of Elizabeth Bennet's life is about a year, from about October to October, the year in which she becomes twenty-one, and we can follow her in the parts of that time. If nothing much seems to be happening at any time we must be concerned for her. "With no greater events than these in the Longbourn family, and otherwise diversified by little beyond walks to Meryton, sometimes dirty and sometimes cold, did January and February pass away. March was to take Elizabeth to Hunsford" (PP 151). In the confines of little beyond the walks to Meryton Elizabeth has got to be doing better than letting the time pass away. To go to Hunsford, for a welcome change, is not what she needs most. What has happened at this point is that the young woman who began this year with all her attractions and excellence of mind has, by a series of unfortunate events and chiefly her own misjudgments, of which she is not yet aware, found herself disappointed. The danger for her is that what has happened will not lead her to rethink what she has been doing, to understand better those people who have not acted as she expected they would, to understand better why she was mistaken, to know herself better and gain in experience and strength. There was a time when she would not, for the sake of one individual, "change the meaning" of principle and integrity or blur the line between selfishness and prudence in matrimonial affairs (135–36). Now she is asking cynically what the difference is between the mercenary and the prudent motive, and where does discretion end and avarice begin. Now she is thankful to be visiting Hunsford, home of Mr. Collins and Charlotte, because stupid men are the only ones worth knowing after all. Now she is finding what she thinks is fresh life and vigor in the prospect of a tour to the Lake country. "What are men to rocks and mountains?" (154). But those journeys become valuable only because they bring into her life not open spaces without responsibility but the surprising impetus of pressing new times.

In Jane Austen time moves softly but certainly, as a natural and inevitable line of life. It is measured by the watch and by the calendar, which mark its divisions, and in those divisions the characters must act appropriately if they are to live with a real fresh life and vigor. In those lives that seem to continue in much the same way from day to day, with little variety of incident, little touched by the world of large action, fixed in one place, there come, again and again, times to make a judgment, times to make a moral choice, and there is a certain amount of time in which to make it, an amount appropriate to know what should be known, feel what should be felt, think what should be thought, do what should be done, neither too quickly nor too slowly for the occasion. There is no choice of standing still. One cannot "dwell." If the Elizabeth Bennet who begins her twenty-first year does not respond properly, as she is faced by the successive events, of the shock of Charlotte's marriage, of the seeming attractiveness and then the defection of Wickham, and so on through the many successive tests that face her, month by month, in this critical year of her life, if she does not learn from their experience more of the world and of herself, and whom she should love, if she succumbs to disappointment, she will not be the same girl in the same place one year older. She will be worse. There are examples of those to whom being in the same place year after year means becoming a vegetable, dozing on a sofa like Lady Bertram; she is innocuous, Lady Bertram, but she does harm by not acting, by not even knowing that she should be acting. Elizabeth is in greater danger and has her example of that close at home, because she has a lively mind; if it cannot grow under the pressures of time it will deteriorate and corrupt. She has seen in her father how a disappointment brought on by his own mistake, in choosing badly when he married, has made him reprehensible. He has abilities Elizabeth respects, she is grateful for his affectionate treatment of herself, but his behavior as a husband, his exposure of his wife to the contempt of her own children, is highly reprehensible. The talents he has, which might have done much for his daughters, in their ill-judged direction are productive of evils. The reader, who can afford to enjoy these talents, and who can see where Elizabeth derives hers, can see the ill-judged direction in which she may move.

Moreover, we know that her life implies another direction for her movement, a certain shape to which she ought to come. There is a completeness of form which is the proper end of living. As we watch Elizabeth Bennet or Emma Woodhouse acting blindly and foolishly there is, as Mr. Knightley would say, an anxiety, a curiosity in what we feel for her; we wonder what will become of her, because there are unused, or abused, powers of mind and spirit in her that will be wasted if they are not rightly fulfilled. There is a true Elizabeth or Emma we want to see come to wholeness in the growth of time.

Nor will that happen in time by chance, because life does not take its shape by chance in Jane Austen's world. Mrs. Bennet may think so: "such things I know are all chance in this world. There is no knowing how estates will go when once they come to be entailed" (PP 65); but the point, of course, is that one knows exactly how they must go. It is a very young and inexperienced girl like Catherine Morland (NA 140–41, 207), or an imaginist like Emma Woodhouse (E 335, 413), not knowing or manufacturing causes, who will see circumstance and chance directing human life. Certainly there are those who are favored, or disfavored, by chance, but that's not the important thing. "Frank Churchill is, indeed, a favorite of fortune," Mr. Knightley says. "Every thing turns out for his good" (428). And Mr. Knightley when he says that, can even envy him in one respect, because Frank, having done everything wrong, still has the affection of a superior woman. But that is not the kind of love the novel offers for our admiration. Frank is "Too much indebted to the event for his acquittal" (445, 447–48). Mr.

Knightley says that to Emma as he reads Frank's letter of explanation, in which Frank describes his own way of doing things. To what did he look forward as a way of determining his action and of finding his happiness? "To any thing, every thing—to time, chance, circumstance," and so forth (437). The principle is immoral; it leads him to use everybody ill, even the woman he loves; it needs the death of someone else for success—that is what he means by "time"; and it means that he has come very near to victimizing himself. When circumstances do not seem to be making for his happiness and he becomes unpleasant, in the climactic scene of the novel, he feels that to act not by real knowledge but by guess and luck will generally mean ill luck. The superiority of the woman he loves, and does not deserve, is in her quiet return: "it can be only weak, irresolute characters, (whose happiness must be always at the mercy of chance,) who will suffer" as he thinks he has been suffering (372–73). It is the self-centered, who measure the world by their own bounds, who are most exposed. A small circumstance that inconveniences Mrs. John Dashwood makes her realize that "one's happiness must in some measure be always at the mercy of chance" (SS 248). It does not improve our opinion of Marianne Dashwood to know that in her own way she is like her sister-in-law, that if a circumstance "through her own weakness . . . chance(s) to prove a source of fresh pain to herself" she throws the blame on others (202). Keeping in mind these examples of how the weak and the selfish do not use their time but blindly abandon themselves to the mercy of chance, we can better feel the enormity of what Charlotte Lucas is doing when she adopts chance as a value. "Happiness in marriage is entirely a matter of chance." Charlotte is sensible and intelligent—and what she says is thoroughly subversive of every value because it removes every basis for moral or feeling or sensible action. There is as good a chance of happiness in marriage, she says, if one marries the man tomorrow or after "studying his character for a twelve-month." Knowledge does not advance felicity; it is better to know as little as possible of the defects of the person with whom you are to pass your life (PP 23). The inevitable irony is that Charlotte, acting on her own principle of chance, schemes with care and delivers her life to the certainty of a dead stagnation.

One more point: the chance of good fortune or ill cannot be made, but the definition of its meaning is the work of time in the life it enters. So even the happily-married endings of the novels insist. All the heroines find happy endings and they all deserve them, as each has, in one way or another, worked, suffered, learned. But if they do not get more than they deserve they often seem to arrive at, or be helped to, the happy ending by a stroke of luck, such as the sudden and fortunate removal of the other woman—Lucy Steele, Louisa Musgrove, Mary Crawford—at the right moment. The happy ending is not guaranteed by their actions. What seems to be more important than the sudden and fortunate event, however, because it precedes the ending again and again, in whatever manner the end is produced, is that the heroine is prepared to accept unhappiness. The endings of Jane Austen's novels are never sentimental because before she will allow the happy result the heroine must face the fact that she has lost—that Edward Ferrars will now marry, or really has married, Lucy; that, after the elopement of Wickham and Lydia, Darcy cannot marry into the Bennet family; that Edmund Bertram is going to marry Mary Crawford; that Mr. Knightley is going to marry Harriet Smith; that Captain Wentworth must marry Louisa Musgrove. The reader may refuse to believe that any of these things will happen because he has been given a different set of expectations, but the heroine must believe. She must not simply see the threat as another obstacle that she can do something about, and she must not despair because, having lost, there is nothing in life for her to do. She must really see it as a loss, absorb it as an irreversible fact, and then come to terms with herself and go ahead with what she must do now. She often finds herself in the same place and in the same company as she was at the beginning, but she cannot be the same person herself because time has made a difference and things will never be the same again. She must in the same place face a new time, and it is very hard. The immaturity of Catherine Morland as a heroine, the relative unseriousness of what her brief story has been, appears, properly, at the end of her story, where she is still unable to reconcile herself to her loss and sit still and do the work before her. The others must accept their unhappiness before they are granted happiness. The reward then is not the essential thing because it need never have arrived; that may well be dependent on chance; what is important is that at the time it is granted the heroine is worthy of a happiness that has a meaning. She would have been worthy of it even if her lot had proved unhappy because in her place she has used her time well, and that is not a matter of chance.

$\mathcal{T}$HERE are, then, coordinates mapping and timing the limits, setting the conditions, demanding action. There is a definable reality, not to be made or unmade, to which Jane Austen's men and women must bring themselves; and it is in proportion to their success that they make or unmake their own lives. What is difficult of definition is, characteristically, painful; if Anne Elliot or Elizabeth Bennet cannot define her own feelings she is in distress. But the means of definition are available to her if she has the sense and the moral will to use them. The precise truth is there if she can bring herself up to the point where she can locate it.

Darcy's letter makes Elizabeth's feelings "acutely painful" and "difficult of definition" because if it is true it means she must change her cherished opinions of what is real, of Wickham's "real character," of Darcy, of herself. What she must do is command herself to "examine the meaning of every sen-

tence" (PP 204–6). In every sentence are the words of meaning which, if correctly used and correctly understood, are the
adequate expression of the reality. There is a language in which
she can move to arrive at its place and give it the proper name.
If that seems simple, it imposes a complex moral discipline. If it
seems to us that the word is inadequate to the complexities of
life, the point is rather that to come to the proper word is to
do justice to the complexities. Anne Elliot sees Captain Wentworth and the Miss Musgroves in an ambiguous situation and
must work, by observation, memory, experience, to find the word.
He is not in love with either of them, she knows. They are more
in love with him; yet it is not love; it is a little fever of admiration. Nor is it his intention to give pain. "He was only wrong in
accepting the attentions—(for accepting must be the word) of
two young women at once" (P 82). That must be the word and
it does exact justice. It defines Captain Wentworth's activity and
state at that moment in that place.

Like Jane Austen herself, admirable characters in her novels
dislike hearing dislocated words that do not meet the reality.
In one of her letters she is offended by a dreadful female who is
unable to pronounce the word *shift* and affects *chemise*. "I could
forgive her any follies in English, rather than the Mock Modesty
of that french word" (L 472). That is a mock preciseness—she
should not only place her quilt in the center, Jane Austen adds
in a geographical parallel, but give its latitude and longitude
and give its dimension by a lunar observation if she chose; that
foolish word is an affectation designed to obscure the reality
of the thing. Mr. Knightley speaks in plain, unaffected, gentlemanlike English (E 448), makes his answers short, decided, full,
distinct (57, 99, 369). Mrs. Elton's idea of what is simple and
natural is not his. "Not quite," as he says (355). He speaks
his plain English to the end, even to the woman he loves, or
rather, especially to her.

A great part of the fun of the juvenilia is that we are put

into a whirling chaos of disoriented creatures where the references of forms, motives, actions have lost their promised meanings and simply dissolve. An eloping couple will choose Gretna Green for their nuptials, "in preference to any other place," although they are already in Scotland and Gretna Green is at a considerable distance (MW 95). In this nonsense, words begin to work against each other in self-contradiction. Myself, "& a few more," a heroine tells us, were my father's "only" children (16). Or we are given an offer of strict definition and then left clutching air: "I found her exactly what her Brother had described her to be—of the middle size" (82). Two lovers (4) "were exceedingly handsome and so much alike" (that sounds hopeful and loverlike) "that it was not every one who knew them apart" (and somehow "alike" has shifted meaning in a startling way). "Nay even their most intimate friends had nothing to distinguish them by" (dear God!) "but the shape of the face, the colour of the Eye, the length of the Nose & the difference of the complexion" (and now, wonderfully, "alike" has exploded into no meaning at all). The delights of this treasure house are at their best when the self-contradiction or the failure of definition betrays a moral leak—where a young lady has many rare and charming qualities "but Sobriety is not one of them" (23), or where it is possible to declare "I *am* very Charitable every now and then" (170). The words slip because the character has no firm footing where he stands. The young man in "Love and Freindship" who has lost his way, proficient in geography though he thought himself, has a correspondent moral confusion and a confusion of language. "My Father, seduced by the false glare of Fortune and the Deluding Pomp of Title," as he says, has insisted on his marrying the Lady Dorothea. "No never exclaimed I. Lady Dorothea is lovely and Engaging; I prefer no woman to her; but know Sir, that I scorn to marry her in compliance with your Wishes. No! Never shall it be said that I obliged my Father." His father is surprised. " 'Where, Edward in the name of wonder (said he) did you pick up this unmeaning gibberish? You have been studying Novels I suspect.' I scorned to answer: it would have been beneath my dignity. I mounted my Horse . . ." (81).

The novels that Jane Austen admires, and wants to write, are written in another language. They display, as she says in *Northanger Abbey,* the greatest powers of the mind, a most thorough knowledge of human nature, the happiest delineation of its varieties, the liveliest effusions of wit and humor, all conveyed to the world in "the best chosen language" (38). Language is a given reality that presents choices and so tests the powers and the life of its users by their ability to make the right choices—as it tests those who hear what is conveyed by their ability to understand its meaning. As time and space are not subject to individual desires but are determinate realities, measurable by public standards, words are the defined means by which men and women speak and hear not a private or imagined meaning but the reality common to society. Nor are words, any more than space and time, the impositions of gross necessity upon the satisfactory expression of life; they are, rather, life's necessary fulfilling form.

To hold a lady to the time by the watch, to insist on the meaning of a word, can be the way of love, for it insists on nothing less than the fullest truth of seeing and saying. Henry Tilney, a pleasant and worthy lover because a pleasant and worthy instructor, is forever pressing Catherine Morland to a definition, correctness of language, propriety of diction; he overpowers with Johnson and Blair, as his sister says. To Catherine *Udolpho* is the nicest book in the world—"but it *is* a nice book, and why should not I call it so?" "Very true," said Henry, ". . . it is a very nice word indeed!—it does for every thing . . . every commendation on every subject is comprised in that one word" (NA 107–8). Catherine is not nice in her choice of words, that one word will do for everything, because she makes no distinctions among things. That will become a serious moral problem, nor will a nice book like *Udolpho* teach her better. But Henry is there, showing her his watch and correcting her language to the very end, as he does in the climactic scene (195–96). Mr. Knightley, in his first scene, insists that Emma look again at her word, at what she has been doing, when she claims "success" in matchmaking for Miss Taylor. "I do not understand what you mean by 'success,'" says Mr. Knightley. He defines the word, makes a distinction and concludes "—you made a lucky guess; and *that* is all that can be said." Emma will not have him quarrel with "my poor word," as she calls it, and tries to skip from the distinction between luck and success; now she claims "a something between" (E 12–13). It is because Mr. Knightley will never let her rest in something between, evade a meaning, that their love becomes possible. He teaches her, eventually, the real meaning of what it is to be "amiable," in English (149). Emma is certain of her command of real meanings, in all senses, spoken or unspoken, serious or lively, is clever even in riddle and in word game. But there is always more meaning than she can control, and when she finds herself in a difficulty she tries to escape responsibility and Mr. Knightley by a denial of meaning. "What I said just now, meant nothing" (288). May he ask, says Mr. Knightley, in what lay the great amusement, the poignant sting of the last word of the anagrams? "'Oh!' she cried in evident embarrassment, 'it all meant nothing'" (349–50). And so to Box Hill, where she encourages the flattery and gallantry of Frank Churchill because, in her own estimation, it "meant nothing, though in the judgment of most people looking on it must have had such an appearance as no English word but flirtation could very well describe" (368). It is a very dangerous moment and Emma is about to meet her crisis. Having loosed herself from the meaning of English words, with a mock ceremony she speaks her cruel words to Miss Bates. Deceived by the manner Miss Bates "did not immediately catch her meaning";

then it bursts and pains. Confronted by Mr. Knightley once again, Emma tries to laugh it off, dares to say Miss Bates did not understand her, but Mr. Knightley will not allow it. "I assure you she did. She felt your full meaning" (371, 374–75). Emma, before she rests, must feel those full meanings that then burst on her in successive explosions of revelation. "Good God! You are not serious? You do not mean it?" "What do you mean— Good Heaven! what do you mean?" "You cannot mean . . . You cannot mean . . . Good God!" (395, 405–6, 471).

There are several quick ways of losing the definition and reality in the meanings of words. One is to fall into a hackneyed expression, the normal style of an affected fool. Mr. Collins is superb here, an absolute master at separating words from their meaning: "And now nothing remains for me but to assure you in the most animated language of the violence of my affection" (PP 106). But the style is one into which the wittiest of us, too, can fall in those weak moments, as when Elizabeth says bitterly of Mr. Bingley that only a few days before he departed he had been a man "violently in love." That expression, Mrs. Gardiner answers, "is so hackneyed, so doubtful, so indefinite, that it gives me very little idea. It is as often applied to feelings which arise from an half-hour's acquaintance, as to a real, strong attachment. Pray how *violent was* Mr. Bingley's love?" Elizabeth tries again. "I never saw a more promising inclination" (140–41).

But there is also a more serious failure of style in which language becomes inadequate to expression because reality itself becomes indefinable. Minds that run to "Sublimity" and "Sensibility" and "illimitable Ardour" are liable to this infirmity and become, by inevitable irony, victims of their own limited, hackneyed vocabulary; Sir Edward Denham of *Sanditon* is the latest example, giving us the 1817 version of "all the usual Phrases . . . descriptive of the *undescribable*," and "all the newest-fashioned hard words" (MW 396–98). Marianne Dashwood is an earlier version. Marianne dislikes commonplace phrases; she detests jargon. She admires landscape scenery but that admiration has become, in others, a mere jargon; everyone pretends to feel and describe with the taste and elegance of the man who first defined what picturesque beauty was, and she refuses to be like everyone. "I detest jargon of every kind, and sometimes I have kept my feelings to myself, because I could find no language to describe them in but what was worn and hackneyed out of all sense and meaning" (SS 97). The real superiority of the feelings, however, is open to question; if she can find no language but the hackneyed and worn, it is not at all clear that the vehemence of the feeling is any indication of depth of taste or meaning. The inadequacy of language for Marianne is her deficiency of feeling. A letter delivered by Mrs. Jennings, converted by Marianne's imagination into a full and convincing explanation from Willoughby, is really a letter from Marianne's mother and so an acute disappointment to Marianne: "The cruelty of Mrs. Jennings no language, within her reach in her moments of happiest eloquence, could have expressed"; tears of passionate violence follow, a reproach entirely lost on its object (202). That which is beyond the reach of her language, the inexpressible, is without shape, in a sense without reality; Mrs. Jennings's cruelty does not exist. Marianne's suffering is real enough, but it is exacerbated by her deliberate cultivation of its limitless repetition, and it will not end until she can find the words that will define it. Her anxiety to avoid the common and the hackneyed for the language of the higher feelings has made Willoughby seem to her worthy of her love, but her mistake is obvious from their earliest acquaintance. What she thinks is the escape from the commonplace notions of decorum which they achieve in their conversation is not more than a small collection of favorite topics which she chooses and in which she sets the style and he returns her own voice to her. Willoughby picks up her cue because he is clever enough and because he is shallow enough, not because his feelings are superior. In his conversation of greatest emotion and sincerity, with Elinor late in the novel, he cannot find words for the occasion. What he felt when he received Marianne's note in London, he says, is "in the common phrase, not to be expressed." In a more simple phrase, perhaps too simple to raise any emotions, he says that his feelings were "very, very painful." The open simplicity is an improvement on his usual speech, but it is still a sadly impoverished language he has for his feelings. As he read Marianne's letter, every line was "in the hackneyed metaphor which their dear writer, were she here, would forbid—a dagger to my heart." To know she was in town was "in the same language—a thunderbolt.—Thunderbolts and daggers!—what a reproof would she have given me!" (325). She would forbid and reprove, no doubt, but it is not a language he can transcend; and if this man, who speaks in the hackneyed language she so detested, was the man Marianne chose to love, then we have a comment on the reach of her own words and emotions.

To be without the word is to be without the thing. Willoughby's vocabulary is limited by his moral weakness. His whole conduct declares, Elinor points out, that "self-denial is a word hardly understood by him" (SS 350). Witty and adroit as they are, and with an agreeable flow of words, Henry and Mary Crawford have the same disfiguring gaps in their vocabulary. In the happy enthusiasm of his love for Fanny and his unforeseen desire to marry, Henry sees moral qualities he has never known before. He has discovered, he says, something unknown to his uncle the Admiral and the hater of marriage; for Fanny is exactly such a woman as the Admiral thinks does not exist in the world, the very impossibility he would describe "—if indeed he has now delicacy of language enough to embody his own ideas" (MP 293). But Henry's awareness of his uncle's gross mind, and its inability to find words for virtues he cannot conceive to be real, measures for us not only Henry's superiority but his own similar obtuseness on another level. Henry has more sense than his uncle, too much sense not to feel the worth of good principles in a wife—"though he was too little accustomed to serious reflection to know them by their proper name." He talks of Fanny's steadiness and regularity of conduct, her honor, the decorum that warrants a man's fullest dependence on her faith and integrity; he is expressing what is inspired by the knowledge of her being well principled and religious (294). The things he can see and describe in Fanny are her social virtues, but what he cannot name properly is the reality he does not know, the source that makes her virtues reliable. Without that source there can be no more dependence on the conduct than there is on Henry's own conduct. The luck that had once led him into the way of happiness cannot last.

His sister has a similar cleverness and sense and a similar inability to know the proper name. She is alive to the meanings and shades of meaning of words as they are used in casual conversation or in making certain kinds of social signals, but not when a major moral distinction must be made. She is surprised at the discovery that Edmund is to be a clergyman when the choice is not forced on him. He asks if she thinks the church itself is never chosen and her reply springs from a quick intelligence and a limited one. "*Never* is a black word. But yes, in the *never* of conversation which means *not very often,* I do think it." There is a liveliness in the mind that picks up his word and trims it to the moment and the purpose; she takes a shade from the blackness by merging it with a social meaning, where the responsibility for exactness presumably is lightened. Before she has completed a few more lines of the same speech, however, she has fallen into that conversational mode as her natural speech: "A clergyman is nothing." Edmund can then pick up her word in reply—"The *nothing* of conversation has its gradations, I hope, as well as the *never*"—but the warning for himself in the language he hears is unheeded (MP 92). A moment later she will not measure distance with him or look at his watch. On an occasion when Edmund is away Mary regrets some of the expressions she has used of the clergy in her conversations. "She wished such words unsaid with all her heart." She tries to convey something of that to him by saying to Fanny, "But you must give my compliments to him. Yes—I think it must be compliments. Is not there a something wanted, Miss Price, in our language—a something between compliments and—and love—to suit the sort of friendly acquaintance we have had together?—So many months acquaintance!—But compliments may be sufficient here" (286–88). This is quite engaging, as Mary so often is, and displays a sensitivity to nuances of feelings that seem to fall between the coarser categories to which words limit their recognition. But then it is not quite so engaging. This is not the only time she tries to use Fanny as an instrument through which she can send or receive messages when the necessary indirection is a sign of their doubtful propriety. Her inability to find a word for what it is she wants Fanny to send, something to suit the "sort of friendly acquaintance" she wants to establish, is an indication of the ambiguity in her own feelings and in her relationships with Edmund. Compliments may be sufficient, she is forced to say, because there is no stronger word short of the love she cannot claim. The fault is not in the language, which is wanting "a something between," but in the state of her own mind and emotion, which cannot define themselves in such a way as to be given a proper name. If the thing were there the word would be there. Edmund's final disillusionment comes in her last interview with him, when he goes to her in a softened, devoted state of mind, finds her serious, even agitated, by the action of Henry and Maria—and then, before he is able to speak one intelligible sentence, she introduces the subject in a manner that shocks him. "Let us talk over this sad business." "Sad," as she is using it, carries no sorrow but, the reverse, is flip and colloquial (cf. 357). Edmund realizes that this is her meaning from her next, more important sentence, "What can equal the folly of our two relations?" This is devastating to Edmund. ". . . no harsher name than folly given!" (454). She has no harsher name to give to sin because her richly endowed mind has been utterly spoiled, perverted. Her "meaning" is not to wound Edmund's feelings with cruelty, he knows. The evil lies deeper, in her total ignorance, unsuspiciousness of there being such feelings. "She was speaking only, as she had been used to hear others speak, as she imagined every body else would speak." Like her brother's, hers are faults not of bad nature or temper, but faults of principle, a corrupted, vitiated mind (456). For all her wit and fluency she can find every word but the right one and the exact one.

In the reality and in the language of Jane Austen there are degrees of exactness that must be found to meet the purposes of life. There is a continuum of words in which the passage from one to another is a passage from one moral state to another; a notation is available to name the steps and the critical moment the misstep is made. But there is no simple lesson for knowing that moment when a quality becomes excessive and a virtue passes over to a fault; finding the propriety in varied circumstances is the test. Such a fool as John Thorpe cannot make the judgments and is always missing the mark; along a scale of social manner, marked civil-easy-impudent, he is always one degree below what he should be: "easy where he ought to be civil, and impudent where he might be allowed to be easy" (NA 45). Civility is a lesser duty of life (SS 347), its demands are not high, and it ought to be within the capacity of most; but to achieve it to the right degree, without falling below, like John Thorpe, or exceeding, like Sir John Middleton, whose kind entreaties "were carried to a point of perseverance beyond civility" (30), requires both proper feeling and intelligence. Mrs. Bennet receives Bingley "with a degree of civility" which makes Jane and Elizabeth ashamed, especially when contrasted with her cold and ceremonious politeness to Darcy; the excess is as wretched as the deficiency which is its simple complement (PP

335). The sensible and the sensitive are always concerned to be certain of the degree (PP 22), to arrange with precision the degree (PP 50), to know the exact degree (PP 360), perfectly understand the degree (E 350), assure oneself as to the degree (E 426), just that degree (P 89). And how lovely to hear Mrs. Elton describe her own performance, in an absurdly accurate misuse of words, as "*mediocre* to the last degree" (E 276).

To achieve the right degree is usually to have avoided excesses and deficiencies, to have attained to fine balance. But the balance is not a facile one for several reasons. For one thing, it is not attained simply by an avoidance, a safe virtue of not doing. The repeated examples of the indolent or irresponsible parent show how there is no possibility of not making a choice, how the avoidance of one alternative is the fall into another. Jane Austen needed advice on how to understand the words of permission to dedicate a book to the Prince Regent: "I sh^d be equally concerned to appear either Presumptuous or Ungrateful" (L 429). There are failures on either side and finding the right way is not to shrink but to make a positive movement that demands intelligent and moral choice. More importantly, the right sort of balance is not only a middle between extremes but an achieved union of excellences. If the balancing of words had become by Jane Austen's day a false form, which she mocked, it was also the form of an admirable reality. To be really "Sensible yet unaffected—Accomplished yet Easy—Lively yet Gentle" (MW 150) is to unite two virtues that are difficult of reconcilement; it is a merit to possess one, but an advantage that can be purchased by the loss of its coordinate. It is part of the attractiveness of the Miss Musgroves that one is lively and one is gentle, but it is part of their insignificance that they divide the honors and it really doesn't make much difference which is which. Captain Wentworth must learn much before the perfection of Anne's character is fixed in his mind as maintaining "the loveliest medium of fortitude and gentleness" (P 241); in the first version of the chapter it is the "just" medium (259). That medium is not attained by having a little of one thing and a little of the other, and now and then, but by a simultaneous completeness of fortitude and of gentleness. Either is easy when it is relieved of the responsibility of maintaining its potential opposite and neither has its full meaning without the other. The just medium does full justice to both values and then a reality so completely realized and defined in its shape becomes lovely. It is neither artless nor artful. The proper mean is art, knowing the limits and the possibilities and using them to their fullest. In a world of real meaning and proper naming, of degree and of balance, definition is limitation, but it is also liberation.

𝒯HE just and lovely words of Jane Austen take power, therefore, not from a narrowness of meaning, fixed and single, but from a certain largeness of scope within which they can move in careful purpose. Going to the eighteenth-century dictionaries and synonymies and to the literary, moral, and philosophical sources that give information toward defining the meaning of her words is often very useful. The reader will find fragments of that reading here and there in the following pages, but only fragments because her words cannot be defined satisfactorily by those external aids. The effect her words have derives from a development of forces; as the relationship of the many parts of a situation, giving shape to the whole, begins to change, so the meaning of the parts changes. Sometimes the result becomes for one of her characters a discovery, as a re-vision brings into view for the first time a "real" meaning. There are few "good" words or "bad" words in Jane Austen's lexicon, as there are relatively few things good or bad in themselves. Persons, places, times, circumstances, manners, motives will determine. Take, as an example, the meaning of such a thing as solitude. It is wrong for Marianne, after Willoughby's departure, to wander by herself, to avoid her sisters, and Elinor greatly disapproves such continual seclusion (SS 85), because Marianne's conduct is injurious to both herself and her family. At the same time it is not a higher form of personal or social virtue in Lady Middleton that leaves her feeling quite alone if she has the company of only three others and requires preservation from such frightful solitude (143). But it is right for Elinor to keep her secret and bear her burden alone, not only because she has an obligation to Lucy but because, knowing her family as she does, by concealment she will save useless distress for both them and herself: she was stronger alone (141). There is a similar dialectic at work in Jane Austen's words, their meaning being dependent on the level at which they are being used. One cannot simply say, for example, that "propriety" is one of Jane Austen's values, but "sensibility" is not, because as they stand those statements have no useful truth or falsity. There is a sense in which either word may be used to claim an unreal value; in this false sense it may well mean, not hypocritically but ironically, the very reverse of the unlimited strength it assumes and represents itself to be. There is another sense in which either word has a real value; and in this true sense it may well be a possession of someone who does not seem to have it, or it may seem to be a weak limitation of its possessor rather than the strength it proves to be. It is this sort of question of definition we will be concerned with.

So many kinds of false freedom from limitation are offered her characters. These false offerings hold forth a life of greater intensity and greater power, of superior vision, a higher activity of mind, feeling, body, a fulfillment of desire. They give a reality of the mind's own making and seem therefore to be dominant. They prove to be false because they are really reductions of life. They do not have more vision but see less, they do not have more power but are inadequate to life, and they do not fulfill desires because they are self-defeating. In the eager expectations of Catherine Morland romance is an art of exciting surprise, its events more eventful, its emotions more moving, altogether a higher adventure than the life she observes. Sensibility, to Marianne Dashwood, is a loftier form of feeling, unrestrained and honest, receptive to more life, warmer than the lives of the people of little feeling or of deliberate calmness and conformity she sees around her. Elizabeth Bennet's quick insights into character give her a superior discernment that makes life more interesting for her than it is for others; most especially they enable her to see at first impression which is the disagreeable man, which the amiable, and to know love in its most interesting mode. Mary and Henry Crawford are extraordinarily lively people, witty and ironic, active, figures of vitality beside that gentle, fatigued, and very proper Fanny Price. Clever Emma Woodhouse has the imagination that gives her truths unseen by lesser minds; it gives her therefore a perfect control of her own life and the power to direct the course of true love for others, always for their good. Captain Wentworth is a strong-minded man, outspoken and decisive, tested by battle and rewarded by success, master of himself and not prepared to suffer weakness in the woman he loves. But Catherine Morland's romance is a false art, without the dignity and without the surprise she seeks, and common life is far more demanding and more interesting; the true art is in common life and in the novel that teaches it. But Marianne Dashwood's sensibility is a false feeling, without the force and integrity she admires, reversing for her the very virtues she wants; the real feeling is in the exertion of Elinor and the achievement of that effort. But the meaning of true affection is what Elizabeth Bennet can learn not by a first interview but only by a much slower development, much more interesting for that reason; and for her that will mean a series of mortifications. But Mary and Henry Crawford do not have a real liveliness that enables them to survive, to make their own lives; they are themselves the ironic victims, while it is Fanny Price who has the real life that endures and gives life to others. But

Emma Woodhouse's is a false imagination, never in possession of what it sees with most certainty, deluded by the truth it creates into disservice to others and disaster for herself, while the real truth moves evenly and unregarded to confront her. But it is not Captain Wentworth and it is Anne Elliot, only Anne, small, submissive, unseen, unheard herself and hearing around her sounds of confusion, who has the real strength. The real freedom is in the life triumphing over the illusion that it escapes those limits which hold smaller spirits; it is in the life that transforms every impediment into an acquisition and fills its room and its moment.

That tight and demarcated little world, which may seem to us so restricted in its scope and in its assumptions about reality, becomes enormously exhilarating and liberating; it offers to those who are capable of exerting themselves to discover its meaning the control of the essential qualities of their lives; it challenges our own narrowness, our assumption of powerlessness or rebellion. The restrictions in the world of Jane Austen's heroines do not make their choices less significant. As boundaries become clear and close and alternatives are few and final, choice becomes more heroic. The more valuable way to approach her novels is not through the list of all the mighty matters and all the odd corners that she omits, as though her primary concern were to reject or withdraw from what she could not or did not want to touch in art. It is not helpful to say, with one critic of many, that she "feels compelled to tidy up life's customary messiness," because to say that is to make an assumption about life that is not hers. She knows, and she shows us in her novels, messy lives, and most people are leading them, even when the surface of life seems proper; but custom is not the first fact of life. Life is not a disorder to be ordered, a given mess on which those of tidy compulsions impose a tidiness. It is not a meaningless heap from which meaning is extracted by reduction and exclusion. Meaning is the first fact. It is obscured by inexperience, by miseducation, by deception, above all by internal blindness, but it is there and it is clear to the opened eye. She does not omit any more than a dancer omits clumsiness, but begins directly with what is essential, as the dancer begins with grace. The form of the dance does not suppress significant motion; by its order it sets free the dancer. Jane Austen's world is full, it has all the parts it needs and all of them are fully given to us as far as they are needed. All parts become luminous in a defining vision. Each part is located, each part can be explained, as far as it must be for purposeful word and action. Strong feelings rise in her characters, rightly and necessarily at moments of crisis, with pleasures and pains beyond what they have ever felt: the characteristic accompaniment of this increase of feeling is an increase in articulateness; they must often struggle for it but their stature is in proportion to their willingness to try for it and their eventual success in achieving the brightness of command.

That definition, clarity of atmosphere, fullness of articulation, with which she gives us the actions of men and women in common life, give her stories such original simplicity that it is understandable why even sophisticated critics have thought of her as a primitive. Her stories have a freshness and firstness, even while what we see seems to have happened many times before, and will happen again, because it is in the inevitable order of things; it is an old story, always beginning, the same story, always different. In that sense hers is a timeless world, where life repeats and renews itself in each well-lived individual life. And in that sense it is a spacious world, in which the measured movement of the dance can be found in every place. "There is nothing like dancing after all," Sir William Lucas says to Mr. Darcy. "I consider it as one of the first refinements of polished societies." "Certainly, Sir," Darcy replies, "and it has the advantage also of being in vogue amongst the less polished societies of the world.—Every savage can dance" (PP 25). Each man is right, of course, but of course each is being foolish in his exclusive statement. There is good dancing everywhere that men and women have mastered the arts of time and space, to move with meaning.

2

The Expectations of Catherine Morland

Catherine Morland presents a difficult problem in art. She is supposed to be a heroine but neither she nor her family will do the heroic thing "as any body might expect." "What a strange, unaccountable character!" (NA 13, 14). The art of the author who must tell the story is continually defeated because it is inadequate to define this very plain family which insists on acting "with the common feelings of common life" (19). As at the opening so at the close of her career, heroine and family refuse to delight the pen of the contriver: a heroine returning in a hack post chaise brings to her author no share in glory, only a humiliation; but to her everyday family, who have different expectations, Catherine's return is an enjoyment of no everyday nature, for a chaise is itself a rare sight in Fullerton and Catherine's appearance is a pleasure quite unlooked for—except by the two youngest children, "who expected a brother or sister in every carriage" (232–33). Even when the telltale compression of the last few pages signals to the reader that we are all hasting together to perfect felicity, that desperate contriver must cast about quickly for some "probable circumstance" to remove an

obstacle: she finds it in a hitherto unmentioned young gentleman's "unexpected accession to title and fortune"; declares him
to be, to a precision, the most charming young man in the world,
thereby making any definition of his merits unnecessary; and,
without mind or meaning, meets the rules of composition by
inventing for him a connection with the fable (250–51). A
superior art, the novel displaying greater powers of the mind,
will be needed to cope with the unexpected, with problems of
probability, and with the common feelings of common life. Jane
Austen's own art is not yet good enough to produce all it seems
to promise—inconsistent as it is in the use of the mock author
and in the stitching together of a story of unequal parts—but
then she is engaged in an adventurous attempt to change the
expectations of readers.

This is a novel that takes the romance out of life. Strange
things may seem to happen, "But strange things may be generally accounted for if their cause be fairly searched out" (16).
Surprise is a foolish thing; as it offers itself in, for example, the
indeterminateness of what is "odd" and as it creates the emotion of an undefined "alarm," it is dissolved; in its stead is a
process of understanding by means of "observation" of what
is and a determination of "probability." "Remember that we are
English," the hero tells the heroine at the climax (197), and
most bitterly did she cry. He has been schooling her in the meanings and the accurate usage of English words and the best, the
only, evidence of her maturity at the end is her attempt to write
adequately a difficult letter. But the art of the novel of common life holds its own surprises, some subsuming and some
exceeding the excitements of romance. It is—unexpectedly—
more interesting.

$\mathcal{O}$NE of the first things Catherine does upon her inglorious
return is to take the well-known road to Mrs. Allen's house.
Not three months ago "wild with joyful expectation" she had

run backwards and forwards there ten times a day, looking forward to pleasures untasted and unalloyed, free from the apprehension of evil as from the knowledge of it; now how altered a being did she return (237). That sounds like a Johnsonian conclusion on the endless human illusion of imagined hopes, and it is that, but, as so much in Jane Austen, it is Johnsonian with a comic resolution of what in Johnson can be resolved only by religion. The eleven weeks, the shortest span in any of the novels, has not and cannot have produced much alteration in the most naive of all the heroines. Nor can she have had much instruction in the company of Mrs. Allen, that happy counterpoint to Catherine, a woman whose intellectual poverty never rises to the possibility of the unexpected ("I thought how it would be"). But Catherine has learned something about expectations. What is the shape of life to be? If expectations are a definition of life, Catherine comes to know something of the making of odd shapes and their emotions of alarm, and of the making of observations and their probabilities.

It is a dependable trait in Catherine that her expectations are almost always mistaken. If her history is less interesting than the histories of subsequent heroines of Jane Austen, one reason is that our own expectations are somewhat dulled by this pattern. Catherine holds our interest, however, because the pattern of her expectation is not fixed and therefore not easily predictable. She is young, ignorant, open. If her brother finds that the limited family fortune will make him wait two or three years to marry, it is no more than he expected, and Catherine is equally satisfied, because her "expectations" had been as "unfixed" as her ideas of her father's income (135). It is Isabella who has expected more and has unpleasant insinuations to offer about Catherine's father; Catherine is free of this selfish demand on events. One of her charms is that she is as likely to underestimate as to overestimate and therefore to be delighted by the event when it exceeds her hopes or conceptions; small things can make her very happy. "The morning had answered all her hopes, and the evening of the following day was now the object of expectation, the future good." Her happiness comes easily and she is often a fool, but it would be churlish not to sympathize with that time of young happiness when life is always outdoing itself in promise. On the evening of that following day she "could not, dared not expect" that Mr. Tilney should ask her again to dance, but her wishes, hopes, and plans all center in nothing less, and of course, when she has given herself up for lost, unable to escape John Thorpe, suddenly Mr. Tilney is there: it did not appear that life could supply any greater felicity (73–75). It is the kind of extravagant felicity that can exist only to be reversed and re-reversed on every occasion. If she goes to a play and finds that she is "not deceived in her own expectation of pleasure" (92), she is then recalled to anxiety and distress in the fifth act by the sudden view of Henry and his father, and then she finds that it all ends delightfully when John Thorpe reports how much the General admires her: "The evening had done more, much more, for her, than she could have expected" (96). And it really has, because Thorpe's conversation with the General will do even more than she can now expect, and through several turns of good and ill. All this engages our sympathy even as it guarantees disappointment and unhappiness for her. She goes to her visit in Milsom street, General Tilney's house, with "expectations of pleasure . . . so very high, that disappointment was inevitable." But she is puzzled to account for this (129).

Catherine at Bath is an artless girl. In their first conversation, hearing in her words and seeing in her face her inability at the simplest disguise of feeling, Henry tells her, with a pleasant irony, that she is "artful and deep" (29). An "artless exclamation" in open praise of Henry's dancing at once surprises and amuses Miss Tilney (72). Her artless style, the fresh feelings of every sort she brings to Bath, the honest relish of balls and plays and everyday sights (79), is a large part of the worthiness and promise seen in her by the two young Tilneys. It is a quality that Henry appreciates not the less because it brings pressure upon him too. A question of hers "thoroughly artless in itself" can be rather distressing to the gentleman because it openly questions his generosity on a point where it should be questioned and it brings him to a better and more intimate response (94).

That her artlessness is also insufficient is soon obvious in her acquaintance with the Thorpes, those determined shapers of life. John Thorpe is one of the difficulties of Bath; he is a transparent fool but Catherine in her ignorance doesn't know how to take him. Thorpe absolutely manufactures reality. He comes on the scene as a "most knowing-looking coachman," with all the vehemence that could endanger the lives of himself, his companion and his horse (44). He begins immediately to remake space and time in accord with his own heroic achievement and he will not allow simple arithmetic to persuade him out of his senses. He is a cause of "alarm" to Catherine by his stories of how spirited his horse will be, but she soon perceives that in fact the horse is by no means alarmingly fast; he frightens her again by his chatter about the dangers to which James and Isabella are exposed in their carriage, but a little reflection makes her conclude that they are in fact perfectly safe and she "therefore would alarm herself no longer" (62–66). She is not in the habit of judging for herself and her general notions of what men ought to be are unfixed, but she is, on her own, learning a little about Thorpe. He is dangerous to her not by his own agreeableness, because she sees and hears by his distortions that he is "odd," and that by his falsifications he makes the Tilneys appear "very odd" to her or she "so strange" to them (85, 87). It is, rather, by his literal making and unmaking of "expectations" that he creates problems for her.

Isabella is a more immediate menace because, more skillful

than her brother, she has a command of shallow artifice which is obvious to the reader but dominant over the artless Catherine; we are interested in seeing how Catherine will be able to understand what she is and how she deceives. Isabella puts a form on every person, including herself, every gesture, every event, designed to make life seem more grandly heroic. Her speech insists on higher feeling by an undifferentiated hyperbole—ten ages, a hundred things, agonies, wild, dearest, prettiest, sweetest, beautiful as an angel. She does nothing by halves, as she says; her attachments are always excessively strong; and this she claims is her nature, this is "real"—those who are really my friends, real friendship, the heart really attached. In her mouth everything becomes "amazing," seemingly raised to a wonder beyond expectation, actually depressed to an identical confusion. If vanity and triviality speak from behind these forms, something worse is there, an egotistical selfishness that is using the forms. Isabella knows how to pursue her own ends by seeming to avoid them, as she pursues young men by seeming to avoid them. Furthermore she uses "real" friendship for her own purposes (39–43).

Isabella, like her brother, leads Catherine into a "strange, wild scheme" (89), or into a situation where Catherine's conduct has an "odd appearance" (104), but these improprieties are easily correctable as soon as Catherine is simply informed by someone like Mr. Allen that she is doing wrong. Isabella is a more serious danger because she can lead Catherine to accept her own false manner of judgment; she can make Catherine feel odd for not thinking like her friend. "It is so odd to me, that you should never have read Udolpho before" (41). Catherine admires her as one who has superior knowledge and arts of understanding, is guided in her reading by her, adopts her diction until corrected by Henry. She accepts the part Isabella chooses to act and tries, as well as she can, to act the part Isabella casts her in. She is "ashamed of an ignorance little expected," when it suits Isabella to consider her as being full of the arch penetration of her friend's secret love for James; Isabella's utterance of a charming sentiment, a grand idea, freely rejecting millions of pounds, the whole world, for love, gives Catherine a pleasing remembrance of all the heroines of her acquaintance (119). Happily Catherine is not successful in playing her own part; she finds, for once, what she thinks is a fine opportunity for really being arch—she observes Isabella's eyes in eager expectation and reassures her that James will soon arrive: by that time circumstances have changed and Isabella is expecting Captain Tilney (143). Happily, too, Isabella can't quite maintain her own role under changing circumstances: "and after all that romancers may say, there is no doing without money" (146).

Catherine is capable of learning. As the artificiality that makes Isabella successful is also self-defeating, the same simple lack of art that makes Catherine Isabella's victim, though it is insufficient, is protective of her and it is teachable. The first time Catherine saw Henry in company with another woman (his sister) she could have played the heroine by considering him lost to her forever, turning deathly pale and falling into a fit; but "guided only by what was simple and probable" it never entered her head that he could be married (53). Similarly, the vacuous general rules Isabella invents about the character of young men do not affect Catherine's conduct: "Well, I never observed *that*" (42). Noting a difference between the professed strength of one of Isabella's emotions and its immediate total suspension, Catherine cannot avoid a little suspicion (57). When Isabella's desires begin to force Catherine from what she knows is right conduct she finds Isabella's words as a friend "strange" and unkind; Isabella appears selfish, regardless of everything but her own gratification; painful ideas cross Catherine's mind but she says nothing (98). Isabella's conduct with Captain Tilney is genuinely amazing; she must be acting unconsciously, Catherine is certain, because to doubt her truth or good intentions is "impossible." Yet her manner is "odd . . . How strange . . . !" (148).

*T*HE small but promising development of the artless Catherine at Bath is then, in the second stage of her career, suspended; more than suspended, it is reversed. So far as *Northanger Abbey* is one more among the unknown delights to which she brings fresh feelings, her response is the same pleasure in finding that it gives more than she asks. She goes off to it wound to the highest point of ecstasy, meeting every milestone on the way "before she expected it" (156). Its grandeur strikes her "beyond her expectation," the multiplicity and convenience of its modern offices impress her "beyond her expectations" (177, 184). Her difficulties arise not from this but from ways in which the abbey falls below what it is she wants it to be. What is "expected with solemn awe" is the glimpse of the massy wall, the ancient oaks, the high Gothic windows, and all the rest, but the low abbey with its smooth, level road will not give her the approach she desires: "She knew not that she had any right to be surprised, but there was a something in this mode of approach which she certainly had not expected"; the absence of alarm strikes her as "odd and inconsistent" (161). So when the abbey will not, again and again, meet her expectation, she begins to make it what will satisfy her. If nothing "within her observation" gives her the consciousness she desires, everything then becomes by her translation "strange" and "odd," an occasion of "surprize" and "alarm." A little reflection had been sufficient to let her know she need not allow odd John Thorpe to alarm her, but now she is seeking those very qualities and feelings, the extraordinary event or character and the extraordinary emotion. Eager to create that shape of a higher life she becomes comically like those least capable of understanding ordinary life.

What is "odd," to take that as the example, becomes significant as that which cannot be brought within the definition of a comprehensible reality. The convention of English humor that oddity is free, warm, and delightful may be one of Mrs. Elton's commonplaces (E 355, 356) but it is not Jane Austen's. Characters in Jane Austen who find things odd are usually simple-minded types. Miss Bates is persuaded there are two steps in the passage at the Crown Inn and finds but one. "How very odd!" She was convinced there were two and there is but one (E 329). Emma may be negligent of Miss Bates and most partial to Harriet, but there is little to choose between the minds of those two ladies or their words. Mr. Martin's birthday is June 8 and Harriet's is June 23, just a fortnight and a day's difference! "which is very odd!" (30). Harriet goes to Ford's shop, the main shop in Highbury, where she and the Martins always go, and there she meets them: "to be sure it was so very odd!" (178). "Things are settled so oddly," Mrs. Bennet says in allusion to the entail of the estate, "There is no knowing how estates will go when once they come to be entailed" (PP 65). Lady Bertram is induced to play an easy game of cards, made easier for her by Henry Crawford, who plays her hand entirely, and she finds it very entertaining. "A very odd game. I do not know what it is all about" (MP 240). These are all ladies who know so little of what it is all about that the simplest matter, however inconsequential or however clear, puzzles their ability to assimilate. But there is less amusement when the inability to understand becomes a weapon of the mind used by the unpleasantly dominant types to dispose of those who do not meet their narrow definitions. Fanny Price, from her arrival at Mansfield Park, is the victim of this tyranny, being only "so odd and so stupid" to Julia and Maria, who have so much information and so little self-knowledge, generosity, or humility (19); and she must face it again in Mary Crawford, who "thought her odd, or thought her any thing" rather than insensible of the pleasure of Henry's attention (278). Lady Catherine de Bourgh sweeps away the Bennet family and the domestic history of its daughters as "very strange . . . Very odd!" (PP 164–65). Elizabeth Elliot, like her father, can clear off whole groups of people not handsome enough for them, "odd-looking men walking about here, who, I am told, are sailors" (P 166). In Jane Austen's vocabulary there is an ominous sound when Emma warns Harriet against the Martins as "odd acquaintance," for it is a grave charge and when not just it tells us much of the speaker; on the same page we are shown the neat and sensible Robert Martin and Harriet's typically more inane reaction, of how "very odd" it is that they should meet, marks the much less innocent usage by Emma (E 31–32). There is a clever incomprehension in Emma that makes many people seem odd to her. Genuinely odd people, those whose character and conduct cannot be defined by reasonable expectations, especially if they have any power or responsibility, like Mrs. Churchill (E 120, 121), are capable of damaging the lives of others. Mr. Collins may be an oddity (PP 64) and remain amusing, though even he is not harmless, but to hear of Mr. Bennet in the conclusion of the first chapter that he was "so odd a mixture" is a warning the joke will not always be funny (5). Willoughby's conduct is odd, a fact that Mrs. Dashwood unfortunately cannot see (SS 81) and Marianne cannot appreciate. "How very odd!" Marianne says with disappointment when no letter arrives; to Elinor it is serious: "How odd indeed!" (165).

If Catherine at Bath had been the simple-minded innocent of undefined expectations, baffled by oddities and just beginning to understand some of them, at Northanger she becomes one who imposes her own defined expectations and thereby creates oddity; it is not an innocent foolishness, either in what it makes of others or what it makes of herself. She cultivates what is odd, strange, and mysterious because she is eager for the strong emotions they produce, for "surprize" and for the heightened surprise of "alarm."

Alarm, to take that as another example, is a response to the shape that is unexpected and uncomprehended, but it is most frequent therefore, contrary to Catherine's intended effect, in the weak-minded. "Mrs. John Knightley is easily alarmed" (E 40). It is what the daughter has in common with her invalid father; the falling of a very few flakes of snow produces in her an "alarm . . . equal to his own"; the "horror" of it—to mark the similarity of language with Catherine's experience—is "full in her imagination" and makes the road just passable for "adventurous people" (127–28). It is a debility that Mr. Woodhouse nurtures, in the magnification of trivial causes; Mrs. Weston feels foolish for having been alarmed by a ten-minute indisposition of her child, but Mr. Woodhouse commends her and only regrets that she had not sent for the apothecary: "She could not be too soon alarmed, nor send for Perry too often" (479). The "alarm" the gypsies occasion in him is the very kind of event to engage most the young and the low, to whom it is "the happiness of frightful news"; poor Mr. Woodhouse, for all his trembling, participates, in his own way, in that sort of happiness, in the pleasure of being comforted by the inquiries of his neighbors after his health and in returning the answer that he and Emma and Harriet are not well, which is not exactly true (336). Mr. Woodhouse's alarms make his own little truths and isolate him effectively, making it virtually impossible that he can ever know what is happening, making him, for all his special difficulties, easy to manipulate. Catherine courts such debility as an art.

If Catherine at Bath was the artless girl who could be deceived by others, at Northanger Abbey she becomes artful. "Well read in the art of concealing a treasure," she knows of the possibility of false linings in drawers as she searches for the manuscript (169). Building her case against the General, she is eager in questioning Eleanor, "blushing at the consummate art of her own question" (180). It would not help Catherine now to see the very coffin in which Mrs. Tilney's ashes were supposed to slumber; "Catherine had read too much" not to be perfectly aware of the ease with which a waxen figure might have been substituted (191). At Northanger Abbey Catherine is not deceived by anyone else: it is all "a voluntary, self-created delusion," in which each trifling circumstance receives importance from "an imagination resolved on alarm," and everything "forced to bend to one purpose" by a mind "craving to be frightened" (199–200). Catherine has been craving a more exciting life, Isabella's style, a grander life of extraordinary events and of emotions violently stirred. It seems to be a life of greater adventure in its oddness, strangeness, and mystery, its willingness to risk the undefined and to feel the unknown alarm. The proper name of that artful vision is "romance." Catherine is now the heroine the author has wanted from the first chapter, the heroine who has at last risen to the expected level. But life at that level of unreality, where all is forced to bend to the expectation, cannot be maintained; the return home is humiliating to the author and things happen that are "dreadfully derogatory of an heroine's dignity" (243). What is also true, however, and more dreadfully derogatory, is that "the visions of romance" (199), while they do last, do not provide the larger life they seem to offer. Romance is really rather dull.

The sad little truth about the romantic heroine is that her dignity is quite false. The adventures of the unexpected which she risks are in fact easily predicted. "This is strange indeed! I did not expect such a sight as this!—An immense heavy chest!" (163). But it is of all things just the thing she did expect; all she has seen is "a large high chest" and the transformation is her own. The artful dominance is in fact a contrived surrender of the possession of her own mind. It is a craving for the stronger sensations of alarm, but it is in fact a surrender to a weaker, simpler, and fixed form. Henry can foresee the form and the circumstantial details of the supposedly fearful experience that awaits her at

Northanger Abbey, "just like a book," not merely because the physical paraphernalia and the kind of event is standard; it is because as romantic heroine Catherine must be the passive victim of events, with a mind and emotions over which she has no control. "Unable of course to repress your curiosity . . . you will instantly," etc. If the real Catherine interjects that she will be too frightened to enter a vaulted room, he knows that there is no such possibility: "No, no, you will proceed . . . Impelled by an irresistible presentiment, you will eagerly advance . . ." (159–60). No choice is given her and she can have no moral life. A more sophisticated romantic mind, Mrs. Dashwood, for example, may feel that she is asserting herself strongly, but she too is delivering herself to an immobility. The indelicacy of Fanny Dashwood's conduct to a woman in Mrs. Dashwood's situation would have been highly unpleasing to a woman "with only common feelings"; but in Mrs. Dashwood's mind there is a sense of honor so keen, "a generosity so romantic" that "any offence of the kind, by whomsoever given or received, was to her a source of immoveable disgust" (SS 6). There is clearly a loss of freedom in that rigidity of response without regard for persons or circumstances. Mrs. Dashwood will not ask Marianne whether or not she is engaged to Willoughby because such an inquiry would be an ungenerous lack of confidence. Elinor thinks the generosity overstrained, considering Marianne's youth, as she always considers particular qualifications, but she urges her mother in vain: "common sense, common care, common prudence, were all sunk in Mrs. Dashwood's romantic delicacy" (SS 85). What is common makes larger demands upon the spirit. And it demands a more difficult art.

*T*HE review of Jane Austen written by Sir Walter Scott turns on the distinction between the romance and the novel of common life. That it was not a review of *Northanger Abbey,* which had not yet been published, but of *Emma,* and also of *Sense and Sen-*

sibility and *Pride and Prejudice,* emphasizes the general importance in her works of the opposition made explicit in *Northanger
Abbey.* Scott does not think of Jane Austen as a timid author or
an author who turns from reality because she places limits on the
kinds of incidents and characters she depicts and on the kind of
appeal she makes to the reader. Rather he thinks of her as adventurous and original and more real. He sees her as writing a new
kind of novel that is succeeding the exhaustion of the romance
and the novels derived from the romance, differing in the conduct
of narrative and in sentiments attributed to characters: "neither
alarming our credulity" nor amusing our imagination by wild
variety of incident or by extravagant characterization. The substitute for these romantic excitements, now worn out, is the art of
copying from nature "as she really exists in the common walks
of life," presenting to the reader a correct and striking representation of that which is daily taking place around him. The author
who adventures upon this task sets a special artistic problem for
himself by making obvious sacrifices and encountering peculiar
difficulties. He is not exempted from the "ordinary probabilities
of life," but places himself within the extensive range of criticism which general experience offers to every reader; furthermore,
since the obvious kind of elevation and surprise has been given
up there must be, to maintain the interest, a depth of knowledge
and dexterity of execution. It is, therefore, no mean compliment
Scott bestows upon Jane Austen when he says that "keeping close
to common incidents" and such characters as occupy the ordinary
walks of life her work has so much spirit and originality we never
miss the excitement of uncommon events or characters. She is almost alone in this, even Maria Edgeworth dealing more with
higher life and the variety of "more romantic incident," where
Jane Austen confines herself to the "middling classes." Her narratives are composed of such occurrences as may have fallen under the "observation of most folks"; and the characters conduct
themselves upon motives and principles readers may recognize

as ruling in themselves and their acquaintance. The kind of moral of her novels applies equally to "the paths of common life" (*Quarterly Review* 14 [1815]: 192–93). Scott's essay is excellent, especially valuable as testimony from an author who might not be expected to appreciate her accomplishment. He points us in the right direction but something more must be said, because though he sees Jane Austen's common life as a question of subject matter and observation, and as a question of artistry and probability, and as having moral consequence, the relationships among these are not drawn closely enough.

There is a sense, it can be well argued, in which the common life observed by Jane Austen is not more real than romance and its extraordinary incidents and emotions; these contain a kind of reality that she does not touch, in their very violence and alarm, which exercise a pleasurable and compelling power over any mind not intolerably stupid; Henry Tilney knows this well. It is also certainly true that above and below the middling classes to which she confines herself there is a reality which she does not include. Furthermore, the probability of her novels encompasses a neatness and even symmetry of shape, no loose ends, and happy endings, that are not common in life. But common life, for Jane Austen, is not simply a question of observation and of probability; these are important as they are necessary in the sort of reality which is common to all men as properly men, and for her that means men as moral beings. What is essential to moral men is the making of choices, deliberate judgments, and in her novels what is essential is that which is within the control of the characters by a reasonable, moral self-command and by a credible means. The observation and the probability have meaning within that moral order. Nothing happens that man cannot meet with his proper ethical humanity, seeing what is right and acting accordingly. What requires, for example, a specifically religious response, such as death, is excluded (though there are religious assumptions, to be noted later). The extremes of romance, the extraor-

dinary events and the characters, the alarming emotions, may or
may not exist somewhere or at some time, but the question is not
worth much consideration because it has no moral importance. It
is not merely that the events and emotions may lie outside the
experiences of most human beings but that they are outside any
meaningful response of careful observation, judgments of probabilities, moral choice. The pure or villainous characters in a romance neither have nor present any problem in doing or judging,
have only a fixed pattern that they must follow. To this sightless,
will-less pattern the reader of romance is asked to surrender his
mind.

Charlotte Heywood of *Sanditon,* in meeting Clara Brereton
"could see in her only the most perfect representation of whatever
Heroine might be most beautiful & bewitching" in the volumes
of the circulating library she has just left: "she c^d not separate the
idea of a complete Heroine from Clara Brereton." Clara's situation makes her seem placed with Lady Denham on purpose to be
ill used: such poverty and dependence joined to such beauty and
merit "seemed to leave no choice in the business." But there is no
"spirit of Romance" in Charlotte herself, a sober-minded young
lady who reads novels to supply her imagination with amusement
but is not at all unreasonably influenced by them; so while she
pleases herself for five minutes with fancying the persecution
"which *ought* to be the Lot of the interesting Clara," she finds
no reluctance to admit "from subsequent observation" that Clara
and Lady Denham appear to be on comfortable terms (MW
391–92). The limitations of this spirit, the sober mind that
uses its imagination for amusement but stops short of being
unreasonable, may well irritate another mode of mind by its
denials, but its virtue is not in the denial but in the strength that
will not permit an attractive self-deception to falsify its own
experience; it returns without reluctance to observation and
makes its beginning there; then the mind is able to separate
ideas.

Of observation then: to make a simple observation is the beginning of knowledge and of moral action and it is a more difficult and noteworthy accomplishment than anything within the powers of the romantic heroine. The temptations are always to distort the vision, to observe only as ministers to the needs of the self. Catherine at Bath had lately begun the difficult work of making observations, watching Isabella closely and trying to understand the results, disagreeable though they were. But she makes her entry to Northanger Abbey quite literally unable to see anything. What she can see is not what she expects so it strikes her as odd, and then a sudden scud of rain driving full in her face "made it impossible for her to observe any thing further." And she observes nothing further. Once within the abbey, on the same page, she finds it delightful to be there but doubts, as she looks around the room, "whether any thing within her observation" would have given her the consciousness of its being an abbey (161). It is a consciousness she makes for herself, fitting the place to her cravings and the selective vision it demands. The old black cabinet may be in a situation conspicuous enough but it does not catch her notice until the right moment: it is "the ebony cabinet which was to escape her observation at first" (168). If the form her fault takes is silly and small, the fault is not and it reappears in more interesting minds. Marianne Dashwood, Emma Woodhouse, Mary Crawford, are all skillful observers of detail systematic in seeing only pleasing preconceptions. *Mansfield Park* has many characters who are inobservant because possessed by their own needs. The powers of observation help define the special kind of suffering and virtue of Fanny Price and of the other quiet heroines, Elinor Dashwood and Anne Elliot: first, that they are superior observers in the midst of those who are blindly pursuing wrong ends, usually those with whom the heroines have deep emotional ties that affect their own happiness; second, that they cannot do much, overtly, to change what they observe; but finally, that their observations are never distorted by the pressures of their own feelings.

From observations follow inferences, most importantly the determination of probabilities, and as she has surrendered her powers of observation, Catherine has surrendered to an order of improbability. "Romantic and improbable"—the phrase is in *Udolpho,* to go no further (1794; 3: 183–84). Emily blames herself for suffering her "romantic" imagination to carry her "beyond the bounds of probability" and is determined to check its rapid flights lest they should extend into madness (3: 3–4). That extreme of improbability which is madness is not common life and not of much interest to Jane Austen, but the probability of common life is a primary and continual interest. Probability in her novels is a technical problem for the novelist because it is a moral problem; if the characters do not live among probabilities they do not live in a moral reality where they can use their own understanding to make judgments and face the consequences. The order of probability at Northanger Abbey has been imported by Catherine from romance, in which no consideration, no effort of mind or spirit is needed; the probabilities are mechanical, often produced by physical objects, to the exclusion of human choice and dominant over it. The appearance of the ebony cabinet that had escaped her observation now strikes her, makes it impossible for her not to apply herself incompetently to its locks, until in the center she finds the small door that secured "in all probability" a cavity of importance (169). The General is assimilated to the same inhuman order, in which, having formed her suspicion she regrets "the impossibility" of thinking well of a man so kindly disposed toward herself; she knows "certainly" that something is concealed by him in the room where Mrs. Tilney died, a room "in all probability" never entered by him since the dreadful scene of the death (185–86). General Tilney says he will stay awake to read pamphlets on the affairs of the nation when the family retires to bed, but Catherine knows that to be kept up for hours by stupid pamphlets is "not very likely"; there must be some deeper cause, "and the probability that Mrs. Tilney yet lived," shut up and receiving from her pitiless husband her nightly supply of coarse food, was "the conclusion which necessarily followed." The suddenness of her reputed illness, the absence of her daughter, "and probably of her other children," at the time, favors the supposition. She goes on, adding details to the "plausibility" of her conjecture, sometimes starting at the boldness of her own surmises, but finding them supported by such appearances as made their dismissal "impossible" (187–88).

That absurdity in Catherine is, again, an elementary problem, but it is, again, and as a reader of Dr. Johnson would know, a type of moral importance. The common life of man turns upon probabilities, a wide realm of many problematic parts in which the best efforts of understanding and the entire strength of character are called up. There are so many parts to be observed, judged, tested against experience, held together in a shapely integrity that makes action possible, when it is always most comfortable to find probability where one would most like it. Emma Woodhouse's easy equation of "desirable, natural, and probable" (E 35, 74) is always tempting. "Are no probabilities to be accepted, merely because they are not certainties?" This is Mrs. Dashwood (SS 78–79), in a characteristic depth of interesting confusion, because, like Marianne, her mind is bright and what she says is so often true, and usually irrelevant. Probabilities must be accepted and acted upon, and in the kind of problem she is discussing, making an early estimate of Willoughby's character, there are no certainties. But she uses the principle to make a facile judgment, not to consider probabilities but to make the probability what it is that she wants it to be; she uses it to bypass the difficulties of weighing all the evidence, in order to seize upon the one interpretation that will suit her and explain away whatever does not. But Elinor will not let desire dictate probability; it would be easy to disbelieve Lucy Steele, a woman on whose veracity Elinor has small dependence, but on serious reflection she cannot, because she sees that the story of Lucy's engagement is supported on every side by "probabilities and proofs, and contradicted by nothing but her own wishes" (SS 139).

It demands a greatness to determine a probability in spite of oneself. Elizabeth Bennet achieves it at the turning point of her life, the moment of self-knowledge, upon the receipt of Darcy's letter, which sets her a complex problem: she wants to discredit the letter entirely and for a while flatters herself that her wishes do not err. But self-command makes her read and reread with the closest attention: "She put down the letter, weighed every circumstance with what she meant to be impartiality—deliberated on the probability of each statement" (PP 205). It is a difficult process and she has little success at first; she must work at it in great detail; to be successful will mean that she must bring herself to a humiliating self-knowledge in the discovery of how her self-flattery has meanly distorted her sight. It requires "giving way to every variety of thought; re-considering events, determining probabilities" and reconciling herself as well as she can to the change (209). To take all of a history into account, all the evidence, adjust all the parts to an understanding of the whole, and judge it rightly asks for magnanimity. There is a special poignancy when Sir Thomas Bertram calls on Fanny to be fair to Mrs. Norris; he thinks too well of Fanny to suppose that she will harbor resentment; her understanding will prevent her from receiving things only in part and judging partially by the event. "—You will take in the whole of the past, you will consider times, persons, and probabilities," and will feel that Mrs. Norris was a friend who meant kindly (MP 313). He is right in principle, and he is right in his estimate of Fanny, but only Fanny knows how wrong he is about Mrs. Norris and how much more he is demanding of herself than he realizes. It is a critical moment in *Mansfield Park* which we will return to.

*T*o take in the whole, to make the observations, determine the probabilities, is what the romantic heroine at Northanger Abbey can never do, whose artfulness reduces the expectation of life to the one wished-for shape. But then neither can the artless girl at Bath whose unfixed expectations leave all shapeless. What she needs is an adequate art, a moral art, an art of common life. What she needs is a capable teacher.

It is the "master of the ceremonies" in the Lower Rooms at Bath who introduces him to her and the value and spirit of that excellent young clergyman she then dances with are apparent in the way he improves the formal opportunity (25). He takes the ceremonies of Bath, an artifice of prescribed behavior, and by making fun of their artificiality he infuses them with grace and converts them to a happy reality, the beginning of a mutual knowledge between himself and his partner. Henry knows how to use art. He dances so well, as Catherine says in her artless exclamation; he drives a horse so well, so quietly, without any parade, without any of John Thorpe's proclamations of a peculiar judicious manner and singular dexterity; and then his hat sits so well and the innumerable capes of his great coat look so becomingly important (72, 157). It takes Catherine a while to appreciate that easy command of art. In their first meeting she finds an archness and pleasantry in his manner which interests though it is hardly understood by her. As he mocks the social artifices—forming his features in a set smile, affectedly softening his voice, saying the set words, pretending surprise at her responses, and then resuming his natural voice, and then returning to the fixed style of "exactly what you will say" and "what you ought to say"—Catherine tries not to laugh or does not know whether she may venture to laugh (25–26). As with so much else in Bath, she does not know how to define what he is doing: he is strange, odd, surprising. The grave way in which he immediately catches and adopts Mrs. Allen's interest in muslins draws her out: " 'How can you,' said Catherine, laughing, 'be so—' she had almost said, strange" (28). She is a little afraid, too, as she listens to him indulging himself in the foibles of Mrs. Allen. At times (113–14) she needs the help of an interpreter in his gentle sister: "Miss Morland is not used to your odd ways," Eleanor says. But Catherine does not require too much reassurance that Henry can never be wrong: "His manner might sometimes surprize, but his meaning must always be just," and she is ready to admire even when she does not understand. The understanding comes because Henry is an excellent teacher; he teaches her the meanings of words, what is really "amazing," what is really "nice," what it is really to "instruct" when Catherine has always thought instruction synonymous with "torment." To teach her to use words with propriety and correctness is to make her see herself and others properly and correctly, to understand the meaning of conduct. The strangeness, oddity, surprise, which elsewhere mark the limits of Catherine's understanding, by her unfixed or by her false expectations, are here the manner of Henry's instruction. Henry knows their proper uses. He uses them as instruments of art, to engage her mind, interest it, shake it, and extend her understanding of just meaning. He uses them to teach her the difficult art of common life.

Catherine cannot understand the actions of others because she does not even know that there is an art to be learned. "How very little trouble it can give you to understand the motive of other people's actions," Henry says. She has just assumed that Captain Tilney's desire to dance with Isabella is very good-natured: seeing her sitting down he fancied she might wish for a partner. "With you," Henry says, "it is not, How is such a one likely to be influenced? What is the inducement most likely to act upon such a person's feelings, age, situation, and probable habits of life considered?—but, how should *I* be influenced, what would be *my* inducement in acting so and so?" Catherine does not understand him. He has begun with a smile and he makes it explicit that it is her own superior good nature that is at work. That promising artless goodness needs the instruction he is offering in the complexities of judgment, in persons and times, in probabilities and surprise. Catherine cannot think how it can happen that Isabella and Captain Tilney are dancing, her friend having been so determined not to dance and, she adds, Henry's brother having been told that Isabella is engaged. "I cannot take surprize to myself on that head," Henry answers. "You bid me be surprized on your friend's account, and therefore I am; but as for my brother, his conduct in the business, I must own, has been no more than I believed him perfectly equal to" (132–33). The lesson is helpful and delicately put; he can speak as an authority on his own brother, and even as he refers to her as an authority on Isabella, he tries to make her understand, gently and wittily, that her surprise should be a warning of what she does not know of her friend.

When she perceives the oddity and strangeness in Isabella's conduct it is a perception that is valuable; it comes neither from a weakness nor from an inability to understand anything that does not fit the measure of one's own mind but from a perception of an inconsistency in what is observed; and it is a spur to the better observation that teaches. Catherine cannot make a connection between Isabella's motive and Isabella's conduct and thinks her friend must be acting unconsciously; but now she cannot help watching closely. "The result of her observations was not agreeable" (149). She sees in private a change of manners so trifling that it might have passed unnoticed, she sees in public an alteration too positive to be passed over. What can be meant by all this is still beyond her comprehension, but her concern for Isabella's conduct, for James, for Captain Tilney, leads her to ask questions of Henry. His answers lead her to make distinctions she has never made: is it his brother's attentions or Isabella's admission of them that gives pain? " 'Is not it the same thing?' 'I think Mr. Morland would acknowledge a difference.' . . . Catherine blushed for her friend." That connection between the observed oddity and the moral judgment is beginning. It is her innocence that makes her go directly to the point of that connection, to the question of meaning of conduct. "But what can your brother mean? If he knows her engagement, what can he mean by his behavior?" "You are a very close questioner." It is a questioning of a sort which a skilled teacher can turn to the best account by making the pupil the self-teacher, not by giving answers but by guiding the questions. "To be guided by second-hand conjecture is pitiful. The premises are before you" (151–52). One of Catherine's premises is still wrong—she has no doubt of the mutual attachment of her brother and her friend—but we see her on the road to an understanding of a real problem of common life.

This is the progress that is interrupted when she enters Northanger Abbey and takes for herself the character of the romantic heroine; her mistakes, while she remains in this condition, are not open to correction, because they are systematically fixed. The blush for one mistake does not prepare her to avoid the next. "Could not the adventure of the chest have taught her wisdom?" have saved her from the humbling adventure of the cabinet? It could not because as long as she maintains her romantic expectation only one kind of experience is possible. "How could she have so imposed on herself?" (173). The question can do her no good until the spell is broken. The end of the self-deception can come, therefore, not by a gradual process but only by the sudden end of the visions of romance.

Our hopes for her are carefully sustained by the novelist, who relieves the succession of misadventures by reminders of the potential Catherine. It is just after the absurdity of the hidden

manuscript that, in one of the more charming passages in Jane
Austen, Catherine's desire to get rid of that subject leads her to
make an announcement: "I have just learnt to love a hyacinth."
It is the Catherine we want to see more of. Certainly Henry does:
"And how might you learn?—By accident or argument?" If it
is Catherine the answer can only be that she was taught: "Your
sister taught me; I cannot tell how" (174). This is the same
Catherine who was introduced as a child in the first chapter with
the information that "She never could learn or understand any
thing before she was taught; and sometimes not even then"
(14). This is a heroine with very little in the way of natural
advantages, often inattentive, occasionally stupid, and, in this
instance, naturally indifferent about flowers. Nothing comes easy
for her and to love a hyacinth is a very little advance, but, as
Henry says, so much the better. "And though the love of a
hyacinth may be rather domestic, who can tell, the sentiment once
raised, but you may in time come to love a rose?" He is pleased.
"The mere habit of learning to love is the thing; and a teach-
ableness of disposition in a young lady is a great blessing" (174).
This is Catherine's one gift and it is one she seems to be for-
saking for romance.

The end of romance requires a special surprise, an ironic
fulfillment and reversal of her expectations, to bring Catherine
out of her delusions. It happens as she moves from the observation of Mrs. Tilney's portrait, which partially justifies her "expectations," to Mrs. Tilney's room. Her first attempt to see the
room is interrupted, to her terror, by the General, and she runs
for safety to lock herself in her own room, "expecting a sum-
mons" from the angry General. None arrives, however, and she
makes her second attempt, to get it over before the return of
Henry, "who was expected on the morrow." She is successful
and beholds what fixes her on the spot and agitates every feature—a handsome and bright modern room. "Catherine had expected to have her feelings worked, and worked they were," but

the feelings are astonishment, doubt, and then, added by a ray
of common sense, shame (191–93). It is a gross mistake she
has made, more serious in its object, more elaborate and longer
in preparation in her mind than her previous miscalculations at
the abbey, more shaming in its discovery, climactic. But that it
is the final mistake, the end of a chapter in her life that will
not be repeated, is assured only by a sudden appearance; this
time it is not her own heart only that is privy to her folly, because she hears footsteps that make her tremble. The romantic
heroine, "She had no power to move." The romantic heroine,
with "a feeling of terror not very definable" she "fixed her eyes"
on the staircase—which gave to her view not the expected General but the unexpected Henry. The romantic heroine, she exclaims in a voice of "more than common astonishment," and
the measure of the moment is that he too is "greatly surprized."
"I am afraid I alarmed you," he says, which is an accurate statement and embarrassingly more accurate than he yet knows because the causeless terror that has moved her is more dreadful
than he knows. All the romantic forces she has set in motion,
by her expectation, surprise, alarm, have gathered to a point and
are now reversed upon her. Henry's lesson is impressive not only
by its substance but by the way he makes his discovery of what
has been going on in her mind blinded by false observations and
absurd possibilities: "looking in her countenance," "earnestly
regarding her," "closely observed her." His questions elicit the
circumstances that have drawn her to Mrs. Tilney's room, including what had been a probability of her own devising and is
now simply offered by her as a fact—that none of the children
were at home when their mother died suddenly. And from these
circumstances, he replies—"his quick eye fixed on her's"—
" 'you infer perhaps the probability of some negligence . . . of
something still less pardonable.' " Catherine raises her eyes
toward him more fully than she has ever done before, and the
force of what he then has to say is addressed directly into those

waiting eyes. It consists of a few clinical facts about Mrs. Tilney's illness, and of the fact that he and his brother were both at home and "from our own observation" can bear witness to the excellent attentions Mrs. Tilney received. The only horror has been the formation of Catherine's mind. "What have you been judging from?" Henry asks. "Remember the country and the age in which we live. Remember that we are English, that we are Christians" (194–97). Catherine is listening and learning and we should not be so foolish as to misunderstand what he is saying.

The subject matter of the novel of common life is the ordinary occurrence, taken from what is open to the observation and understanding of most people, with characters acting on motives and principles readers can recognize, because that is the realm in which man leads his moral life by making choices. In one sense, what constitutes an ordinary occurrence will change from age to age or place to place; the Advertisement to *Northanger Abbey* entreats the public to bear in mind that thirteen years have passed since the work was finished and many more since it was begun, and that during that period places, manners, books, and opinions have undergone considerable changes (12); in that sense of everyday subject matter, common life changes and Jane Austen's is not ours. But that difference does not change what is for her the unchangeable point about common life, that it is always the locus and the moment of daily and ordinary moral life. Henry's admonition to Catherine, which may seem terribly parochial, or even blindly self-satisfied, as though a happy exemption from serious moral problems were granted God's Englishmen, is, rather, an active direction that she rouse herself to the reality of moral problems. It is she who has been blind, not seeing what is before her, unable to make judgments; she has imposed a single mode of explanation upon her experience, deriving it not from the complexities of the life around her but from a much simpler fiction, out of time and space, requiring no effort. Henry directs her to remember where and when she lives. His insistence is that she use her mind and her faculties for fullest understanding. "Consult your own understanding, your own sense of the probable, your own observation of what is passing around you" (197). The works of Mrs. Radcliffe and even of her imitators are charming, Catherine now knows, but it is not in them perhaps that human nature "at least in the midland countries of England" is to be looked for. She has learned her lesson so well that she is not prepared to generalize beyond her limited experience. For all she knows Mrs. Radcliffe may be right about the Alps and Pyrenees: "Catherine dared not doubt beyond her own country, and even of that, if hard pressed, would have yielded the northern and western extremities"; but it is in the "central part of England" that she lives. Catherine is one step on in life, still comically limited in what she knows, but the note of the "midland" counties and the "central part," and the yielding of the "extremities" is an insistence on that common area where the moral life of humanity proceeds. In that central part moral problems must be met by human means and cannot be created or put aside by simple mechanical devices. In the same mode, and more significantly, at the extremes there are, perhaps, no mixed characters, and those who are not spotless as an angel may have the dispositions of fiends; but in England, where she must live, it is not so, and there she must be prepared for "a general though unequal mixture of good and bad" (200). The inequality of the mixture demands a fully awakened mind to make the distinctions and judgments necessary. When Jane Austen said of novels that pictures of perfection made her sick and wicked she meant just what she said (L 486–87). Pictures of perfection are more than insipid, are immoral because they falsify that central, common life of man.

Was Jane Austen concerned that a parson's young daughter from Wiltshire really might think she was a romantic heroine? Not more perhaps than Cervantes was concerned that an elderly hidalgo of La Mancha really might think he was a knight errant. But, like Cervantes, she probably was concerned that authors really might go on writing romances, as though they were greater or more interesting than common life. For her, common life is of universal interest because to live it in the proper way is the proper goal of all men. Their successes and failures vary as their qualities of mind and feeling, as their dispositions and educations, so that none is without interest. None is incapable and none is relieved of responsibility. But then to live beautifully in common life is what very few spirits can do and theirs becomes an extraordinarily interesting achievement. Young Catherine is not yet one of those great heroines, facing as she does only modest challenges and gaining only a modest success, but there are really not many who can learn as much as she in her brief time. Not many can do properly what all men should properly do. To live well in common life is uncommon. That is a simple paradox, hard to learn, and the next step for Catherine.

$\mathcal{T}$HE visions of romance were over. Catherine was completely awakened" (199). That is the end of the second stage of her story. It is a weakness of the novel that the episodes at Northanger Abbey are, unavoidably, inferior to the episodes at Bath, as Catherine is occupied by lesser problems; nor are the causal connections between the reading at Bath under Isabella's guidance and the mischief at the Abbey well established and they must be supplemented by some patching. But the retrogressive movement of the heroine's mind and its resultant shock, handled so much better in the later novels, is the necessary awakening for her progress. "The anxieties of common life began soon to succeed to the alarms of romance" (201). That is the beginning of the third stage of Catherine's story, and it is the conquest of her own delusion which she has just made under Henry's teaching that enables her, with the same help, to make her next and more important advance.

The line of action that had begun with Isabella is resumed but it is resumed by a Catherine who is now a better learner. The absence of a letter from Bath had been a subject of discussion between her and Henry in her moment of shame; then it had been introduced by him only as a tactical diversion, but in such a way as to remind us that Catherine has another unresolved misunderstanding and that it too is the problem of a mind laboring in false expectations and a related weak grasp of meanings. She has had no letter, "and I am very much surprized. Isabella promised so faithfully to write directly." Henry picks up the misuse of words in what seems a rather pedantic way, especially at such a moment. "Promised so faithfully!—A faithful promise!—That puzzles me.—I have heard of a faithful performance. But a faithful promise—the fidelity of promising!" But the point is that the missing faithfulness that has surprised her doesn't exist, either as a real quality in Isabella or in accurate usage. Moreover, he adds, it is a power little worth knowing since it can deceive and pain her (195–96). The end of the deceit by Isabella follows the end of Catherine's self-delusion. When she resumes her action in common life she is still confident (though in more accurate language) of Isabella's scrupulous performance in fulfilling a promise, which makes the nonappearance of the letter "so particularly strange" (201). The letter from James with the tale of Isabella's deceit, and James's warning to Catherine to beware how she gives her own heart, follows directly upon the tears of shame in her first discovery; and it produces an equally valuable self-questioning administered to her by Henry.

Her initial attempt at not revealing the contents of the letter—and then, before she gives it to Henry, her hesitating to do so, as she recollects with a blush James's warning to herself—and then her blushing again that she had blushed before—are all in the best manner of Catherine's artlessness. The direct contrast with Isabella, produced by the immediate situation, is now of immediate interest to the family at Northanger. If Isabella is to marry Captain Tilney, Eleanor must prepare herself, Henry says, for such a sister-in-law as she must delight in: "—Open, candid, artless, guileless, with affections strong but simple, forming no pretensions, and knowing no disguise." Catherine, a moment ago so afraid that Henry will see a personal application in James's reference to her heart, is innocently oblivious, but Eleanor, with Catherine before her, smiles in acknowledgment that such a sister-in-law she should delight in. Catherine still does not understand the mistake she has made in Isabella's character and it is only Henry's quiet pressure that makes her realize, by her own reflection, that her friend is unprincipled. It is something of a crisis for her: "I never was so deceived in any one's character in my life before." If Catherine has been deceived by a false art there is a better art that can teach her more truly: "Among all the great variety that you have known and studied," Henry responds, always with that right degree of insistent irony; he recognizes that the exclamation for all its artlessness has a pretense to experience, in its extravagance and romantic turn of phrase (206). Catherine's experience has been limited and it is not in the reading she has done, as she has realized earlier in this chapter, that a knowledge of human nature is to be looked for. What she learns now, as far as her limits will allow, is the lesson not of a romance but of a novel, "in which the most thorough knowledge of human nature, the happiest delineation of its varieties, the liveliest effusions of wit and humour are conveyed to the world in the best chosen language" (38). She is made to have a more thorough knowledge of human nature, to understand she is only beginning to see its varieties, to learn this from an instructor of lively wit and humor, and one who insists on the best-chosen language.

The very next thing he does is make Catherine, by choosing her language, understand more of herself. She must define what it is she is suffering at the moment in the realization of Isabella's deceit: "You feel, I suppose, that, in losing Isabella, you lose half yourself: you feel a void in your heart which nothing else can occupy. Society is becoming irksome; and as for the amusements in which you were wont to share at Bath, the very idea of them without her is abhorrent." As he goes on with this language, its set phrases, its extravagances, its romance-like and Isabella-like manner, he is forcing Catherine to examine honestly and precisely what it is she does in fact feel. "You feel all this?" Catherine takes him quite seriously, as she should, because for her it is a real question; it requires a few moments' reflection before she says wonderfully, "No . . . I do not—ought I?" The truth comes slowly but exactly: "To say the truth"—no mere formula, she means just what she says—"though I am hurt and grieved, that I cannot still love her, that I am never to hear from her, perhaps never to see her again, I do not feel so very, very much afflicted as one would have thought" (207). The need for the "very, very" in the attempt to locate the degree of affliction is still the language of a young girl, but the careful distinction of the "hurt and grieved," and the location of their causes, from the "afflicted" is excellent. The language is chosen ("*Affliction* is much stronger than *grief,* it lies deeper in the soul, and arises from a more powerful cause," etc. George Crabb, *English Synonymes,* 1816, p. 56); the choice has required not only feeling, because Catherine's feelings have always been good, but refinement of feeling, reflection, self-examination, an important moral effort, a beginning of maturity. Henry's compliment and encouragement are earnest and to the point. "You feel, as you always do, what is most to the credit of human nature.—Such feelings ought to be investigated, that they may know themselves." Catherine, "by some chance or other," finds her spirits relieved by the conversation; not chance but art, Henry's and the beginning of her own, has produced the effect (207).

The confirmation follows a few days later, when the letter from Isabella finally does come, though now both its appearance and its content make it "very unexpected." Catherine can now handle an unexpectedness of this sort which originates not in her own false impositions but in Isabella's. Captain Tilney has left her, Isabella writes, though he had been "amazingly" disposed to follow her, the greatest coxcomb she ever saw, "amazingly" disagreeable, and so forth, in a series of familiar words designed to make Catherine the instrument in repairing the engagement with James. There is no chance of it. "Such a strain of shallow artifice could not impose even upon Catherine." Isabella has never had any art. She has thought of herself as exercising power, but except for her brief dominance over the innocent Morlands, brother and sister, she has never had any power; it was Captain Tilney who played with her in her ignorance, for though he may be now, as she says, the last man whose word she would take, she once had swallowed it whole; and even with the Morlands her foolish devices were self-defeating. As Catherine reads the letter its "inconsistencies, contradictions, and falsehood, struck her from the very first." Isabella has not changed in any way, because the same lying artifice has been apparent in her words to Catherine "from the very first." Isabella can never change, can never respond to a different situation with a different letter. It is Catherine who has learned a little of art and who is now ashamed of Isabella and ashamed of having ever loved her. "So much for Isabella," she says, putting a term to that intimacy and that part of her life. "She must think me an idiot, or she could not have written so." It is only fair to Isabella to say that she would not have been so wrong a few weeks ago, but, as Catherine says rightly, "perhaps this has served to make her character better known to me than mine is to her" (216–18).

$\mathcal{C}$ATHERINE'S story might have ended there. Having learned her lesson of the delusions of romance and having graduated to her lesson of the deceptions of common life, she would seem to have completed the course set for her when she departed from home. Her defeated author who wanted to write a romance about her has been superseded by the novelist of common life whose instrument has been Henry and whose superior art has made the whole. Expectations have been revised, turned from the strangeness of surprise to the understanding of probabilities. Now, when there is a noise in the night of something close to Catherine's door, a slight motion of the lock that proves some hand must be on it, she may tremble a little but is resolved not to be again overcome by trivial appearances of alarm or a raised imagination. She steps quietly forward and opens the door. And she finds a surprise.

It appears at first to be Eleanor's distress, and for the first time we see Catherine administering to another, giving attention and affectionate solicitude, able to reverse roles with someone to whose superiority she has been indebted (222–23). The greater distress is to be her own, however, in the unlooked for return of that General whom she had formerly expected to find everywhere. His action suspends every hope, "every expectation" from Henry, at least for an unknown period, and this was a real expectation. Now something genuinely incomprehensible and hurtful has occurred to her. "From what it could arise, and where it would end, were considerations of equal perplexity and alarm." That is a real alarm, something beyond the possibility of present understanding. It leaves her, as on her first arrival in the same room, to a night of agitated spirits and unquiet slumbers, but now the source of her inquietude is mournfully superior in "reality and substance." Her anxiety has "foundation in fact," her fears "in probability." Her mind is now occupied in contemplating an actual and natural evil, leaving no opportunity for the self-induced emotions; though the wind is high and often produces "strange and sudden noises," she hears it without curiosity or terror (226–27). What has happened to Catherine in her last trial is something new. Having been deceived by Isabella, in her ignorance of common life, having then been willfully self-deluded in her romantic scenes at Northanger Abbey, she has now innocently and involuntarily become a cause of delusion in the General, who makes her his victim. She is ejected alone into the world by a tyrant who separates her from the man she loves, for no apparent reason. It seems very romantic, but to read the ending as a glimpse of the violence lurking below the surface, a rebuke to the complacent expectations of common life, a vindication of imagination, etc., misses the point. The point is more simple, that the event only seems romantic, and more complex, that Catherine, without knowing what it is, must face it with the resources of common life. She never has understood the General and he is just the man to put her to this test.

When Mr. and Mrs. Morland hear how the General has forced Catherine on her long and lonely journey it does not make them suffer "any romantic alarm," but they see that he has certainly acted without honor or feeling for no known reason and "he must be a very strange man," "he must be a very odd man" (234, 237). He *is* an odd man, and Catherine has had much opportunity to see this. She has even heard him try to explain why "it may seem very odd" that he acts as though money interested him; but with her mind occupied, as it is in the same conversation, with how "odd" it is that he takes a walk in the morning (176, 177), and as it has been and continues to be occupied by the various other oddities of her own creation, her romantic vision never allows her to see the reality. She wrongs him by her horrid suspicions and she allows him liberal virtues he never has. When she learns why he has acted so badly to her she feels that in suspecting him of murdering or of shutting up his wife she has scarcely sinned against his character or magnified his cruelty; but if her pique is understandable she is still comically mistaken, because he has never been a grand character in any sense, and her ejection has been a bit of poetic justice for her. The explanation for the General's strange conduct, before and after, is not romantic, for the General is a mean-minded little man, common enough in common life. He is misled by James Thorpe because, for all the differences in outward appearance, he is much like Thorpe. He has an air of dignity and politeness at the opposite extreme from Thorpe's manner, but, like Thorpe's, the manner is always a false art and, like his, it always makes Catherine feel uncomfortable; she ought to have examined that feeling more. He does not tamper with clocks as Thorpe does, to make them say what he wants, and on the contrary insists on the strictest punctuality; but that opposite extreme is again a force he uses to shape life to his own desires at the expense of others, dictating to the quarter-hour when, as he says to Henry, "you may expect us" (210). He is a man incapable of meeting a surprise, a ready victim of Thorpe's exaggerations because they meet or upset his own expectations. He seems so strong, dominant, he seems to Catherine such an overwhelming figure, but he is as weak as herself in her most foolish romantic delusion, both in understanding and in feeling; if she is grossly mistaken in her calculation (193), he is hurried on by false calculations (246); and if the result for her is terror (194), he is not less terrified (246). Both are their own victims.

What the odd General does, then, in maltreating Catherine, is to act like a rigid romantic character. The last lesson of the novelist's art for her is that probabilities produce surprises; and that though strange things can be accounted for, common life will always be presenting what is never expected, when the strange moment must be met before it is understood. It is good that this moment happens to Catherine and forces her to act as she never has before. "It is always good for young people to be put upon exerting themselves," her mother says (234). The conquest of romance Catherine made at Northanger Abbey then helped her to understand Isabella as a problem in common life; now it makes her capable of facing in common life the seemingly romantic difficulties of the conclusion. She does the best she can in this new reality and substance, fact, probability, actual and natural evil. Her return to Fullerton in the hack post chaise is the humiliation of her author but for the family a time of joyful love that awakens the best feelings of Catherine's heart: she finds herself soothed "beyond any thing she had believed possible" (233), so that unknown sources of happiness, too, are forthcoming from the experience. But family love and self-sufficiency have their limits, too; in accounting for the cause of her distress her parents do not think of her heart, which for parents of a young lady of seventeen, just returned from her first excursion, "was odd enough!" (235). Catherine must do what she can by herself and what she must do is solve a problem in the moral art of common life. The first thing she must do is write a letter, to Eleanor Tilney. She has been treated with insolence in her dismissal and rightly and strongly feels the injustice; but she also feels that in her departure she has been cold and has not valued Eleanor's merits and kindness. Never had it been harder for her to write than in addressing Eleanor. "To compose a letter which might at once do justice to her sentiments and her situation, convey gratitude without servile regret, be guarded without coldness, and honest without resentment—a letter which Eleanor might not be pained by the perusal of—and, above all, which she might not blush herself, if Henry should chance to see," is a frightening difficulty. If she is not yet up to it she does determine sensibly, "after long thought and much perplexity" to be brief and affectionate (235–36). The art needed to compose that letter must find the controlled form that will do justice to the complexity of the sentiments of this young woman in this situation; it must find the right way between a series of closely related but critically different moral qualities, the proper words. That Catherine sees what ought to be done, and concludes by doing well what it is she can do toward the end, is a Catherine as close to maturity as we can expect or will see.

The accomplishment is still a small one, Catherine is still

young, she has not yet attained a happy control of herself, the novel must cut things short. But she has learned well of Henry and she has earned him, and so he comes to her. If Henry's affection originated in nothing better than gratitude—a persuasion of her partiality for him had been the only cause of his giving her a serious thought—that is "a new circumstance in romance" and dreadfully derogatory of a heroine's dignity, "but if it be as new in common life," we are told, "the credit of a wild imagination will at least be all my own" (243). But it has been the designing imagination of a novelist that has promoted the heroine to a new dignity.

3

The Sensibility of Marianne and the Exertion of Elinor Dashwood

"Sweet SENSIBILITY! . . ." said Hannah More,

> Thy subtile essence still eludes the chains
> Of Definition, and defeats her pains. . . .
> To those who know thee not, no words can paint,
> And those who know thee, know all words are faint!
>   ("Sensibility," in *Sacred Drama*, 1782, p. 282)

Sensibility interested Jane Austen from her earliest work to her last. It is a lingering affliction of some of her silliest creatures: Sir Edward Denham of *Sanditon,* we have seen, is still playing the Man of Feeling who must, in a tone of great Taste and Feeling, run with energy through all the usual phrases "descriptive of the *undescribable* Emotions" excited in the Mind of Sensibility (MW 396). That a sensibility is indefinable and its emotions indescribable is of the subtile essence, for a defining shape would be a limitation upon its liberated energies; would be the imposition of a conventional form upon higher feelings and conduct that are not to be contained by art; would be the clog of a mediating process upon what is natural, instinctive, swift.

An unbounded sensibility is the more fully alive, completely and instantly open to refinements of feeling, ecstasies or sufferings, that do not touch other minds. It sees itself as powerful, free, generous. To Jane Austen it was of special interest as a carefully cultivated loss of control. Her best burlesque of it is in "Love and Freindship," which the heroine opens with a list of her own "Perfections" of person and of mind, every accomplishment and every virtue: "A sensibility too tremblingly alive to every affliction of my Freinds, my Acquaintance and particularly to every affliction of my own, was my only fault, if a fault it could be called" (MW 78). Such a ready instrument of self-appreciation offers quick opportunities for contempt of others who lack "that interesting Sensibility" and its ritual language and gestures, the members of "that Inferior order of Beings with Regard to Delicate Feelings, tender Sentiments, and refined Sensibility" (82–84). In this mode all problems, whether of judgment or action, are solved because there are no parts of the mind, or of the body for that matter, that can come into conflict in a system that has only one part. "She was all Sensibility and Feeling" (85). Mind and body are wholly abandoned to the overpowering force: "a Blow to our Gentle Sensibility—we could not support it—we could only faint" (89). "But never shall I be able so far to conquer my tender sensibility as to . . . ," as to take any action whatever that may put an end to the pleasant suffering it entails; rather every slightest occasion is absurdly twisted to increase the wound (97–98).

Transparently this kind of sensibility is, at every point, the reverse of what it claims to be. It sees and feels not more but less, because it is conventional, selfish, and weak. What is offered as natural and instinctive is a conduct learned from books and the product of a most elaborated art. The claim of freedom from ordinary social forms is resolved into a limited set of automatic responses. The claim of living by a higher law becomes actions according to a lower law. The vulnerability to suffering is not merely compensated by self-approval but overpaid by an imposition of the self upon others and a taking from them. In "Love and Freindship" this form of taking is simple robbery. "Whether it was from this circumstance, of its being easily taken, or from a wish of being independant, or from an excess of Sensibility (for which we were always remarkable) I cannot now determine, but certain it is that when we had reached our 15th year, we took the Nine Hundred Pounds and ran away" (MW 107). Sensibility is available therefore to more consciously selfish people as a simple disguise under which they can attain their own ends at the expense of others. It is one of the weapons in the battle plans of Lady Susan, who declares that she is going to win her sister-in-law's heart through a pretense of emotion for that lady's children: "I . . . am going to attach myself with the greatest sensibility to one in particular . . ." (MW 250). Emma Watson is distressed by the languishing tone of voice with which her sister Margaret says things designed to please, and she doesn't like it any better when she hears that Margaret has also another voice, a sharp quick accent totally unlike the first, with which Margaret says the unpleasant things she really means: the last is her common voice, the other her "tone of artificial Sensibility" (MW 351).

The other fact to be noted is that Henry Tilney, Mr. Knightley, Jane Fairfax, Fanny Price, Jane Bennet, Anne Elliot, are all of them, explicitly, men and women of a sensibility that is "real," "strong," "great." If there is a false sensibility that is vain and reductive there is also a true one, unpretentious and valuable. It is the "real sensibility" of Henry Tilney when he meets Catherine's mother (NA 241): he is embarrassed, he apologizes for his presence, because he acknowledges that after what has happened, Catherine's eviction from Northanger, he has little right to expect a welcome; the sensibility here is a feeling recognition of the rightful claims of others and of one's own responsibilities. The mark of this sensibility is a heightened perception of feelings in a complex social moment and it is accompanied by a moral response, an increase in life. Believing Emma to have been badly hurt by Frank Churchill, Mr. Knightley comes to her, with no selfish view but endeavoring to soothe and counsel, draws her arm within his, presses it against his heart, and speaks low "in a tone of great sensibility" (E 425). With an affectionate heart and a strong desire of doing right, Fanny Price has, as Edmund sees early, "great sensibility of her situation" (MP 17); hers is a difficult situation that makes difficult demands on the heart and desire. Hers is a sensibility which, when he can see it, increases her value in Henry Crawford's eyes. When he sees the meeting with William, sees her glow, brightness, absorption in an affection for another, he understands her better: the "sensibility" beautifies and illuminates her; he no longer doubts the capabilities of her heart, he knows she has feeling, genuine feeling, and he knows it would be something to be loved by such a girl (235).

In such people as these the sensibility is an accession of strength. It does not render them feebler, self-concerned and disabled for action, but makes them larger human beings, alive to more, capable of loving more fully because more understanding of others, able to do more when the need is there. This is possible only with people who are not "all sensibility," or possessed of an excess of sensibility, but who are complete in character and possessed of sensibility among other and coordinate qualities. Mr. Knightley speaking low in a tone of great sensibility is authentic because we already know that there is nothing faint in him, and that he is capable of speaking quite loudly when he sees occasion, quite able to drown out someone else's voice if necessary. His own qualities enable him to judge a virtue in Jane Fairfax. She has feeling, he says, "Her sensibilities, I suspect, are strong—and her temper excellent in its power of forbearance, patience, self-controul" (E 289), and the thing to notice in this short and pointed description is that both the sensibilities and the controls have strength and power. This real sensibility is neither a weakness to be compensated by a more active virtue nor an excess in need of a curb.

$\mathscr{I}$N looking, then, at *Sense and Sensibility,* we should be surprised to find that sensibility, or any strong feeling simply because it is strong feeling, is an object of attack; or that Marianne Dashwood, if she is a character of sensibility, is for that reason an object for unfavorable comparison with a sister who is better for being free of sensibility. The failure of the novel is Edward and that affects the representation of Elinor, but Elinor's feelings are no less than Marianne's, as the entire novel insists, and as the choice of words emphasizes at key moments. Elinor is "sensible" in more than one sense. At the conclusion of Volume I she is informed by Lucy Steele that Edward and Lucy are engaged and the effect is devastating, an emotion and distress beyond anything she has ever felt before. It takes a while before she is convinced, because Lucy is not trustworthy and Elinor is certain of Edward's love; therefore as she learns the truth, step by step, the effect upon her is all the greater by her very strength of mind and therefore she is "most feelingly sensible" of every fresh circumstance that favors Lucy's veracity (134). And again, near the beginning of the third volume, when Colonel Brandon commissions Elinor to present Edward with the offer that will seal her own unhappiness, she must say, with complete honesty and necessary irony, "I feel the goodness of Colonel Brandon most sensibly" (285). So the meaning of sensibility is determined by its quality, by the occasions that call it forth, its relationship to the whole character, its effects upon other people. Robert Ferrars has "his own sensibility" (298–99), which makes him pity his brother for the engagement to Lucy, but it is as affected and ridiculous and contemptible as the man. When he himself later marries Lucy his sister Fanny suffers "agonies of sensibility" (371), but as hers is all selfishness it is a comic suffering that can give us only pleasure.

There is an additional pleasure in those last words, coming at the end of the novel, because they are then familiar to us and have a certain flavor from our knowledge of Marianne's career. They are also reflexive, now that Marianne has come so far from her starting point, and increase our affection for her while sharpening our judgment upon her serious errors. We never take the same sort of pleasure in Marianne's sufferings, because at their most painful times they are real, with deep causes and consequences, because she has been betrayed, and especially because we always feel that she is worthy of a better fate. But she is worthy because there are better qualities in her than those that chiefly move her, and there is often amusement in watching her when she is no one's victim but her own. The abilities of mind and goodness of heart are a potential that she misuses. The "excess of . . . sensibility" (7) that we meet in the first chapter will not lead her to the absurdity of stealing nine hundred pounds from her own family, but it will impose moral problems for which her own family will have to pay and it will often be comic. The excess, the lack of moderation, the lack of prudence, is a deliberate moral choice, and a choice of weakness. Mrs. Dashwood values and cherishes that excess in her daughter and they encourage one another in the "violence" of their affliction upon the loss they must face in that first chapter; the "agony of grief" that their sensibility entails overpowers them and is voluntarily renewed, sought for, created again and again; they give themselves to it and resolve against admitting consolation. This early loss and Marianne's reaction, contrasted with Elinor's reaction to the same event, which also afflicts her deeply, give us in the first chapter a short preview of the main action; and our later responses to Marianne's agonies of sensibility are prepared by it. When she later "almost screamed with agony" at Willoughby's desertion (182), she has a much greater cause for her reaction, and Elinor too has just given way to a burst of tears which at first was scarcely less violent than Marianne's; but the degree of sympathy we can offer is tempered by our knowledge of the agonies displayed, with less justice, on earlier and smaller occasions, and we must watch her with Elinor until this excess of suffering spends itself. She has left herself with almost no room for emotion adequate to serious grief. The violence of Elinor's burst of tears is unusual, because indeed the occasion is unusual.

Violence, however, is Marianne's normal way. She can be acute enough in disposing of the "violent screams" of a spoiled three-year-old, and the excessive affection and alarm of the adults who encourage those agonies of no reality (121–22), but she herself produces an equal violence in circumstances real and unreal. Violence attracts her. A slight rheumatic feel in Colonel Brandon's shoulder reduces him in her eyes, but a "violent fever" would make him interesting (38). The "violent" cold and fever (306) she later brings on herself is the sickness she has been seeking. It attracts her as a life of greater color and strength, but it leads near to death because it is an attempt to bring all feelings and time to the same level; it not only cannot be supported (83) but it drains life from herself and her objects. Violence becomes the sign of the weak mind, without self-control: no one in Jane Austen is so consistently violent as Marianne but the one who comes closest is Mrs. Bennet, whether delighted or alarmed (e.g., PP 11, 306, 375). The other and related trait Marianne shares with Mrs. Bennet is a nervous "irritability" (PP 113, 134, 306; SS 155, 180, 201, 211, 212, 346): there is little delicacy or power of feeling in the mind that reacts equally to every touch, but both ladies are subject to violent irritation (PP 306; SS 212).

Marianne thinks of her sensibility as a force that gives her freedom and power, gives her depth of emotion, gives her an ability to judge herself and to judge others. It does none of these things and it makes her often the opposite of what she thinks she is. Upon Willoughby's departure from Devonshire, though she expects no more than a brief separation, she is afflicted: there are many tears, no sleep, no food, all as evidence of the power of her feelings, which move beyond the limited responses of other and lesser people. Actually her conduct is following a rigid form which she must fill at all costs. Marianne would have thought herself very inexcusable had she been able to sleep and would have been ashamed to look her family in the face the next morning (83). The feelings that move her are not her immediate and personal moment but the anxiety for the code, the "duty" (77) she must meet: it is the feeling which would have made composure a disgrace which insures that she will be unable to sleep. "Her sensibility was potent enough!" (83). Her conduct is not an innocent indulgence either. For one thing, it has an effect on others, giving pain every moment to her mother and sisters. For another, the effect on herself is destructive: the potency of her sensibility makes her morally impotent; her small degree of fortitude is overcome, she is without any power because she is without any desire of command over herself and the slightest mention of anything relative to Willoughby overpowers her in an instant; the anxiety of her family to comfort her must be self-defeating because it is impossible for them, if they speak at all, to keep clear of subjects connected with her feelings for him (82). That, too, gives Marianne a quality in common with the characters of "Love and Freindship," where the sensibility of the sufferer is wounded by the most well-meaning efforts to change the subject and the comforter is forced into silence for fear of inflicting distress: to call attention to a beautiful sky in which the azure is charmingly varied by delicate streaks of white is a cruel reminder of Augustus' blue satin waistcoat striped with white (MW 98). We remain more interested in Marianne than in the character of "Love and Freindship" because she is obscuring the finer qualities in herself that we want to see flourish, but in the meanwhile her indiscriminate tenderness is absurdly reductive. Ironic reversal of her meaning closes every move.

ARIANNE thinks she has an instrument of superior perceptivity that enables her to make better distinctions of judgment than others. Elinor is surprised that Marianne should have gone to Allenham while Mrs. Smith was not there and with no other companion than Willoughby. Marianne's response is anger, typically the large emotion, the one that raises her morally above her interlocutor, because she has never spent a pleasanter morning in her life. Elinor makes the distinction that the pleasantness of an employment doesn't always evince its propriety. Marianne immediately collapses the distinction: on the contrary, nothing can be a stronger proof, "for if there had been any real impropriety in what I did, I should have been sensible of it at the time, for we always know when we are acting wrong, and with such a conviction I could have had no pleasure" (68). The finer morality here is altogether more blunt in its easy identification of feeling and knowing, and the selfish convenience with which pleasure is the sufficient test. Ten minutes of earnest thought restores her good humor and brings a partial admission that perhaps her act has been ill-judged; but our interest in her is touched with a poignancy, too, because the pity of this ingenuous self-regard is that it is insufficiently self-regarding. There is large suffering in store for a girl so vulnerable. She cannot judge her own conduct or that of others and she does not know where real pain waits.

To Marianne one of the pains of life is the lack of sensibility in others, the "horrible insensibility of the others," for example, to her performance at the pianoforte (35). She hears lines of Cowper which have frequently almost driven her wild now read by Edward with calmness and she sees his performance borne with composure by Elinor: "But it would have broke *my* heart had I loved him, to hear him read with so little sensibility" (18). She is not in fact a good judge. Even where she is not wrong— Sir John and Lady Middleton *are* insensible to music—there is little credit for her: it takes no special skill to discover this much about the Middletons, and the principle on which Marianne makes her judgment is more likely to lead her into misjudgments when she is faced with more complicated people, because it is the simple test of their effect upon her. She feels more respect for Colonel Brandon at this moment, and again she is right, but only for the half-right reason, half-wrong as it is self-centered, that he pays her the compliment of attention; he is estimable in contrast to her other listeners, but she thinks him still deficient so far as his pleasure in music does not amount to her own ecstatic delight. Her judgment of Edward tells us nothing about him—we can form no idea, from her report of how he reads, except that his taste does not in every point correspond with hers. About Elinor she is certainly wrong; because Elinor does not talk Marianne's language Marianne thinks of her indignantly as "Cold-hearted Elinor" and "worse than cold-hearted" because ashamed of being otherwise (21).

Now the matter of being cold-hearted is important in this novel. One reason why we can be sympathetic with Marianne is that there are some heartless people at work whose coldness makes her warmth, however misdirected, a hopeful human possibility. In the first chapter, before we learn anything about the characters of Mrs. Dashwood or Elinor and Marianne, we are introduced to John Dashwood. We are told that he "had not the strong feelings of the rest of the family"—which lets us know quickly enough that there is no virtue in not having strong feelings—and that he was not an ill-disposed young man, "unless to be rather cold hearted, and rather selfish, is to be ill-disposed" (5). Whatever hopes there are of shaping this disposition, still given to us with comparative qualifications, are gone by the end of the paragraph, when we hear of his wife; the marriage which might have helped him, had his wife been more amiable and a corrective influence on him, has only reinforced his faults: Mrs. John Dashwood is a strong caricature of himself, "more narrow-minded and selfish." The whole of the second chapter shows us this couple in action, the wife killing by inches whatever stir of generous feelings the husband may have toward his mother and sisters; so that by the end of chapter 2 we have seen more and know more of this combination than of the Dashwood mother and sisters who are being victimized by this cold selfishness, and we are prepared to feel kindly to almost any opposing feelings. Lady Middleton, if not so actively selfish—only passively because of the invariable sameness of her spirits—is a woman of a "cold insipidity" particularly repulsive; in comparison with her Colonel Brandon's gravity and even the boisterous mirth of Sir John and Mrs. Jennings are interesting (34). Her affinity with Mrs. John Dashwood is made explicit when the two of them meet briefly in the middle of the novel and are equally pleased: "There was a kind of cold hearted selfishness on both sides, which mutually attracted them" (229).

If all this makes Marianne more sympathetic it also makes her accusation against Elinor more foolish and more a sign of her own imperceptiveness and abuse of words. Her values are sensibility, and she cannot bear insensibility and cold hearts and selfishness, but she cannot, except in the most obvious instances, recognize them when she sees them. When Willoughby appears he is exactly formed, in person and in mind, to engage Marianne's heart. His society becomes her most exquisite enjoyment, talking, singing, or reading: "and he read with all the sensibility and spirit which Edward had unfortunately wanted" (48). But the fact is she never sees or hears him. She takes the most superficial signs and uses them to satisfy her ideas of perfection: Willoughby is all her fancy had delineated (49), not a real man she finds by a superior refinement of insight but a figure she welcomes to a prepared role by dulling her own faculties. What is worse, he knows it too, and we know, from their first conversation, that he is playing the part she has given him. All is mutuality and general conformity; she examines his opinions, proceeds to question him

84

on books, brings forward her favorite authors and dwells on them with so rapturous a delight "that any young man of five and twenty must have been insensible indeed, not to become an immediate convert to the excellence of such works, however disregarded before" (47). Insensible indeed. So the sensibility she finds in him is her own irresistible and obvious creation and Willoughby, from the beginning, is charmingly, but dangerously, a fake. The language has the touch of extravagance that puts it just above reality, when their taste is "strikingly" alike, when the same books, the same passages, are "idolized" by each. And it is undercut by the real cause of this extraordinary identity: "—or if any difference appeared, any objection arose, it lasted no longer than till the force of her arguments and the brightness of her eyes could be displayed. He acquiesced in all her decisions, caught all her enthusiasm" (47). Marianne is not only unaware of what is happening but absolutely mistaken. When Elinor remarks that there has been an extraordinary dispatch of every subject, Marianne thinks that in Elinor's eyes her fault has been too much frankness, not enough commonplace, that she has been open and sincere where she ought to have been reserved, spiritless, deceitful. What she misses is that the conversation has had few of the virtues she prizes and many of the vices she scorns. Willoughby is not the man she thinks he is, not simply because he has less sensibility than she fancies—he has a quickness there superior to her own—but because, more precisely, he is insensible.

That is his own evaluation, in his last scene, with Elinor, when his experience has taught him enough to see what he has been. Then his heart becomes astonishing to him, as he reflects on what Marianne's affection and loveliness were at the beginning of their acquaintance—"It is astonishing . . . that my heart should have been so insensible!" (320). Moved by vanity, careless of her happiness, mean, selfish, cruel, he amused himself by engaging her feelings: until, characteristically, he found himself "by insensible degrees" fond of her (321). That development, so far as it was not self-regarding, not an insensibility to the feelings of others but an uncalculating sincerity, was for Willoughby an improvement and it was that which made him learn as much as he did. But it could take him no further than unhappiness for himself as well as for others because the same causes that led him to Marianne led him from her; and these causes are the extravagance and vanity that have made him "cold-hearted and selfish" (331). The words are hard for Marianne to hear when she learns from Elinor what Willoughby has been, and accepting them is the last and most difficult thing for her, even after she has declared herself perfectly satisfied and wishing for no change. His feelings have been so selfish, Elinor points out to her, that even if he had married her the result could never have been happy. "Marianne's lips quivered, and she repeated the word 'Selfish?' in a tone that implied—'do you really think him selfish?' 'The whole of his behaviour,' replied Elinor, 'from the beginning to the end of the affair, has been grounded on selfishness.' " It was selfishness that made him begin the affair and made him end it (351). Marianne agrees to the truth, but it is the last and worst recognition for her because it means that she had given herself to what she most abhorred, to insensibility, coldness of heart, selfishness.

The lesson is harrowing, and Marianne has been almost destroyed by its working out. There is that in her, in mind and heart, and in the possession of a loving sister, that saves her, but what she learns has gone even deeper than a recognition that she loved a man who was all she thought him furthest from. She learns that she herself has been what she least thought, that she had much in common with Willoughby, wrongly, in a way she never suspected, ironically.

On some points she had the evidence before her but it did her no good. Elinor has, in conversation with Willoughby and Marianne, pointed directly to Willoughby's lack of "candour"

(51), a matter of some importance. Candor, in this sense, is a virtue of the generous mind, it is kind and forgiving to human failings, it is good-natured, it is what one should expect from a mind of sensibility, and had been so much affected in the eighteenth century that it had even come to be a subject for joke. Sheridan's Lady Candour is one instance of the last, Jane Austen's own early parody of Pope's line—"Laugh where we must, be candid where we can"—is another (MW 154). "The affectation of candour is not uncommon," Henry Austen said, but his sister Jane had no affectation; she was not unkind to the frailties and follies she saw in others ("Biographical Notice," NA 6). Perhaps he was quoting, not too appropriately. "Affectation of candour is common enough," Elizabeth Bennet says, and it is therefore wonderful to her that her sister Jane has the real thing, that she is "candid without ostentation or design," that she is, to Elizabeth, unique (PP 14). The wonder to Elizabeth is that Jane has good sense and yet is honestly blind to the follies and nonsense of others, and it is obviously a lovable fault that she sees. But if it is a fault, and we see that it is so far as it makes Jane a victim of Miss Bingley, it is also something that Elizabeth would do well to learn by way of correcting her own tendency in the opposite direction. Candor is a charity that can be the rebuke of the weak to the strong, as it is in *Emma* at Box Hill. There Mr. Knightley, remonstrating with Emma, tells her that she had been unfeeling to Miss Bates, that in insolence and pride she has laughed at and humbled a woman without defenses. When Emma tries to laugh it off and dares say that Miss Bates didn't understand, Mr. Knightley assures her that Miss Bates has understood: she has felt the full meaning and her response has been—I wish you could have heard, Mr. Knightley says—"candour and generosity" (E 374–75). It is a moving moment for Emma, a turning point in her life. At the turning point in her life Elizabeth remembers humbly the candor of Jane. Jane is not hasty in censuring, she takes the good of everyone's character, her "mild and steady candour always pleaded for allowances, and urged the possibility of mistakes" (PP 138). She can be right where Elizabeth is wrong: on the particular point for which she is pleading, a suspension of judgment on Darcy when Wickham has been destroying his character, she is right while everybody else is condemning Darcy as the worst of men. Elizabeth, "partial, prejudiced, absurd," is the quickest in censure. After she has received and understood Darcy's letter and knows most of the truth, Elizabeth recognizes her failure; she has acted despicably, she says: "I, who have prided myself on my discernment . . . who have often disdained the generous candour of my sister" (208).

Marianne and Willoughby join in being "prejudiced" against Brandon, for no reason at all, except that he is, unlike themselves, neither lively nor young, and they seem resolved to undervalue his merits. Willoughby, with Marianne's complete support, thinks the less of Brandon because he is approved by Lady Middleton and Mrs. Jennings, who lack the discernment which Willoughby and Marianne are sure they themselves possess. Elinor must point out that if the praise of Lady Middleton and her mother is censure, "your censure may be praise, for they are not more undiscerning, than you are prejudiced and unjust." The contempt of Marianne and Willoughby comes only from their refusal to see the man's value, their deficiency of "candour" (50-51).

Candor does not come easily to most people. The false variety, which is comon enough, turns up in *Sense and Sensibility* in Robert Ferrars, who speaks "candidly and generously" of Edward and himself, as he accounts for his own superiority and his brother's misfortune (251). Candor does not come at all to most people and, apart from a unique instance like Jane Bennet, those who have it must work for it, as Elizabeth does. In *Sense and Sensibility* Elinor wants to make allowances for Willoughby, in her early suspicions of him, because "it is my wish to be candid in my judgment of every body" (79). Shortly thereafter, when Edward too is bent on leaving Barton for no open reasons, though Elinor is disappointed and vexed she finds an excuse for him and is well disposed on the whole to regard his actions "with all the candid allowances and generous qualifications, which had been rather more painfully extorted from her, for Willoughby's service, by her mother" (101). Elinor turns out to be right in her suspicions of Willoughby and her candor toward Edward, but the excuse she finds for Edward—his mother's opposition—is wrong; Elinor knows so little of Mrs. Ferrars at this stage that the lady's character can be convenient explanation. A true candor requires knowledge as well as generosity, both head and heart in good order.

The unhappy fact about Marianne, which makes us interested in her and anxious for her, is that she has both head and heart superior to most of the world, being both clever and good, with excellent abilities and an excellent disposition, but she makes no use of her superiority, or rather abuses it, because she is "neither reasonable nor candid" (201–2). She has little toleration not merely for vulgarity but for inferiority of parts, or even difference of taste from herself, and reacts to them with "coldness" of behavior (127). She is neither reasonable nor candid where she expects others to have the same opinions and feelings, that is, minds and hearts like her own, and she judges their motives by the immediate effects of their actions on herself. If, as we have seen, it is by Marianne's weakness that Mrs. Jennings chances to pain her, then Mrs. Jennings's heart is sunk still lower in her estimation; but Mrs. Jennings has been governed by an impulse of the utmost good will. Marianne is unjust to her as she and Willoughby had been unjust to Colonel Brandon, by the irritable refinement of her mind and the too great importance she places on "the delicacies of a strong sensibility, and the graces of a polished manner" (201–2). The combination of those phrases show how much Marianne's notion of sensibility dwells upon surfaces. Marianne's goodness of heart is a special and limited kind. As there is coldness in her on occasion, there is also, and again like Willoughby, a hard heart. The incident with Mrs. Jennings which elicits Marianne's mistaken sensibility, her lack of reason and candor, is produced by her own inability to believe in Mrs. Jennings's ability to have compassionate feelings: "Her heart was hardened" against the belief (201). The similarity with Willoughby is made immediate, because we have just heard Elinor describe him accurately on the previous page: "in some points, there seems a hardness of heart about him" (200). When Marianne arrives at a better self-knowledge and reviews what her conduct has been, part of the realization is that she has been ungrateful to Mrs. Jennings, insolent and unjust to every common acquaintance, "with an heart hardened against their merits, and a temper irritated by their vary attention" (346). Even John and Fanny, she says, little as they deserve, she had given less then their due. It is both pleasant and instructive to see that "in her new character of candour" Marianne is prepared to think that if they really do interest themselves in an act of reconciliation, even John and Fanny may be not entirely without merit (372).

One must say of Marianne, therefore, that she gave her affections to a man who was not what she thought he was, not a man of sensibility but a man selfish, cold, and hardhearted, because she herself was too much like him. She is insensible. For all her eager receptivity to nature, to poetry, to music, to emotions, for all her responsive ecstasy, Marianne does not know what is happening around her. Having no visit or letter from Willoughby she sits careless, indifferent, lost in her own thoughts "and insensible of her sister's presence" (175). Meeting Willoughby again a few hours later she is in an agony that affects every feature, she expresses her feelings instantly, her face is crimsoned over, she exclaims in a voice of the greatest emotion. But it is all misdirected emotion, betraying itself to everyone present and mistaken in its supposed sources in Willoughby. It is that misdirection of emotion that makes her even at her earnest moments not only wasteful of good feeling but makes her, unknowingly, with good intentions, productive of pain. She cannot bear that Mrs. Ferrars should praise Miss Morton's art at the expense of Elinor, and though she has not any notion of what is principally meant by the praise, she is provoked to speak with warmth. But neither knowing nor caring to know anything of Miss Morton or what it is that her name means to several people present and the relationships among these people, she stirs up anger, bitterness, and fright in what is already a most unpleasant collision. Elinor, whom she thinks she is defending, is in the middle of all this, very much aware of what is going on and why, and Elinor is much more hurt by Marianne's warmth than by what produced it. Colonel Brandon, in love with Marianne, sees only the affectionate heart; and Marianne, whose feelings do not stop with her first speech, thinking that Elinor is in such distress as her own wounded heart teaches her to think of with horror, is urged "by a strong impulse of affectionate sensibility" to put an arm around her sister's neck, to tell her in an eager voice not to be made unhappy (235–36). What her sensibility misses, for all its touching affection, is that Elinor's heart and mind and circumstances differ from hers and that for Elinor she has worsened the moment by taking it in the only way that she can, as her own. The impulse concludes with the dominance of her own feelings when her spirits are quite overcome and she becomes not the comforter of Elinor but, as usual, the one in need of comfort; the supporting arm around her sister's neck becomes her sister's problem, she hides her face on Elinor's shoulder and bursts into tears. Everybody's attention is called to her and almost everybody is concerned for her.

If Colonel Brandon can see in this only what is amiable, we are made to see more, and in a scene that follows a few pages later (238–45) we see that this "sensibility" which expresses

itself as insensibility can turn the tears quickly to a comic foolishness. It is one of the most comic scenes in Jane Austen and it
is Marianne who brings the richness. It begins when Lucy Steele
comes to Elinor to celebrate the triumph of the flattering treatment Mrs. Ferrars has just granted her and denied to Elinor.
Elinor is trying to handle this with as much civility as she can
when suddenly the door is thrown open and Edward walks in.
It is a very awkward moment and all look exceedingly foolish.
What they wanted most to avoid has befallen them, for now
they are all together and without the relief of another person.
Elinor is the one best able to extract herself from being a fool by
the efforts she makes to help the situation. Edward is too embarrassed and Lucy is determined to make no contribution to
the comfort of others, but Elinor acts. After a while she even
leaves the other two by themselves under the pretense of fetch-
ing Marianne. Marianne's entry should give the very relief of
another person's presence that all had desired, but the effect,
Marianne being Marianne, is to intensify the foolishness.

Every word she speaks is designed to express strong affection
and every word is a comic error, a mistaken warmth, and a cause
of distress. It is a moment of great happiness, she cries, that
would almost make amends for everything. The everything, of
course, is her own unhappiness but for Edward the immediate
situation is his unhappiness and he cannot return her kindness
as it deserves. He notices that she is not looking well and is
afraid London has not agreed with her. "Oh! don't think of me!"
she replies with earnestness, though her eyes fill with tears;
and it is a laudable attempt to put the concerns of another before her own; the problem, however, is that at this moment the
others want nothing less than to have their own affairs at the
center of the conversation. She tells Edward not to think of her
health because, as he sees, Elinor is well and "That must be
enough for us both." Unfortunately this is a remark not calculated to make him or Elinor more easy nor to contribute to the

good will of Lucy. Edward, who is willing to say anything to change the subject, asks her if she likes London. It does him no good, because for Marianne there is only one subject: the faithlessness of Willoughby and her need to insist on Edward's consistency. She expected much pleasure in London but found none: the sight of you, she tells him, is the only comfort London has afforded her "and thank Heaven! you are what you always were!" She pauses—no one speaks. There is nothing any one of her listeners can say to ease the embarrassment of that unlucky shot. But she can add to it by proposing that Edward take care of her and Elinor in their return to Barton, trusting, as she says, that Edward will not be very unwilling to accept the charge. Poor Edward, who now must reply and cannot reply, mutters something and what it is nobody knows, not even himself. Marianne sees his agitation, but, in her style, can "easily trace it to whatever cause best pleased herself," and is perfectly satisfied. Now she changes the subject, but the change is not a relief.

Up to this point Marianne's blind hits have been excusable to the degree that her intentions have been good and she knows nothing of the facts that have made her audience squirm; of course her chances of ever realizing what she has been doing are hopelessly reduced by her tracing the signs of the effect she is producing to whatever cause best pleases herself, but she is not behaving badly. Her next subject has no excuse in ignorance. She tells Edward of their visit of yesterday to Mrs. Ferrars; so wretchedly dull, she lets him know, but she has much to add which cannot be said now. In this conversation this reticence has been her first and only attempt at discretion, but Marianne's discretion, as the ironic admiration of the narrator indicates, only emphasizes her dislike of the relatives she and Edward have in common and her particular disgust with his mother; additionally, the discretion of deferring the details until they are more in private is an uncivil exclusion of Lucy Steele from the conversation. The consequence is that when Marianne presses Edward

to explain why he did not meet them at his mother's, then refuses to accept his brief evasion that he was engaged elsewhere,
Lucy is eager for revenge: perhaps, she cries, Marianne thinks
young men never stand upon engagements if they have no mind
to keep them, little as well as great. This is a direct and vicious
insult aimed at the pain of an unhappy girl. Elinor feels it for
her and Elinor is very angry. But Marianne, so susceptible to
suffering upon small occasions, courting it in all the forms in
which she knows it should present itself, is now "entirely insensible" of the sting that has answered her obtuse attempt at
discretion. She is entirely insensible because her mind is occupied
by her praise of Edward, according to a form of her own creation which answers her need of finding him a pattern of fidelity.
Seriously speaking, she says, she is very sure that conscience only
kept him from the visit to Harley Street; she really believes he
has the most delicate conscience in the world, the most scrupulous in performing every engagement, however minute and however it may make against his interest or pleasure. Her language
is extravagant, but what gives it a cutting force is that what she
says is basically true and, with complete confidence in her own
certainty, entirely misdirected; the only engagement that holds
the conscience of the scrupulous Edward, against his interest and
pleasure, is his engagement to Lucy. She continues in the same
high line of painful praise of Edward's fear of giving pain or
wounding expectation. She refuses to accept his apparent modesty
in the face of these compliments, insisting that he must listen if
he will be her friend, for those who accept her love and esteem
must submit to her open commendation. And so they must: her
love and openness are their secret burden; the generous gen-
eralities so powerfully misapplied are particular wounds. Her
commendations in the present case are ill suited to the feelings
of two-thirds of her auditors, and to Edward, whose heart she
has been trying to lift, they are so unexhilarating that he soon
gets up to go. She will not let him make an easy exit, tries to

keep him, whispers that Lucy cannot stay much longer, which does not encourage him.

When both he and then Lucy have gone Marianne delivers herself of her annoyance with Lucy's intrusiveness and refusal to leave when it was obvious they wanted her gone; it is the irritation to Edward's feelings that concerns her especially. Elinor, who knows the truth but cannot disclose it, tries to do as much as she can to correct Marianne's error by speaking of Lucy as a friend of Edward's, of even longer standing than themselves, whom he would naturally like to see. It is another opportunity for Marianne's grand and foolish nobility. She thinks Elinor can only be playing the coy maiden and, quite blindly, Marianne looks at her steadily: this is the kind of talking, she tells Elinor, that she cannot bear; if Elinor only hopes to have her assertion contradicted, as Marianne must suppose to be the case, then Marianne is the last person in the world to do it; she cannot descend to be tricked out of assurances that are not really wanted. It is a lofty integrity of feeling and character she knows she is displaying, in contrast to Elinor's transparent, commonplace trickery. But, as we know, the genuine integrity, the pain, the obligation to submit, is all Elinor's, and Marianne's is spurious.

Marianne's failing is not that her sensibility is too great, for it is that only in a narrow sense: giving herself up to those feelings on those minor occasions as are dictated by a convention; or using her feelings unfeelingly in contempt of others; or, in matters of major importance at critical moments, not gaining strength from her feelings, neither for those she loves nor for herself, but falling weakly beneath them, unable to sustain suffering, in near self-destruction. In that sense she lacks strength of feeling. It is absurd to talk of her as the passionate "burning human heart," or to use any of the more recent variants of that phrase. Her excess of false sensibility is a deficiency of real sensibility; the deadly fever she creates for herself reduces her to "an heavy stupor" (313). She is neither the girl of strong feeling whose sensibility (resisting the novelist's intention) makes her the true heroine of the novel, nor the girl of too much sensibility who (following the novelist's intention) must learn to feel less strongly. Her story requires most of the discussion because it has most of the problems, but it is important and interesting because it is part of another story.

Sense and Sensibility is the story of Elinor Dashwood. The action of the novel is hers; it is not Marianne's and it is not equally divided between the sisters; it is Elinor's. The whole of Marianne's story is included within Elinor's: Marianne's begins later and it ends earlier. The entrance of Marianne's young man, who begins her serious complications, by her love, follows the entrance of Elinor's young man; Marianne's discovery that she has lost her love and must suffer pain follows Elinor's discovery and pain. But the satisfactory resolution of Marianne's crisis, which is her self-understanding, has been reached before Elinor's problem has been satisfactorily resolved in her marriage to Edward. Marianne's marriage to Colonel Brandon, which is an unsatisfactory anticlimax if Marianne is the main character, or an equally important character, is, in this light, an appropriate completion of Elinor's happiness, one last wish, like better pasturage for the cows of Delaford parsonage. Nor has Elinor any illusions about Marianne's marriage; she has never thought seventeen and thirty-five are well matched for matrimony (37), and, heard only by the reader, she has not agreed with her mother's certainty that Marianne will be happier with Brandon than she could have been with Willoughby if Willoughby had been really amiable (338). The whole of the story comes to us through Elinor. There is no part of Marianne's story except what is also a part of Elinor's. There may be things that Elinor doesn't know—what it is that Willoughby and Marianne say to each other when no one else is present, whether those two are engaged or not, and so on—but if Elinor doesn't know, it worries her and affects her. And if she doesn't know, we don't know and it affects us as it affects her. We are concerned for Marianne because Elinor is concerned, because what we are asked to be interested in, as the novel is presented to us, are the several difficulties that Elinor must face, of which the greatest is Marianne. Marianne comes to us always as the heaviest burden Elinor must carry, the one that must occupy most of her attention, her loving care, while she must carry her own life. Marianne's story could not be resolved except for what Elinor does, advising her, protecting her, providing her an example, revealing to her at critical moments information that will do her the most good; even the two men in Marianne's life are understood by the reader, and by Marianne, as they speak to and are interpreted by Elinor. There is no part of Marianne's story that is not a part of Elinor's, but there are large and important parts of Elinor's story that are not part of Marianne's. The whole of the Lucy Steele business enters Marianne's story only long after it has begun and only as it is summarized for her by Elinor; it is then presented to her in a form designed by Elinor to meet the problem Elinor must resolve in Marianne's unhappiness. The details of the matter, the immediate impact of Lucy's revelation, the several subsidiary conversations Elinor has with Lucy and with other characters, in relation to this and to other incidents—conversations with Mrs. Jennings, Colonel Brandon, John Dashwood, Anne Steele—are quite outside Marianne's knowledge and the reader's interest in Marianne. Even the major formal divisions of the novel point us in the same direction. The ending of Volume I is the wretchedness of Elinor, mortified, shocked, confounded by Lucy's surprise to her and to us; Volume II ends with Elinor, for the first time, sharing some of Lucy's expectation, for Lucy is being taken into the Harley Street home of Mrs. John Dashwood and everything looks bright for Lucy and dismal for Elinor. The structure of the novel, in all senses, turns our attention to Elinor. There is an important unresolved problem in the effective representation of Elinor (p. 281 below), but if that weakens it does not invert the novel's central interest in Elinor. It is only by importing a different order of concern into the novel and taking Marianne's emotions with a different order of seriousness that we can make the novel hers or equally hers. What the novel asks us to watch is Elinor's exertion for herself and for others, and the best effect it has on others is to bring Marianne to exert herself.

*T*HERE is only a specious show of life in a sensibility that makes easy claims to a higher morality because it has higher feelings, for it has neither. The moral life in Jane Austen makes greater demands on the human spirit, the greater strength of considered feeling needed for the strength of effective doing. The moral life is a purposeful and powerful pursuit, a life of activity, of usefulness, of exertion. Frank Churchill, Emma argues, may have as strong a sense of what is right as Mr. Knightley can have, without being able, under his circumstances, to act up to it; but Mr. Knightley allows no nonsense: "Then, it would not be so strong a sense. If it failed to produce equal exertion, it could not be an equal conviction" (E 148). Mr. Knightley, a complete man, will allow no sentimental distinctions between feeling and doing. The test of the inner quality is the quality of the exertion. One exerts powers by choice and it is for that reason exertion is so important to Jane Austen. And as the mere feeling is not real sensibility so the mere activity is not real exertion. The right kind of feeling productive of useful action is an unusual achievement, for it must begin with the first and most difficult exertion, self-command.

When Fanny Price visits Portsmouth, her disappointment in her mother is that she had hoped for much and found nothing; Portsmouth, she finds, is not home, either emotionally or physically, and those two deficiencies have their origin in the moral failure of Mrs. Price. It is not that Mrs. Price is unkind or immobile, but her capacity to feel or to do is so shallow. She spends her days, in a fine phrase, "in a kind of slow bustle"; always busy without getting on, always behindhand and lamenting it, without altering her ways. She remains at the level of ineffective desire, wishing, dissatisfied, but unable to do anything about her home because she is unable to do anything about herself. She is incapable of "exertions" (MP 389–90). Fanny thinks of her mother's two sisters, those sisters whose luck in marriage had begun the novel. There had been no discernible reason why they had made matches productive of such different fortunes; but what Fanny sees at Portsmouth are the family resemblances and differences that have made the differences of fortune important. Mrs. Price is much more like Lady Bertram than Mrs. Norris. Mrs. Price's marriage had made her a manager by necessity, without any of Mrs. Norris's inclination for it or any of her "activity." Her disposition was like Lady Bertram's, naturally "easy and indolent," and a situation of similar affluence and do-nothing-ness would have been more suited to her capacity than the "exertions and self-denials" required by her imprudent marriage. Fanny's mother might have made just as good a woman of consequence as Lady Bertram, but Mrs. Norris would have been a more respectable mother of nine children on a small income (390). That presents a refined judgment on each, and it is especially just to Mrs. Norris, for whom so little can be said. There is something to be said for exertion, if only in the sense that a frenzy fit is better than a swoon. Bodily "Exertions," as the heroine learns in "Love and Freindship," circulate and warm the blood, but lying totally inactive on the ground exposes one to all the chilling damps (MW 101). Lady Bertram is as close to nonexistence as a living being can be, which is amusing enough in her dozing and in her inability to see or hold her own cards, but it is less amusing in its moral result. To her astonishment (a height of emotion) she can do very well without her husband as long as her son supplies his place in carving and in doing whatever else needs doing and in "saving her from all possible fatigue or exertion in every particular" but that of directing her own letters (MP 34). The consequences for her children are wretched.

Mrs. Bennet is a busier mother—the business of her life is to get her daughters married—but this nervous irritation is not exertion. The fact is plain in a time of crisis, when one of her matrimonial devices has produced an elopement; Mrs. Bennet in a crisis is the same Mrs. Bennet with all her faults magnified; she becomes ill and stays in her room: "Could she exert herself it would be better," Jane writes to Elizabeth, "but this is not to be expected" (PP 275). She becomes then a wearisome load upon others, "a mother incapable of exertion, and requiring constant attendance" (280). Her husband is the more culpable as one who knows better the faults of his family but contents himself with laughing and "would never exert himself" to restrain the wild giddiness of his youngest daughters (213). Even when the catastrophe hits him, and Mr. Bennet recognizes his responsibility, and he moves himself, literally, as he never has before, the difference is very little. He goes to London to seek his daughter, leaving an anxious family behind, but he writes not a line to them. They know him to be on all common occasions a most negligent and dilatory correspondent, "but at such a time, they had hoped for exertion" (294). He suffers from Lydia's action, for once in his life feels how much he is to blame, but the moment is a brief one for him. He knows himself well enough to realize that. The matter is settled, by Mr. Gardiner as he thinks at first, with little cost to himself, and that it is to be done "with such trifling exertion on his side, too, [is] another very welcome surprise," for his chief wish is to have as little trouble as possible. The first transports of rage have produced his "activity" and when it is over he returns to his former indolence (309).

If "indolence" is the deficiency of exertion, its excess is "offi-

ciousness." "I admire the activity of your benevolence," Mary
Bennet observes, "but every impulse of feeling should be guided
by reason; and, in my opinion, exertion should always be in
proportion to what is required" (PP 32). As with much of what
Mary says it is generally true and specifically stupid. Elizabeth
is feeling really anxious about Jane's illness, is determined to go
to Netherfield, jumping over stiles and springing over puddles
"with impatient activity," exactly in proportion to what is required by her affection and her sister's needs. Mary's judicious
declaration is her substitute for feeling and acting. Those who
talk most of exertion are not always those who are active, and
those who are active are not always useful in action. Mrs. Norris
would have been a more respectable mother in Mrs. Price's situation, but having no children and living at Mansfield she uses
her "spirit of activity" (MP 4) in mean or minor ways that become destructive of what she thinks she is protecting. To Sir
Thomas she has a great deal to insinuate in her own praise "as
to *general* attention to the interest and comfort of his family,
much exertion and many sacrifices" in a host of inconsequential
details; but on the main point, of the propriety of the theatricals,
she has been blind and has done nothing. Her greatest glory in
this misdirection is that she has formed the connection with the
Rushworths. "If I had not been active," she says, going on to
more and more agonizing details of her moving heaven and earth
and her walking uphill to save the labor of the horses, nothing
would have come of that connection. And she is right, to the
lasting sorrow of Sir Thomas, Maria, and herself (188–89).
When her false activity ends in Maria's sin, and Mrs. Norris is
really touched by affliction, her "active powers" are all benumbed
(448). Mrs. Elton is another who is prepared to do a vast deal
because she dares to act; to admire "incredible exertions" directed
to trivia (E 306); and, worse yet, to call upon Emma for a
joint endeavor to do something for Jane Fairfax: "we must
exert ourselves" (282). It is an exertion that is designed for

her own self-importance and exacerbates Jane's unhappiness; it is also a reproach to Emma that her own inattention to Jane leaves the field open to Mrs. Elton. But probably the best instances of false exertion are the Parker sisters of *Sanditon*—"excellent useful Women," their brother calls them, with so much energy of character that where any good is to be done "they force themselves on exertions which to those who do not thoroughly know them, have an extraordinary appearance" (MW 385). Charlotte Heywood comes to know them and hears what they are doing for people they do not know and who have never asked for their services. "The words 'Unaccountable Officiousness!—Activity run mad!' " pass through her mind, and they are the right words, for which, when she speaks, she must substitute the civil words "very great exertions." Diana Parker takes the opportunity to deliver her own panegyric on her strength of mind, her exertions to be of use to others and to do her duty (410). Her words are all misplaced, because she has none of what she asserts. She is not only of no use to anyone but is blindly self-centered. The Parker sisters have charitable hearts and amiable feelings but "a spirit of restless activity, & the glory of doing more than anybody else, had their share in every exertion of Benevolence— and there was Vanity in all they did, as well as in all they endured" (412–13). These exertions do not rise from a moral command of themselves and a fulfillment of duties to others but from a lack of control, a kind of madness.

What exertion means, then, whether it is judged to be too little or too much, lost in indolence or in officiousness, becomes an elemental revelation of character. In Mary Crawford's judgment if Sir Thomas attempts to do anything by way of leading Maria from her adulterous life, instead of being quiet and letting things take their course, if "by any officious exertions of his" Maria is induced to leave Henry, Sir Thomas will be injuring his own cause (MP 457). The moral base from which she uses these words to indicate the right degree and kind of exertion is deeply corrupt. Her brother's corruption is deeper still. Unlike her, Henry can appreciate an exertion that is not within his own character, and he can even exert himself; but the motives from which he judges and acts are so selfish as to pervert the value of what he does and, in the last incident, to destroy himself. Listening to William Price's account of the bodily hardships William has gone through, the proofs of mind he has given, Henry sees that the "glory of heroism, of usefulness, of exertion, of endurance" make his own habits of selfish indulgence appear in shameful contrast. They do, but it is the glory rather than the work that attracts Henry and the wish that he had been a William Price is rather eager than lasting (236). He does do something for William, in getting him a commission—"I know he must have exerted himself very much," Mary says (364)— but, for all its real good, the action is still suspect, and causes distress, because it is done to advance his own ends and to bring himself credit. Henry is capable of exertion, and in his subsequent visit to his estate there is evidence, Fanny sees, that he has been useful, performed a duty, acted as he ought to do. But even then he attempts to turn it all to his own advantage with Fanny. Moreover, it is as he leaves Fanny, intending, as he knew he ought, to return to Everingham, that he is flattered into meeting Maria once again. His curiosity and his vanity are engaged, Maria receives him with a coldness he finds mortifying and he cannot bear that: "he must exert himself to subdue so proud a display of resentment" (467–68); and thus, ironically and perversely, Henry Crawford, making the only exertion of which he is finally capable, creates his own wretchedness.

The failures are many, the successes are few. There are simply not many useful people in the world because there are not many with the integrity for the right kind and degree of exertion. The usefulness is an earned virtue that rises from a conquest of self over a period of time, often a continual striving in the face of new and increased pressures. Fanny Price is one example—"Time

did something, her own exertions something more" (MP 418)
is very much the pattern of her life. It is a grace in Emma, for
all her faults, that from the earliest scene we see she "spared
no exertions" in tending her father (E 9), and it is edifying to
hear her give Harriet excellent advice on the comprehensive motives and rewards of exertion (268). But it is more impressive
to see her at the end, under many bitter feelings for the loss
of Mr. Knightley, and to find that the bitterness is not turned on
Harriet but rather makes "the utmost exertion necessary" (411).
It is more impressive to see her still tending her father, but now
"by exertions which had never cost her half so much before"
(422). The beautiful example of Anne Elliot we will save for
the later chapter.

In *Sense and Sensibility* the force of exertion is a major part
of the novel. There it operates, at each level in a varied form,
in the motive power of the minor characters and in the shaping
of the lives of the major characters. Lady Middleton is one of
those nonentities like Lady Bertram who dwells outside the moral
life, unnoticing, unperturbed, accepting and never giving. It is
only when a mild reality, like a conversation on a pregnancy,
seems to intrude upon her calm that her inability to endure it
leads her to exert herself so far as to change the subject (108; see
also Chapman's note to 66). John Dashwood, with the guidance
of his wife, is a less passive creature, whose action is concentrated
upon the careful reduction of moral obligation. When he has
brought himself to the point of thinking that all he is required to
do for his widowed mother is help her remove her furniture
to another house, he is exceedingly sorry that the distance of her
new house will keep him from being of any service. "He really
felt conscientiously vexed on the occasion; for the very exertion
to which he had limited the performance of his promise to his
father was by this arrangement rendered impracticable" (26).
There is a happy little pathos in seeing John Dashwood lose the
one meaningless exertion that would enable him to discharge his

conscience. He and his wife are specialists in the inconsequential exertion that costs nothing because selfish interest has been protected and in fact nothing will be done. Mrs. John Dashwood attempts cordiality to Elinor after she discovers that it is not Elinor who may marry her brother. Heretofore she has carefully excluded Elinor but now she even proceeds so far as to be concerned that Elinor and her sister are leaving town when she hoped to see more of them, "—an exertion in which her husband, who . . . hung enamoured over her accents, seemed to distinguish every thing that was most affectionate and graceful" (300). But it is not comic to see Willoughby, who is too weak to do what he knows he should, gathering his strength only to carry off his betrayal, under the pain and embarrassment of his public meeting with Marianne: catching the eye of his wife-to-be "he felt the necessity of instant exertion," recovered himself and delivered the blow (177). Having been given whatever credit he deserves by his later explanation of his behavior he is justly written off by the information that though he repented, envied, and regretted, his life was not inconsolable: "He lived to exert, and frequently to enjoy himself." He had a wife not always out of humor, he had horses, he had dogs (379). And that was the limit of Willoughby's exertion. Colonel Brandon, able to make painful exertions on Marianne's behalf for small reward, will be a more worthy husband (207, 216). That is part of the lesson Marianne must learn and it is through Elinor that she must learn it. It is Elinor who must exert herself to bring Marianne to the point where Marianne is capable of performing her own essential acts of exertion.

In the prefigurative opening chapter, already noted, Marianne and Mrs. Dashwood build upon their agony, renewing it, seeking it, creating it, resolving against admitting consolation, and so on (7). The weight of emotions that require so much labor and so little struggle is suspect. Within a few months Mrs. Dashwood's volatility moves her in a different direction; in her affliction the sight of every well-known spot at Norland has raised the violent emotions which she has desired, but when that ceases, when her spirits begin to revive and her mind becomes "capable of some other exertion" than heightening its own affliction, she is impatient to be gone (14). Elinor too is deeply afflicted by her father's death, but "still she could struggle, she could exert herself." She can act in response to her brother and sister-in-law, as she will in other situations respond to others, and, as she will in other situations with her mother and Marianne, she can "strive to rouse her mother to similar exertion" (7). For example, Willoughby's departure from Barton, though he is expected to return shortly, is sufficient to produce a violent oppression of spirits in Marianne; she is without any power because without any desire of command over herself, she gives pain every moment to her mother and sisters, indulges her feelings, nourishes her grief. But such violence of affliction could not be supported and sinks in a few days (82–83). It is again Elinor who, seeing the dangers of the seclusion Marianne seeks, takes action: and at length Marianne "was secured by the exertions of Elinor" (85). They are still silent as they walk together, for Marianne's mind cannot be controlled, and her continued self-deception appears immediately in her seeing Willoughby where it is really only Edward who has come; but Elinor has gained at least one point and must wait until she can attempt more.

Elinor's major test in her own life begins at the end of Volume I with Lucy's disclosure and the series of emotions of rising intensity that come upon her. She replies with "an exertion of spirits, which increased with her increase of emotion" (130). That is the point to be grasped, that the exertion is powerful in proportion to what is required, because it is that dynamic relation of exertion and emotions that makes Elinor's sensibility credible. There is increasing pain for her as her security sinks with each confirming detail in Lucy's explanation, "but her self-command did not sink with it" (131). She is "most feelingly sensible" of every new piece of evidence in Lucy's favor, until she can no longer doubt there is a positive engagement between Lucy and Edward; for a few moments she is almost overcome, her heart sinks, she can hardly stand; "but exertion was indispensably necessary, and she struggled so resolutely against the oppression of her feelings, that her success was speedy, and for the time complete" (134). Her success will require continual renewal of effort. Her emotion and distress are beyond anything she has ever felt before (135) and the struggle will be great, but she has begun it. Elinor's emotions are not less than Marianne's; that they do not come as easily and violently as Marianne's on all occasions makes them and their causes more significant when they are aroused; the attempt to control and conceal, rather than encourage and display them, gives them a greater integrity and force, more feeling sensibility. Her emotions are greater than Marianne's and her exertions are greater.

She is now obliged to "unceasing exertion" by the necessity of concealing what she has been told. The information has been entrusted to her in confidence, for selfish reasons and with the intention of wounding, to be sure, but that does not lessen Elinor's obligation. By not revealing her secret she can save her mother and Marianne from the affliction of her own suffering. And, they being what they are, she could receive no assistance from them, only additional distress; her self-command could not be strengthened by their example or their praise (141). Every obligation, to one she has most reason to despise, to those most near to her affection, to herself, makes exertion her best and only way, a strength necessary to hold herself and her world together.

It is in this set of tensions that she must watch and protect Marianne, and it is through Elinor's eyes that we see what is happening and what must be done. She must be prepared to observe Willoughby and if the results of her observation are unfavorable she must open her sister's eyes; should the results be favorable, "her exertion would be of a different nature" and she must then learn to avoid every selfish comparison with her sister's happiness (159). The discovery of Willoughby's treachery, which makes Elinor give way to a burst of tears at first scarcely less violent than Marianne's, requires still another kind of action from her. Edward is in her mind, by comparison with Willoughby, though he has no connection whatever with the affair other than what her heart gives him with everything that passes. But the need she must attend to is Marianne's misery, a torrent of unresisted grief, and the need is to bring Marianne to an understanding of what it is that must be done, the essential act: "Exert yourself, dear Marianne . . . if you would not kill yourself and all who love you . . . you must exert yourself." The appeal is serious and urgent; Marianne, whose body and mind both have been weakened by what she has been doing, will come near to killing herself. She cannot do what Elinor asks, she can only exclaim how easy it is "for those who have no sorrow of their own to talk of exertion!" To her Elinor is happy, happy Elinor who can have no idea of what Marianne is suffering; and if Elinor denies it, the reach of Marianne's feeling can go no further than "I know you feel for me" (185). Marianne is the weight Elinor must support while under the mounting pressures of her own secret; she has always "more to do," must "force" herself, with "another struggle, another effort," to see that in more and more difficult tests with Edward and Lucy "her exertions did not stop" (241). Only at the beginning of the third volume can she explain to Marianne the pain she has borne since the end of the first volume. Even then it is a difficult explanation, because Marianne thinks that the resolution and self-command have been easy only because Elinor never has felt much. It is only by an account of the varied and continual struggle she has made for four months that she can make Marianne understand: the enforced solitude, the triumph of Lucy, the loss of Edward without being able to think him less worthy of her love, the punishing unkindness of his mother and sister brought against her for possessing an advantage which in fact she did not enjoy—and all this while she was bearing Marianne's unhappiness. If Marianne can think Elinor ever capable of feeling, she must see now that she has suffered. That composure of mind and consolation have not been the gift of deficiency or mere temperament, nor did they spring up of themselves; they have been the result of long moral effort; they "have been the effect of constant and painful exertion" (263–64).

The immediate effect on Marianne is not altogether salutary. It makes her hate herself, in extravagant language, for her injustice to Elinor; and though she does, admirably, try to carry out the succeeding promise of acting in a lesser matter with more discretion, listening to Mrs. Jennings as well as she can, at the cost of only a spasm in the throat, she disappoints Elinor's larger hope. Marianne feels all the force of the comparison of her own conduct and Elinor's, but not in such a way as "to urge her to exertion now." She feels it with the pain of continual self-reproach, regrets most bitterly that "she had never exerted herself before"; but this brings only the torture of penitence without the hope of amendment; her mind is so much weakened that "she still fancied present exertion impossible" and she is therefore the more dispirited (270). This is the middle of Marianne's story, the necessary passage if there is to be any valuable change, the stage in which she recognizes how wrong she has been; but the recognition reduces her to despair; she is convinced of her incapacity for ever doing that which she has never done.

Elinor, however, must go on to her own severest test. Colonel Brandon comes to make his offer of the living of Delaford to Edward, which will remove the last obstacle to the marriage of Edward and Lucy, and he gives to Elinor the office of informing Edward. His motives are excellent and his choice of her as his agent arises from his delicacy in conferring an obligation. What he cannot know is the difficulty he creates for her. There is a bit of byplay during this incident, as Mrs. Jennings watches the conversation between Brandon and Elinor and hears snatches of it in the intervals between the music Marianne is playing on the pianoforte. Marianne, as usual, is oblivious to what is happening. Mrs. Jennings has decided before this time that there must be a match between the Colonel and Elinor and she hears the scene as his proposal; her misconception continues to the end of the next chapter, to the end of Elinor's subsequent conversation with Edward. Even the reader, who knows that Mrs. Jennings must be wrong, does not know for a while what really is happening. It is one of the few times that we do not see things through Elinor's eyes. The comic cross-purposes at this moment seem rather mistimed, though they do keep the scene and its effect from becoming heavy and potentially sentimental; but they do so only because Elinor's character makes it possible by converting the scene dramatically. She is not receiving an offer of marriage, as Mrs. Jennings thinks; on the contrary, the man she loves is now enabled to marry another woman and she, of all people in the world, is fixed on to bestow the means. The emotion that Mrs. Jennings sees in her rises from a different cause but it is only Elinor who knows this, who does not allow her own less pure, less pleasing, feelings to become more than minor to the occasion either in the eyes of others or in her own feelings of strong and warm esteem for Brandon's benevolence. When we know what has really happened, the gratitude she expresses can be seen to be not less reasonably excited nor less properly worded than if it had arisen from an offer of marriage (280–84). This is admirable, but not yet enough, because she must still inform Edward, by a letter. The particular circumstances between them make it difficult for her to express herself, when to any other person it would be the easiest thing in the world; she is equally afraid of saying too much or too little. The perplexity is great but she can congratulate herself that however difficult the letter will be it is at least preferable to giving the information by word of mouth: and as she does so, Edward himself enters—"to force her upon this greatest exertion of all" (288). It is a moment of astonishment and confusion, but Elinor is equal to it, to the greatest exertion of all, accepting her loss, conferring a benefit, doing it directly in the most difficult way, by the word of her own mouth.

That she does eventually marry Edward is a bit of luck. It is entirely in Lucy's character to have dropped Edward when her self-interest provided a better chance, but there was nothing Elinor did or could or should have done to effect that. All she could do was to have been deserving of the happiness she achieved; but her real achievement was to have been worthy of her fate whatever it brought her. There is another episode of cross-purposes at the end, in a deception designed by Lucy with a flourish of malice to make it seem that she really has married Edward. It is, as ever, Marianne who becomes hysterical though it is Elinor who is really suffering. The necessity of the event is that Elinor must find the difference between the expectation of an unpleasant event, however certain the mind may be told to consider it, and certainty itself. She must find that in spite of herself she has always admitted a hope that something could occur to prevent his marriage and assist the happiness of all and she must rid her heart of the lurking flattery. It is in that certainty that the last thing she does before she is told the truth is to meet Edward once more with the determination that she will be calm, will be mistress of herself, and will speak to him of his wife— "resolving to exert herself, though fearing the sound of her own voice" (359). Only then does the action end.

$\mathcal{T}$HE end has been immediately preceded by the conclusion of the change in Marianne; the midpoint had been her recognition of how mistaken she had been, without the strength to act upon that recognition, with, in fact, a mind so weakened that she fancied exertion impossible; the end of Marianne's action is that time when, in the whole of Marianne's manner, Elinor can trace "the direction of a mind awakened to reasonable exertion" (342). The awakening has come as a result of the sickness that brought her near death, a self-induced sickness as she realizes, and the seriousness of language with which both Elinor and Marianne speak of it gives to the change a religious weight.

It is one of the few times in Jane Austen that there is explicit statement of what is elsewhere assumed, that right action is dependent on a right state of mind which must rest finally on a religious ground. A contemporary like Archbishop Whately understood that at first sight, it being more immediately know-able than the correct spelling of her name: "Miss Austin" had the merit, in his judgment most essential, "of being evidently a Christian writer." Evidently, "her religion being not at all obtrusive," "rather alluded to, and that incidentally"; but evi-dently, it would seem, from the evidence of the story, just as her moral lessons too "spring incidentally from the circumstances of the story," not forced on the reader but recognizable by him without any difficulty (*Quarterly Review* 24[1821]: 359–60). It seems also true that for her contemporaries some of her words at certain times were capable of a religious force that is not now immediately felt. "Serious" is certainly one. Serious subjects, whether in her private writings or the novels, are usually reli-gious (e.g., Prayers, MW 456; L 422; MP 87, 340, 350; P 156, 161; also "Biographical Notice," NA 8). When Emma or Anne Elliot is serious in thanksgiving or gratefulness to have received a happy ending (E 475, P 245), they are of course in prayer. "Principle," important especially in *Mansfield Park,* is a word of similar religious weight. "Duty" is another example. Of the three duties, to God, to one's neighbors, to oneself, specified in the Book of Common Prayer and innumerable sermons and moral essays, duty to God would not be for Jane Austen the proper subject of the novelist; but the other duties are, and they become gravely important, not as they might be in a later nineteenth-century novelist, because they are substitutes for religion, but because they are daily expressions of it in common life. "The common Duties of common Life," said Archbishop Secker, "make far the greatest Part of what our Maker expects of us" (*Lectures on the Catechism of the Church of England,* 1769, and frequently reprinted, well into the nineteenth century, 2: 288); Jane Austen read sermons and knew Secker's explanation of the catechism (MW 232n), but she could have found the point made by many moralists, notably Dr. Johnson.

And in *Sense and Sensibility* "exertion" is another serious word. Like the other words it has the social and secular meanings to which this sort of vocabulary would soon be exclusively given, and sometimes it is certainly limited to them; what is important, however, is that in Jane Austen this is a language that still retains another force which keeps working quietly to charge the meaning of ordinary events and, at critical moments, can become explicit. In real life in moments that call for a specifically religious response, as at the death of Jane Austen herself, Cassandra speaks of the "pious exertions" of the mourning members of the family; at the death of a sister-in-law Jane Austen writes that it is too early to think of moderation in the grief of the bereaved young daughter but that soon we may hope the girl's "sense of duty" to her father "will rouse her to exertion"—to the best proof of love, trying to be tranquil and resigned (L 516, 221).

Exertion becomes the outward and social manifestation of the inward and religious conquest; in that sense it is the perfection of manners. The *OED* lists "manifestation, display," the action of putting forth, as an obsolete sense of "exertion" and offers as one of its last two instances a sermon by Secker, who speaks of "a proper Exertion of that Chearfulness, which God hath plainly designed us to shew, on small Occasions, as well as great" (*Sermons on Several Subjects,* 1770, 1: 221). The last instance in the *OED* is from *Sense and Sensibility* and is Elinor's exertion of spirits which increased with the increase of emotion. The point, again, is not that Secker is her source, he obviously is not, but rather that she assumes a reader who will recognize a public meaning. In the next chapter of the novel as we hear of Elinor's pains and tears and the need for unceasing exertion and self-command, we hear too, as we must, of "her appearance of cheerfulness," as invariable as it was possible to be (141). That kind of cheerfulness is the social appearance of the religious mind which takes as its aim to be content in itself, in amity with others and grateful to God. Cheerfulness as the sign of piety would be recognized by any reader of, for example, the *Spectator* (No. 381), or *Sir Charles Grandison,* or *Rambler* essays by several different authors (Nos. 44, 97, 127). "So calm!—so cheerful!" Marianne cries when she learns how long Elinor has borne a painful secret; "—how have you been supported?" "By feeling that I was doing my duty" (262). Anne Elliot, who knows what it is to do one's duty, could have been eloquent on a "cheerful confidence" which does not "insult exertion and distrust Providence" (P 30).

It is the end of Marianne's action when Elinor sees in her a "calmness of spirits," a composure of mind which is the result of "serious reflection" and must therefore eventually lead to "contentment and cheerfulness" (341–42). She sees in the manner the "mind awakened to reasonable exertion," a mind with much painful emotion but with firm resolution. Marianne says very little, but "every sentence aimed at cheerfulness" and if a sigh sometimes escapes "it never passed away without the atonement of a smile" (342). When she is prepared to talk the flow of her self-reproving spirit is rapid and it is clear. Her illness has made her think, has given leisure and "calmness for serious recollection" (345), has made her reflect on the moral failure that almost led her to the grave. Had she died it would have been self-destruction. The feelings that those reflections gave her make her wonder at her recovery, wonder that the very eagerness of her desire to live "to have time for atonement to my God" and to those she wronged did not kill her at once. The cheerfulness she now strives for, the atonement of a smile, is then evidently the manifestation of a serious atonement. Her heart, she says, had been hardened, she had turned away "from every exertion of duty or friendship" (346). Now the spirit is humbled, the heart amended, and she will show that she can practice "the civilities, the lesser duties of life," with gentleness and forbearance. And here again it is evident that the civilities properly practiced rest upon a deep base. As for Willoughby, the remembrance cannot be overcome, but it shall be regulated, it shall be checked "by religion, by reason, by constant employment" (347). It is now possible for Elinor, who has done so much, to tell her what she must know about Willoughby, enough to restore Marianne's self-respect and to help her overcome the remembrance.

4

Affection and the Mortification of Elizabeth Bennet

The first time Elizabeth Bennet sees Mr. Darcy, before they have ever spoken to each other, he mortifies her. It is the beginning of their action. His character has been decided already, by all the principal people in the room; Bingley has such amiable qualities as must speak for themselves, but—what a contrast between him and his friend!—Darcy is the proudest, most disagreeable man in the world. Before the action ends Elizabeth will have to discover that this is a really amiable man, to whom she must give her affection. She will have to define the differences between the agreeable and the amiable and to define the foundations of affection; and he will have to become worthy of that process of painful definition. It will be a mortifying experience for both of them. Elizabeth has wit and intelligence, a mind that runs with rapid play and liveliness. She finds life more amusing than others do because she is superior in discernment and abilities, so quick in observation and decisive in judgment at the first interview; she will discover a slower and seemingly "less interesting mode" far more interesting, more full of real life.

$\mathscr{I}$T will be a long time before she can say of Darcy that he is
an "amiable" man, because it is a long time before she knows
what the word means. It is a word that can be used lightly, as
she has been using it, but not by those who weigh their words.
Before Frank Churchill comes to Highbury Emma and Mr.
Knightley are arguing about him and the argument, as Mr.
Knightley attempts unsuccessfully to give it some precision,
turns upon a definition. Emma has called Frank "an amiable
young man" (E 148). Not only is she unacquainted with him
but she is, when she uses the phrase, offering a general proposition about a young man of a certain type; to Mr. Knightley it is
a weak, indecisive type. There is in some weak people an amiability that is an inactive, docile good temper; it is what Mr. Woodhouse has (7) and Isabella, the daughter who is more like him
(92); it is the kind of thing Captain Wentworth finds in
Henrietta Musgrove (P 86) and, when he knows her faults
better, in Louisa (182). But that is not what Mr. Knightley
means by real amiability. Nor is it quite what Emma meant, who
had something more agreeable in mind and, without realizing
it, something more dangerous. Emma is surprised at the heat of
the reaction she has provoked in Mr. Knightley, for several reasons, but she had spoken the word casually, as a conventional
epithet of praise. It had pervaded the fiction of the late eighteenth
century, densely populated by "amiable," "more than amiable"
and "most amiable" heroines and heroes.

Some awareness of this novelistic jargon adds a delight to a
reading of Jane Austen's juvenilia, because it adds force to the
parodic use of the word. One meets an absurdly endless number
of amiable characters, like the landlady of the little alehouse in
Evelyn, "who as well as every one else in Evelyn was remarkably amiable" (MW 180); one meets characters who are, over
and over, "the amiable Rebecca" (notwithstanding her forbidding squint, greasy tresses, and swelling back) (6 ff.). Part of

the joke of the "History of England" is the application of the novelistic adjective to kings, queens, and entire realms, with a scholarly exactness: in the reign of Charles I ("This amiable Monarch") "never were amiable men so scarce. The number of them throughout the whole Kingdom amounting only to *five . . .*" (148–49). The historian herself may be partial, prejudiced, and ignorant but we must take confidence in the value of the History from her own assurance that she is "my no less amiable self" (147). If we are told, in one of these early pieces, that a character is amiable we know it to be perfect: "perfectly amiable," like the young man who was addicted to no vice (beyond what his age and situation rendered perfectly excusable) (74). It is a happy thing to hear in a young lady's account of her education that "I daily became more amiable, & might perhaps by this time have nearly attained perfection" (17). The progress of the young Catherine Morland, from an unsuccessful romantic heroine to a rather more sensible observer of humanity, can be traced: from her beginning point, when she was surprised that she had reached the age of seventeen "without having seen one amiable youth who could call forth her sensibility" (NA 16); through her exceeding love for Isabella, as she swallows whole James Morland's estimate of that "thoroughly unaffected and amiable . . . most amiable girl" (NA 50); to the end point where she can clear General Tilney from her grossly injurious suspicions of villainy and still be able to believe, upon serious consideration, that he is "not perfectly amiable" (200). The charming Augusta Hawkins, before she is ever seen by Highbury, is discovered to have every recommendation of person and mind, to be handsome, elegant, highly accomplished, and, it follows by the formula that denotes not a real person but a fiction, "perfectly amiable" (E 181). The vapid amiable character, familiar to Jane Austen and no danger to her from her earliest years, remained a staple product of novelists and it was one of the dangers she had to mark out for that beginning author, young Anna Austen.

A character in Anna's manuscript is at first interesting to Jane Austen "in spite of her being so amiable" (L 387), obviously an unusual accomplishment; but Anna could not maintain that pitch, so, in a second letter, her aunt loses interest in that character and finds still another who worries her: "I am afraid [he] will be too much in the common Novel style—a handsome, amiable, unexceptionable Young Man (such as do not much abound in real Life)" (403).

To stupid Mr. Collins, a self-conscious master of complimentary terminology that has not much to do with real life, the word is a valuable all-purpose superlative. Miss De Bourgh, he rapidly informs the Bennets, is "perfectly amiable" (PP 67), though the details of her he has offered bear another tale. His cousin Elizabeth, as he tells her with clocklike solemnity during his proposal, also qualifies for the word, though, as he also assures her, there are many other amiable young women in his own neighborhood (105, 106, 107, 108); and when he transfers his affections to Charlotte he transfers the word as easily (128, 139). What is more amusing is that in Elizabeth's difficult brief period, following her rejection of Mr. Collins, Charlotte seems to her to be "very amiable" in accepting his attentions (121); she is thankful to her friend Charlotte for this obliging kindness. Elizabeth has something to learn about amiability. It is something important enough to consider in multiple illustration because it keeps returning in almost all of Jane Austen's writing. To Mr. Knightley it is a point of reality that helps define the national character.

What Elizabeth has to learn is important, because there is a true amiability, not an insipid fictive perfection that offers itself for immediate admiration but a reality that frequently takes time to disclose itself or to be discovered by an observer who is unable to see it. An intelligent young woman, unlike a romantic heroine, will not meet much perfection in her experience but she may well make mistakes in understanding what is more difficult: the difference between those who are truly "amiable" and those who are only "agreeable." That is "an important distinction," Dr. Gregory warned his daughters, "which many of your sex are not aware of" (*A Father's Legacy to His Daughters,* 1774, and many later editions, into the nineteenth century, p. 37). Jane Austen makes the distinction in two of her letters, writing about the same young man: first in a passing observation to her sister Cassandra, and then, more than a year later, to Fanny Knight, on a critical occasion, which validates the large significance of the words. Mr. John Plumtre, she tells Cassandra, is someone she likes very much: "He gives me the idea of a very amiable young Man, only too diffident to be so agreeable as he might be" (L 342). He is lacking in the social manner that would make him complete, but a completeness cannot be expected often, and when there are choices to be made it is always the amiable that is to be chosen. Mr. Plumtre then attaches himself to Fanny Knight and Fanny encourages him until she finds that perhaps she has mistaken her own feelings; Jane Austen, as her aunt, tries to give her the best possible advice, not telling her what to do, but clarifying for her what the alternatives are. There is a strong case to be made for Mr. Plumtre, "above all his character—his uncommonly amiable mind, strict principles, just notions, good habits . . . *All* that really is of the first importance." His manners are not equal to this excellence, but a comparison between him and Fanny's own "agreeable, idle Brothers" will show Fanny that it is Mr. Plumtre who has the sterling worth. He is not perfect, because he has a fault of modesty, and if he were less modest "he would be more agreeable, speak louder & look Impudenter," but it is a fine character of which this is the only defect (L 409–10). The conclusion is not that Fanny should marry him—and we'll come back to Mr. Plumtre— but her aunt's advice will lead her to understand her choices and enable her to decide for the right reasons, not reject a man of uncommonly amiable mind and all that is really of the first importance because she thinks it more important that the man be agreeable.

If agreeable men are likely to be suspect characters in Jane Austen there is good cause. Their agreeableness might be an initial value but it would improve upon acquaintance and reveal the mind, principles, notions, and habits that make the moral character, so that the agreeableness of manner and person would not remain the most notable quality. Mr. Elliot of *Persuasion* is that "exceedingly agreeable man," who makes his impression even before his identity is known, who is, in his regard for Anne, a source of agreeable sensation to her; he is offered as a suitable match. "Where could you expect a more gentlemanlike, agreeable man?" (P 104–5, 159–60, 196). But well before she learns the full story of his life Anne has real doubts because she can never find anything more in him. "Mr. Elliot was too generally agreeable," deliberately pleases even where he is contemptuous: even Mrs. Clay "found him as agreeable as anybody," a note in passing that makes the ending of the novel less surprising and more enjoyable (P 160–61). Henry Crawford is more interesting because he is a man who makes an effort to change himself to something better, from "the most agreeable young man" the Miss Bertrams had ever known (MP 44) to a man deserving of the affection of an amiable woman. There is much byplay at Mansfield Park about the mutual agreeableness of the Crawfords and the young Bertrams and even Sir Thomas is impressed by Henry's "more than common agreeableness," the address and conversation pleasing to everyone (316). Mrs. Price at Portsmouth "had never seen so agreeable a man in her life" (400). It will take more than this to win Fanny but she sees in his visit to Portsmouth that there are ways in which he really is acting differently. In his account of where he has been and what he has been doing there is more than the "accidental agreeableness" of the parties he has been in; he has done good work in performing a duty, for the first time, among the tenants of his estate, thereby securing "agreeable recollections for his own mind"; that is certainly a better kind of agreeableness than he has ever known (404). She sees that he is much more gentle, obliging, and attentive to other people's feelings than he had ever been at Mansfield: "she had never seen him so agreeable—so *near* being agreeable" (406). Fanny is using the lower word in her own high sense, because he is now near being amiable, and she is making a fine distinction; but she is right, because the good impulse now moving Henry will not be enough. He lacks the principle to maintain the habit of right action. His moral character cannot rise above the agreeable manner. His story ends when he goes to the house of the family at Twickenham where Maria has grown intimate—a family of lively, "agreeable manners, and probably of morals and discretion to suit," for to that house Henry had constant access at all times (450). What he threw away when he entered that accessible house was the way of happiness, working for the esteem and tenderness that leads to "one amiable woman's affections" (467).

To recognize the one amiable woman, or man, is the first simple perception in making a marriage. In fact few can do it. The lady for whom Willoughby has jilted Marianne is very rich, Elinor learns, but what Elinor wants to know is what kind of woman she is: "Is she said to be amiable?" (SS 194). That is the question because it will determine what can be said for him and what are his chances of happiness, but it was never a question that touched his mind. Edward Ferrars is a better man because the question did concern him, but he had not been able to answer it: Lucy Steele had been successful with him because she "appeared everything that was amiable and obliging" (362). She was not really so, as Elinor has always known (129, 238), and the mistake he made could have been ruinous in time. The perception of a real amiability requires time. Mrs. Dashwood is correct in her opinion of Edward but her opinion is without much meaning: "It was enough for her that he appeared to be amiable"; to say that he is unlike Fanny Dashwood is enough: "It implies every thing amiable. I love him already" (15–16). Elinor's measured answer is the right one: " 'I think you will like him,' said Elinor, 'when you know more of him,' " because time and knowledge measure possible degrees and truths of feeling. If, therefore, Edward had married Lucy he would have entered a future of great peril. The man who marries an un-amiable woman may be made unhappy, but that is not the worst; if he falls in with her manner he may be happy, but he will be-come an unworthy man. It happened to John Dashwood, who "had he married a more amiable woman" might have improved, "might even have been made amiable himself," for he was very young when he married and very fond of his wife; but Mrs. John Dashwood was a caricature of himself, more narrow-minded and selfish (5). It happened to Mr. Elton. Emma recog-nizes that when she sees him as an old married man, to use his own phrase, deliberately hurting Harriet while smiles of high glee pass between him and his wife. "This was Mr. Elton! the amiable, obliging, gentle Mr. Elton" (E 328). He is not quite so hardened as his wife but he is growing very like her. There is a littleness about him that Emma had not discovered.

Emma's discovery is a long time in coming because the ability to recognize an amiable man is dependent on the ability to per-ceive with a moral clarity of definition. Harriet can look forward to being happily married to Mr. Elton, Emma assures her, be-cause "here is a man whose amiable character gives every assur-ance of it" (E 75). With the advantage of her long intimacy with Miss Taylor Emma should be able to recognize a "truly amiable woman" (17); but if she can then say of Harriet that she has never met with a disposition "more truly amiable" (43) the word can have no real meaning for her. She finds Harriet very amiable because of that early and easy deference to herself (26). Emma cannot distinguish the amiable from the agreeable, uses the words indiscriminately. She has no doubt she has given

Harriet's fancy a proper direction when she makes her aware that Mr. Elton is a "remarkably handsome man, with most agreeable manners" (42); but that is also the language of the talkative Miss Nash, head teacher at Mrs. Goddard's, telling Harriet that beyond a doubt Mr. Elton has not his equal "for beauty or agreeableness" (68). The question Emma puts to Harriet about Robert Martin is precisely the wrong one: "if you think him the most agreeable man you have ever been in company with, why should you hesitate?" (53). The intention of the question, as she points out, is to put another man into Harriet's mind, and it is successful, unfortunately. But it takes a blunt John Knightley to point out an obvious truth: "I never . . . saw a man more intent on being agreeable than Mr. Elton" (111); Emma has been willing to overlook the labor and the affectation and the working of every feature because it fits her pleasure to think he is a man of good will. Only after he has astonished her by his proposal does she judge him "not . . . so particularly amiable" (138), because at that point it is a great consolation to think so.

Emma needs the agreeable so that she can continue to be comfortable, think a little too well of herself, create her own world without being disturbed by examining it or herself too closely. It is Mr. Knightley, angry with her for misguiding Harriet, who prompts her better self by making things uncomfortable and being "very disagreeable" (E 65). It is he who gives her hints that she is being neglectful in not visiting the Bateses, not contributing to their scanty comforts, and some hints have come from her own heart—but none is equal to counteract the persuasion of its all being "very disagreeable" (155). When she does call on them, with Harriet, it is not to bring comfort to them but to get rid of what is now the more tiresome subject of Mr. Elton.

The mistake with the agreeable Mr. Elton also makes her rejoice in the coming of Frank Churchill; she hopes to find him agreeable. It was the hope that she was defending against Mr.

Knightley when she elicited his critical definition. She has called Frank amiable, but Mr. Knightley makes the distinction for her: "Your amiable young man," if he has not been following his duty instead of consulting expediency, "is a very weak young man." The young man writes fine flourishing letters but he has never exerted himself to pay the proper attention to his father and especially to Mrs. Weston, upon their marriage, so that he has all the external manner and none of the reality of action: "No, Emma, your amiable young man can be amiable only in French, not in English. He may be very 'aimable,' have very good manners, and be very agreeable; but he can have no English delicacy towards the feelings of other people: nothing really amiable about him." But those smooth, plausible manners will be enough, Emma says, to make him a treasure at Highbury, where "We do not often look upon fine young men, well-bred and agreeable"; we must not be nice and ask for virtue too. Her idea of him is that he can adapt his conversation to the taste of everybody and "has the power as well as the wish of being universally agreeable." If he is anything like this he will be insupportable, Mr. Knightley says (E 148–50). But when Frank arrives Emma's vanity gives him every support. She is directly sure that "he knew how to make himself agreeable," as he certainly does; he talks of Highbury as his *own* country and says he has had the greatest curiosity to visit: that he should "never have been able to indulge so amiable a feeling before" passes suspiciously through Emma's brain, but it passes (191). She only feels that he is agreeable and the rest must wait. The danger to her of the man who knows how to make himself agreeable but who is not amiable multiplies as the story progresses. He even arrives at the point where he is sick of England, which means that in self-pity he is prepared to run from the obligations he owes to the feelings of others. He is, Mr. Knightley had guessed correctly, a weak young man; on the day at Box Hill Jane Fairfax has come to recognize that fact and recognize that he therefore puts his own happiness at the mercy of chance, and hers too. For Emma the moral dangers are even greater because she is readily susceptible to, desirous of, his agreeableness and blind to the rest. In the climactic two hours at Box Hill, when to amuse her "and be agreeable in her eyes" seems all he cares for, Emma is ignorant of his motives and is not sorry to be flattered (368). As the pitch of the scene rises, in response to his lead Emma loses self-command and insults Miss Bates, pains her, is herself unfeeling. There is an extraordinary pathos and irony when Miss Bates can only reply, "I must make myself very disagreeable, or she would not have said such a thing to an old friend" (371).

The really amiable man, Mr. Knightley teaches us, is the man who is strong in his action because fine in his emotion, who habitually exerts himself to do his duty because he has a delicacy for the feelings of others. He will be a man capable of love and worthy of love. The happiness of Elizabeth Bennet turns upon her ability to recognize the really amiable man; one way of marking her fortunes and progress is to follow her accuracy in assigning the right adjective to the right man and all that it implies of quality of vision. Darcy, we have said, enters the novel with a character quickly determined by the assembly room at the first ball, when his fine person and fortune draw admiration and then, just as quickly, his manners give a disgust. He is discovered to have "a most forbidding, disagreeable countenance." "He was the proudest, most disagreeable man in the world (PP 10–11). The immediate contrast is between him and Bingley, whose "amiable qualities must speak for themselves": Bingley soon makes himself acquainted with all the principal people in the room, is lively and unreserved, dances every dance, talks of giving a dance himself at Netherfield. The evidence on either side is hardly existent and Elizabeth will have to do better than all the principal people. She will have to do so in spite of the man himself, in spite of herself, and of their mutually disagreeable introduction. Bingley tries to interest Darcy in Elizabeth as someone very pretty "and I dare say, very agreeable," but he is not tempted (11). To her Darcy is then "only the man who made himself agreeable no where, and who had not thought her handsome enough to dance with" (23). When, some weeks later, he does ask her to dance she is surprised into accepting him and she frets. "I dare say you will find him very agreeable," says Charlotte, with a small echo. "Heaven forbid!—*That* would be the greatest misfortune of all!—To find a man agreeable whom one is determined to hate!—Do not wish me such an evil" (90).

Bingley, it does develop, is "truly amiable," as Elizabeth later calls him (82); but even at the time she says that she doesn't know enough of him, and her opinion is still to undergo changes, because Bingley's is a soft amiability that makes him dependent on chance, susceptible to interference by others with his own happiness and therefore with the feelings of the woman he loves. More importantly, Elizabeth's praise of Bingley is offered to emphasize the contrast between him and Darcy and it is delivered to Wickham for that purpose. In response to Wickham's questioning the very first thing she had said of Darcy was "I think him very disagreeable" (77). For that reason she is ready to accept Wickham's story and to think of Darcy as cruel, malicious, unjust, inhumane. Wickham himself she trusts: he is a young man, she says to herself, "whose very countenance may vouch for your being amiable" (80–81); and if she thinks of herself as a better judge of character than Jane, she has done no better than Jane will do the next day: "it was not in her nature to question the veracity of a young man of such amiable appearance as Wickham" (85). Jane's less confident nature at least preserves her from Elizabeth's error of deciding the matter against Darcy. More than that, Jane has a good reason for suspending judgment for it is difficult to believe that an intimate friend like Bingley can be so deceived in Darcy's character. The very thought had just occurred to Elizabeth as she listened to Wickham and declared Bingley's amiability but, like several other true thoughts that had come and gone, it did her no good. She is not in love with Wickham, she tells Mrs. Gardiner, "But he is, beyond all comparison, the most agreeable man I ever saw," and the possibility of affection interests her (144–45). For all her superior intelligence Elizabeth is more blind than Jane. When Jane thinks that Bingley has departed from her life she has the steadiness not to repine though he "may live in my memory as the most amiable man of my acquaintance" (134). When Elizabeth parts from Wickham, who may now be marrying Miss King, she is convinced that "he must always be her model of the amiable and pleasing" (152). Only Jane has any evidence of the real character of the man she is talking about and Elizabeth has confused the most agreeable man with the model of the amiable. Jane has been crossed in love by the loss of Bingley, which gives her, says Mr. Bennet, a sort of distinction: "Let Wickham be *your* man." "Thank you, Sir," Elizabeth replies, "but a less agreeable man would satisfy me" (138). He would and he does. What she has still to discover is the identity and amiability of that less agreeable man.

Where Wickham has been able to deceive her by false information he has done what he could. As he was maligning Darcy he was also shaking his head over Miss Darcy, professing pain because he could not call her "amiable"—but she was too like her brother in being very, very proud (82); some months later, in Derbyshire, Elizabeth is prepared to see a "proud, reserved, disagreeable girl," then finds that Miss Darcy is "amiable and unpretending" (284). But Wickham's ability to mislead her where she has never seen the object of his lies is a small thing. The great humiliation is the discovery that she has believed all he says of Darcy because she has been pleased by his preference and offended by Darcy's neglect, therefore courted prepossession and ignorance and driven reason away. The discovery she makes in the receipt of Darcy's letter is less in the new information he offers than in a self-discovery that allows her to see what has always been before her. What she now begins to comprehend is a reality to which she has blinded herself because the appearance was so much more pleasing. That agreeableness, that false amiability of Wickham, had been a charm: it was a countenance, a voice, a manner; as to his "real character" she had never felt a wish of inquiring. She tries now to find some moral reality in her recollection of him, "some instance of goodness," some trait of integrity or benevolence, virtue; she can see him instantly before her in every charm of air and address, but she can remember no "substantial good" beyond the general approbation of the neighborhood or the regard that his social powers had gained him (206).

The substantial good evaporates as one seeks it in Wickham; as it does in Willoughby, with his uncommonly attractive person and lively manner, which it was no merit to possess (SS 333); as it does in Mr. Elliot when Anne finds him sensible and agreeable but is still afraid to answer for his conduct (P 160–61). Anne has her own reasons for prizing a man of more warmth and enthusiasm, but the truth about Mr. Elliot's real character, that he has no feeling for others (199), is the truth about all the very well-mannered and very agreeable young men who, in Mr. Knightley's distinction, have no delicacy toward the feelings of other people, nothing really amiable about them. They can separate their agreeableness from their feeling, so that the pleasing sensations they offer turn terribly chilling. To miss the distinction, then, to be drawn to the agreeable, is shocking, is both an easy and a dangerous temptation, because it is to fall into that pleasing sensation of the unreality that flatters the self. The agreeable imitation of feeling becomes the instant welcome deception. But the real feeling of the amiable man expressing the principle of a life can be known only by the evidences of an earned experience. It may be hard to find that reality, when its appearance is not readily pleasing, and to acknowledge it, however disagreeable to the self.

It was this reality Elizabeth had denied Darcy, as she rejected him and grew more angry and told him directly, in the last sentence that drove him from the room: his manners impressed her with "the fullest belief of your arrogance, your conceit, and your selfish disdain of the feelings of others" (193). As she begins to make the discovery about her blindness she remembers that she has often heard Darcy speak "so affectionately of his sister as to prove him capable of *some* amiable feeling." It is a minimal fact but it has meaning as it follows a new realization of his character—that however proud and repulsive his manners, her acquaintance has given her an intimacy with Darcy's ways and she has never seen anything that betrayed him to be unprincipled or unjust, anything that spoke of irreligious or immoral habits. It has meaning as it precedes her new realization that had his actions been what Wickham represented them, there could be no friendship between anyone capable of those actions and "such an amiable man as Mr. Bingley" (207–8). She realizes now, when she receives his letter, that she has no evidence to bring against him; as she learns more of the history of his life, when she visits his home, she learns more positively what his behavior has been as child and man. Mrs. Reynolds can testify to his goodness of disposition and to his goodness of action as landlord to tenant and as master to servant. It is a new light on his character. "In what an amiable light does this place him!" Elizabeth thinks, ". . . so amiable a light" (249, 265). But above all she then knows by his conduct to her, who has given him such cause to be an enemy, his capacity for love. She questions him at the end of the story, wanting him to account for having ever fallen in love with her, when her behavior to him had been at least always bordering on the uncivil and when she never spoke to him without rather wishing to give him pain: "Had you not been really amiable you would have hated me for it." He knew no "actual good" of her, she adds; but in fact he did, certainly in her "affectionate behavior" to Jane in need

(380). They are both of them people who are capable of actual good, of affection, really amiable, worthy of love. She knows what he has done for her and her family. By the time Darcy has made his second proposal Elizabeth has learned enough of him and his family (339, 369) to be able to answer her father's doubts of that proud, unpleasant man: " 'I do, I do like him,' she replied, with tears in her eyes. 'I love him. Indeed he has no improper pride. He is perfectly amiable' " (376). It is astonishing praise, and a daring phrase for Elizabeth to use. It is a sign of the pressure of feeling upon her, because her earlier misjudgments and immoderate expressions have forced her into this awkwardness, that she should be so extravagant as to use a kind of novelistic jargon; and it is a sign of Darcy's real excellence that he does not sink under the weight of it. He really is amiable.

The accomplishment of amiability is unusual; it is earned by moral and intelligent effort and it cannot be distributed sentimentally as a reward. The narrator wishes it could be said that Mrs. Bennet's accomplishment of her earnest desire in marrying off her daughters produced so happy an effect as to make her "a sensible, amiable, well-informed woman"; but that could not be, and perhaps it was lucky for her husband, who might not have relished domestic felicity in so unusual a form (385).

$\mathcal{T}$HE form in which domestic felicity comes to Elizabeth and Darcy is unusual and it is there not by luck. It comes, first, because both are amiable and that is a necessary foundation, but it comes because on that is built something more. Above all, as Elizabeth knows, there must be love, or to use the word Jane Austen prefers in such contexts, there must be "affection." It is the quieter, more general word, for an emotion of slower growth and more lasting therefor; but it is, in this context, a strong word for a deep emotion. It is the word Emma uses at the moment of her insight into her own heart when she is ashamed of every sensation but one, "her affection for Mr.

Knightley" (E 412); it is the word Anne Elliot uses to describe her feelings for Captain Wentworth, when he is once again desirous of her affection: "her affection would be his for ever" (P 190, 192). It is, in general, Jane Austen's chiefest instance of how without the appropriate emotion there is no moral action; specifically it is the love that every marriage must have and without which no married life can stand. Elizabeth Bennet's closest friend calls it into serious question, both in talk and in action, with grave result both for herself and for Elizabeth.

To Charlotte affection is of no importance, except as an appearance that may be useful for getting a husband. She has advice for Jane Bennet, who is very much on the way to being in love but whose composure and cheerfulness do not disclose her real strength of feeling; her advice has nothing to do with the needs of that reality and of the particular characters of Jane and Bingley, for Charlotte's concern is the general method of exploiting the opportunity to fix a man by helping him on with a show of affection. "In nine cases out of ten, a woman had better shew *more* affection than she feels." The love may or may not follow the marriage, but if it does it is a casual supplementary decision that does not require any thought or feeling. "When she is secure of him, there will be leisure for falling in love as much as she chuses." In a word, affection has no real existence for Charlotte. The minor practicality of her advice is that she is right about Bingley's need for encouragement, but she would apply that to any man because the larger need of understanding one's own thoughts and feelings and a mutual understanding of character is what she denies in marriage. The time needed for a developed love is meaningless. To marry tomorrow, to marry after studying character for a twelvemonth, is all the same. "Happiness in marriage is entirely a matter of chance." Knowledge does not advance felicity and it is better to know as little as possible of the defects of the person with whom you are to pass your life. Elizabeth refuses to take her seriously, finds the opinion laughable because it is not sound, because Charlotte knows it is not sound and because Charlotte would never act in that way herself (21–23). But Charlotte acts precisely in that way.

There can be no question of any "affection" for or from Mr. Collins, a man to whom the word is known, and known only, as a word which it is customary to employ during a proposal. We have heard him declare himself to Elizabeth shortly before he is secured by Charlotte. "And now nothing remains for me but to assure you in the most animated language of the violence of my affection," where the words and the meaning of the sentence are so marvellously contradictory (106). Charlotte marries him. "I am not romantic you know," she tells Elizabeth. "I never was." She asks only a comfortable home and considering what she will get with Collins she is convinced that her chance of happiness with him is as fair as most people can boast of on entering the marriage state. Elizabeth's astonishment is so great that it overcomes the bounds of decorum and she cannot help crying out, "Engaged to Mr. Collins! my dear Charlotte,—impossible!" She could not have supposed it possible that when Charlotte's opinions on matrimony were called into action she could have sacrificed every better feeling to worldly advantage. It is, to Elizabeth, a humiliating picture (124–25).

One must not be misled by Charlotte's quiet declaration that she is not romantic to think that she is acting in a sensible way in a most difficult situation. What Charlotte does is wrong. But then what ought Charlotte do rather than marry Mr. Collins? She is without much money, she is not handsome, she is no longer young, and to be an old maid without money or position will be an unfortunate life. Miss Bates of *Emma* is an instance and Mr. Knightley lectures Emma on the special consideration Miss Bates's misfortune demands. Miss Bates is in worse condition than Charlotte would be because she has no abilities that can give her respect; Charlotte is intelligent. But that intelligence increases the magnitude of Charlotte's defection, because it makes her match with Mr. Collins the more unequal. He is stupid. He is neither sensible nor agreeable; his society is irksome; and his attachment to her must be imaginary. "But still he would be her husband." And that and his establishment are his total charm. Charlotte is interested in neither the man nor the relationship, only the marriage; and it is not the narrator's but Charlotte's reflection on marriage that "it was the only honourable provision for well-educated young women of small fortune, and however uncertain of giving happiness, must be their pleasantest preservative from want" (122–23).

There is more than enough evidence, elsewhere in Jane Austen and in this novel, to make clear how mistaken Charlotte is in a decision to marry without affection. The problem of that type of decision returns several times, in minor works and in major, and even in the letters, and the answer is always the same. It is in the first conversation Emma Watson has with her oldest sister. Elizabeth Watson tells bitter tales of their sister, Penelope, who has acted with rivalry and treachery to Elizabeth in the pursuit of a husband, for there is nothing Penelope would not do to get married; at present she is in pursuit of a rich old doctor attacked by asthma. Emma Watson's reaction is sorrow and fear and more than that: to be so bent on marriage, to pursue a man merely for the sake of a situation is shocking to her and she cannot understand it. "Poverty is a great Evil, but to a woman of Education & feeling it ought not, it cannot be the greatest.— I would rather be a Teacher at a school (and I can think of nothing worse) than marry a Man I did not like." Emma Watson is surprised because she is inexperienced, but there is no question that her principles are quite right and that if Elizabeth Watson thinks her too refined it is because Elizabeth herself is, though good-hearted, coarse. Elizabeth's reply, "I think I could like any good humoured Man with a comfortable Income," is one of many signs of her deficiencies (MW 318). In *Mansfield Park* the great temptation of Fanny Price is to accept the proposal of Henry Crawford, for which every pressure is brought to bear upon her and by those she loves most. But she knows she is doing right in refusing him and she hopes that her uncle's displeasure with her will abate when he considers the matter with more impartiality and comes to feel, as a good man must feel, "how wretched, and how unpardonable, how hopeless and how wicked it was, to marry without affection" (324). We never have any doubt that she is right in this refusal and indeed the whole novel turns on it. It is wicked to marry without affection.

One of Jane Austen's more interesting letters is the advice she wrote to Fanny Knight in 1814 (just after the publication of *Pride and Prejudice* in 1813 and of *Mansfield Park* in 1814), that same letter about the amiable Mr. Plumtre. In it she replies to her niece's anxiety over a grievous mistake, because Fanny has encouraged the young man to such a point as to make him feel almost secure of her—and now her feelings have changed. It was a common mistake, her aunt comforts her, one that thousands of women fall into: he was the first young man who attached himself to her and that was a powerful charm. Furthermore, unlike most who have done the same, Fanny Knight has little to regret, because the young man is nothing to be ashamed of. Jane Austen then goes on to point out all his excellences— his mind, his principles, and all qualities which, as she says, are really of the first importance; the more she writes about him the warmer her feelings grow and the more strongly she feels the sterling worth of such a young man and the desirableness of Fanny's growing in love with him again. She takes up certain objections that Fanny has to him and tries to show her that they are false, that what her niece thinks are faults in him are really unimportant or even advantages. At that point, after such a lengthy, thoughtful, and feeling argument on behalf of the young man, Jane Austen puts into the other side of the balance the one thing that outweighs everything else:

—And now, my dear Fanny, having written so much on one side of the question, I shall turn round & entreat you not to commit yourself farther, & not to think of accepting him unless you really do like him. Anything is to be preferred or endured rather than marrying without Affection; and if his deficiencies of Manner &c &c strike you more than all his good qualities, if you continue to think strongly of them, give him up at once. (L 409–10)

To return, then, from Jane Austen's "my dear Fanny" to Elizabeth Bennet's "my dear Charlotte" and Jane Bennet's "my dear Lizzy" (as they are all addressed in moments of similar crisis): when Elizabeth receives her second proposal from Darcy and accepts him, she seems to the intelligent members of her family, to her father and Jane, to be in a situation similar to Charlotte's when Charlotte accepted Mr. Collins. The similarity is emphasized by a verbal identity. Elizabeth's astonishment had been so great when Charlotte informed her of the engagement to Collins that she could not help crying out, "Engaged to Mr. Collins! . . . impossible!" (124). When Elizabeth is engaged and opens her heart to Jane, the reaction is, untypically for Jane but understandably so, absolute incredulity: "engaged to Mr. Darcy! . . . impossible" (372). Jane's disbelief, unlike Elizabeth's reaction to Charlotte's match, is not that she thinks Darcy without a single quality to make him a desirable husband; on the contrary, nothing could give Bingley or Jane more delight than such a marriage. But she thought it impossible because of Elizabeth's dislike, and even now she cannot approve, however great and desirable it seems, if Elizabeth does not really love him quite well enough. The appeal is direct and deep, and very like Jane Austen's words to Fanny Knight: "Oh, Lizzy! do any thing rather than marry without affection. Are you quite sure that you feel what you ought to do?" (373). So the answer to the question of what Charlotte Lucas ought to do rather than marry Mr. Collins is—"any thing." To be an impoverished old maid is a misfortune, but to marry Mr. Collins is immoral.

Nor is it true that because she has not made the romantic choice, Charlotte has made the practical choice for the comfortable home. The antithesis is false. She had said, in general, that happiness is entirely a matter of chance and she says, in particular, that considering what Collins is, in character, connections, and situation, her chance of happiness with him is as fair as most people can boast on entering the marriage state. But her chances are not even uncertain. That point emerges most convincingly because Charlotte makes the very best of her marriage state and manages it admirably. Elizabeth thinks that it will be impossible for her friend to be tolerably happy (125), but in her visit to Kent she sees how well Charlotte can do. Charlotte maintains her comfortable home and her married life by excluding her husband from it as much as she possibly can. She chooses for her own common use an inferior room with a less lively view because he is less likely to appear in it; Elizabeth gives her credit for the arrangement (168). She encourages her husband as much as possible in his gardening, to keep him out of the house. When he says something of which she might reasonably be ashamed, which certainly is not seldom, she sometimes blushes faintly, but in general she wisely does not hear (156). The necessary wisdom for living with Mr. Collins, which Charlotte accepts, is to give up a piece of herself, suppress her shame, lose her ears, see less, diminish her life. As Elizabeth leaves her, at the end of the visit, Charlotte does not ask for compassion, but her prospect is a melancholy one. Her home, housekeeping, her parish and poultry have not yet lost their charms (216). Not yet. Neither is it a comforting later little note to hear that Mr. Collins's dear Charlotte is expecting a young olive branch. She no doubt will do the best she can, but the children of mismatches without respect or affection do not begin life with advantage.

With her eyes open Charlotte has miscalculated, because there are no fair chances of happiness in an inequality that makes affection impossible. Elizabeth's father can advise his child of this. Like Jane, Mr. Bennet may be mistaken in his facts but not in his principle when he warns Elizabeth to think better before having Mr. Darcy. He knows she cannot be happy or respectable unless she esteems her husband, that an unequal marriage would put her in danger, perhaps discredit and misery. "My child, let me not have the grief of seeing *you* unable to respect your partner in life" (376). He and his daughter know the living experience that speaks in these words. Captivated by youth and beauty and the appearance of good humor they generally give, he had married a woman whose weak understanding and illiberal mind "had very early in their marriage put an end to all real affection for her" (236). The results have been before the reader since the first chapter and before Elizabeth, with less amusement and more pain, all her life. She has felt strongly the disadvantages that must attend the children of so unsuitable a marriage, and Lydia's disaster has confirmed her judgment.

Lydia's affair is, for one thing, what can happen to the child of a marriage without affection. It is, for another, itself an instance of a marriage where neither person is capable of affection. "Her affections had been continually fluctuating" and it required only encouragement for her to attach herself to him in particular (280). His fluctuations have been apparent to Elizabeth from personal experience; his affection for Lydia, just as Elizabeth had expected, is not equal to hers for him (318) and it is only in fulfillment of the obvious that we hear at the end how "His affection for her soon sunk into indifference" (387). His last private conversation with Elizabeth, in which she makes embarrassingly clear that she knows all about him, ends as he kisses her hand "with affectionate gallantry, though he hardly knew how to look" (329): a very pretty touch that leaves his affection exposed for what it is in a shallow and losing gesture. But, furthermore, the affection of Lydia's Wickham was once something that interested Elizabeth for herself (144–45, 153), so that her own understanding of the meaning of affection has not always been what it is at last; it has taken time. If Charlotte Lucas thinks time is unimportant because affection is unimportant, Elizabeth has flirted with another mode in which time is unimportant because affection is so quickly seen. Lydia's affair helps her sister to better understanding.

The validity of the marriage between Darcy and Elizabeth is established by the time in which their affection grows, and by the capacity of the affection to withstand and to be strengthened by the proofs of time and crisis. Elizabeth is certain that the immediate effect of Lydia's disgrace will be that her own power with Darcy must sink, that everything must sink under such a proof of family weakness; it makes her understand her own wishes, and never has she so honestly felt how much she could have loved him as now when all love is vain. The whole of their acquaintance, as she can now review it, has been full of contradictions and varieties and she sighs at the perverseness of her own feelings, which have so changed. In the mode of romance Elizabeth's change is unreasonable or unnatural in comparison with the regard that arises on a first interview and even before two words have been exchanged; but she had given "somewhat of a trial" to this "method" with Wickham and its ill-success might perhaps authorize her to try the other "less interesting mode of attachment." The ironic language sounds like the language of experimental method, and it is that, in the sense of tested experience of common life as opposed to romantic prejudice, but the reality here is the reality of tried emotions. "If gratitude and esteem are good foundations of affection"—and the hypothesis has been tried by Elizabeth's mind and emotions—then the change of sentiment will be "neither improbable nor faulty" (279).

Henry Tilney had come to be sincerely attached to Catherine Morland, he felt and delighted in all the excellences of her character and "truly loved" her society, but, as we know, "his affection originated in nothing better than gratitude." That may be a new circumstance in romance, but not in common life (NA 243). "Gratitude" here is the response to the feeling of another, the natural obligation in return for having been thought worthy of being loved. It was this that led Fanny Knight into her mistake with her young man, whose powerful charm was that he was the first young man to attach himself to her. John Gregory, giving fatherly advice to his daughters, warns them that what is commonly called love among girls is rather gratitude and partiality to the man who prefers them to the rest of the sex, so that such a man they often marry with little personal esteem or affection. But the difference between Fanny Knight or Dr. Gregory's daughters and what happens to Elizabeth Bennet is the difference between the young miss and the woman who knows the meaning of affection. In the one the gratitude is the first pleasing stir of a self-love that confuses its object, in the other it is the feeling that initiates a self-discovery. The feeling develops if, as with Darcy, there is a continuing revelation of a character whose actions build more powerful causes of gratitude and if, as with Elizabeth, there is a continuing increase of a character who can perceive and respond to that revelation. Elizabeth's gratitude develops in a heightened vision of him, and in a properly chastened revision of her self-love. That irony, the coolness and detachment of her language, as she recollects how she has arrived at her present feelings by the less interesting mode of attachment, is directed not at her feelings but at herself. She sees in her affection the complicated history of herself. The slow preparation of the foundations creates for an affection its depth of interest and is the guarantee of its reality of meaning in a life. Four months earlier at his declaration of how ardently he admired and loved her she had not been willing to grant Darcy even the conventional gratitude: "In such cases as this, it is, I believe, the established mode to express a sense of obligation for the sentiments avowed, however unequally they may be returned. It is natural that obligation should be felt, and if I could *feel* gratitude, I would now thank you. But I cannot—I have never desired your good opinion" (190). Now she knows by extended experience what his good opinion is worth and what the value of his affection is. Having seen him at Pemberley in a new light, an amiable light, there was then above all, above the respect and esteem, another motive within her, the gratitude she felt for his love of her. It was gratitude not merely for his having loved her, but for loving her still well enough to forgive the petulance and acrimony of her manner in rejecting him and forgive all her unjust accusations. A man who had reason to be her enemy has been eager to preserve her acquaintance, solicit the good opinion of her friends, make her known to his sister. Such a change in such a man excites gratitude, for this is a man who knows something of love, of ardent love (265–66).

Furthermore, Darcy's response to the event which she fears has put an end to their acquaintance then becomes the severest test of his affection. He arranges for the marriage of Wickham and her sister and he does it because of "his affection for her" (326). At first she rebukes her vanity for putting so much dependence on the force of that affection, but she has underestimated it. It has remained unshaken (334), unchanged (366); when, at last, he can tell her of his feelings, they prove how important she has been to him, and they make "his affection every moment more valuable" (366). That is what enables her to answer her father's doubts of Darcy with "absolute certainty that his affection was not the work of a day, but had stood the test of many months suspense" (377). She is "in the certain possession of his warmest affection" (378).

$\mathcal{T}$HEY have come to that happy moment because each has suffered a change. If he has no improper pride and is perfectly amiable when she accepts him, he was not so when she rejected him. And if she is capable of the kind of affection she feels when she accepts him, she was not so when she rejected him. Each has changed because each has worked a change on the other. The happiness is deserved by a process of mortification begun early and ended late. Charlotte Lucas suggested at the start that Darcy is a man who has some right to be proud, and Elizabeth agrees. "I could easily forgive *his* pride, if he had not mortified *mine*" (20). As Mary Bennet, on the same page, draws upon her reading of synonym dictionaries to define pride, we can get some help from these sources in understanding mortification. It is more than the mere vexation of a contradictory will, it is a force that cuts into the understanding and evaluation of one's self. Mrs. Bennet is easily vexed—"You take delight in vexing me," she says in the first chapter. "You have no compassion on my poor nerves" (5)—but she cannot be mortified. Elizabeth will have to make the distinction. Vexation arises from the crossing our wishes and views, says Crabb's *English Synonymes* (1816, p. 760), "*mortification* from the hurting our pride and self-importance."

The hurt may not be significant when it is simply a proper return for the excessive self-opinion of a fool who is deceived but who will never be improved by the event: as, at the end of *Persuasion,* Elizabeth Elliot is mortified when Mr. Elliot withdraws, or both she and Sir Walter are "shocked and mortified" by the discovery of Mrs. Clay's deception (P 250, 251). Deliberately to inflict mortification on others is significant as the action of a small mind desirous of hurting another to gratify its own pride and insulting importance. It appears in "Volume the Second" in an early sketch for Lady Catherine de Bourgh (MW 158). Mrs. Ferrars and Mrs. John Dashwood of *Sense and Sensibility* are "anxious to mortify" (233). To be the victim of such mortification when one's conduct has not merited it is more significant, because that is a severe test. Elinor Dashwood cannot now be made unhappy by this behavior of Mrs. Ferrars, though a few months ago it would have hurt her exceedingly; a few months ago was before she had learned from Lucy of Edward's engagement. She cannot now be hurt because she is the mistaken object of attack, but she is stronger also because she had met successfully that earlier undeserved and much worse mortification. In Lucy's revelation she had faced an emotion and distress beyond anything she had ever felt before: "She was mortified, shocked, confounded." That is the effect on Sir Walter and Elizabeth at the end of *Persuasion,* but for Elinor this is early in the action, the end of only her first volume, and she exerts herself to struggle resolutely and to gain strength (SS 134–35). (It makes more comic, incidentally, our recollection of how Marianne blushes to acknowledge her sister's lack of strong affections—and the striking proof Marianne gives of the strength of her own affections by her ability to love and respect that sister "in spite of this mortifying conviction" [104]; the incident improves Marianne's opinion of herself.)

Misapplied mortifications, felt by those who do not need them, not understood by those who do, can be a source of touching, piercing emotion. In *Mansfield Park* the mortifications are almost always distorted. Some of them are gratuitous insults inflicted on Fanny, by the Miss Bertrams or even Sir Thomas (20, 33); she is undeserving of them, there is nothing she can do to improve under them, and she feels too lowly to be injured by them; it is altogether painful and helps define the pain peculiar to *Mansfield Park.* Even Edmund, under the spell of Mary Crawford, mortifies Fanny when he turns from her, in their congenial moment of enthusiastic contemplation of nature, turns his back and rejoins Mary; the failure is not Fanny's and only the sigh is hers—and a scolding from Mrs. Norris (113). She who is pained by others is put in difficult circumstances where it is she who must bear the burden of not giving pain: if she does not wear the amber cross William has given her it might be mortifying him (254); but a few pages later if she does not wear Mary's necklace, Edmund says, it would be mortifying Mary severely (263). Always it is Fanny who feels for others what they are unable to feel for themselves; when she finds out that Henry has not changed as much as she had thought, that he is still the acquaintance and perhaps the flirt of Mrs. Rushworth, "She was mortified. She had thought better of him" (436). Those who most need the benefits are incapable of the pain. They feel it on the wrong occasions, for the wrong reasons, as when Maria, having lost the barouche box to her sister takes her seat within, "in gloom and mortification" (80). Mary Crawford, when Edmund refuses to accept the temptation that he take part in the play, moves away from him "with some feelings of re-sentment and mortification" (145); when she hears later that he is soon to take orders, this too "was felt with resentment and mortification" (227). The combination, emphasized by the identity of reaction on the two occasions, is especially bad, be-cause it means that Mary cannot learn; she is thinking only of her own importance and far from turning the experience valuably upon herself she turns it weakly upon him, expends her emotion not in revising her own faults but in anger at his for making her think less of herself. Henry is worse. When, at the end, he is received by Mrs. Rushworth with a coldness that ought to have been repulsive and final, he is "mortified" because he can-not bear to be thrown off by the woman he had once commanded; "he must exert himself" to subdue her "resentment" (468). There is a devilish reversal of terms.

Sweet Anne Elliot knows much of the poignancy of the lonely mortification. It is only Anne who has been able to see the morti-fications hanging over her father and sister (P 212, 215), with-out being able to help because of their obtuse vanity; it is Anne who has to bear the mortification of their conduct (226) because they are insensitive to the effect of their own action. She has had long practice in bearing lonely feelings. Nobody appre-ciates her music, but Mr. and Mrs. Musgrove's fond partiality for their daughters' performance and total indifference to hers gives her more pleasure for their sake than mortification for her own (47). Anne bears the pain even when it is cruel, even when there is no way that she can respond by changing herself to avoid it. When she hears that Captain Wentworth thought her so altered that he should not have known her, a wound has been inflicted. But "Anne fully submitted, in silent, deep mortification" (60–61), a sentence in which every word is important and to which we will return. There is nothing Anne can do to reverse time, but she can accept the blow fully as it tells her a truth about herself that she must live with.

But the mortification that leads to a truth has its fullest value when it is part of an extended learning process, simple or complex. The tale of Catherine Morland is a tale of "hopes and fears, mortifications and pleasures" (NA 97) that are an initiation into the ways of life and the proper responses to it, though their interest, of course, is limited by the simplicity of the heroine. She cannot be aware of the full meaning of her actions or of what is done to her. When she is turned out of the Abbey, "It was as incomprehensible as it was mortifying and grievous" (226), so that there seems to be little she can do to meet it. Still, the little that Catherine does do is sufficient for her purposes. In the Upper Rooms at Bath "one mortification succeeded another" and from the whole she deduced a small but "useful lesson," about the anticipations and the realities of going to a ball (55). She is teachable, and one of the best signs of this is that she does not answer mortification by trying to return it. Having been put by the Thorpes into a situation in which she has been impolite to Eleanor and Henry Tilney, she calls upon Miss Tilney to explain and be forgiven; she is told that Miss Tilney is not at home, only to see her walk out a moment later. Catherine's response to the denial is a "blush of mortification" and her response to the sight of Miss Tilney is "deep mortification" (91–92). Miss Tilney's conduct has been angry incivility, Catherine thinks, and she could almost be angry herself in return; "but she checked the resentful sensation; she remembered her ignorance" (92). That is a virtue and we can augur well for Catherine. At the end her "mortified feelings" at General Tilney's insolence are controlled in her letter to Eleanor, which is just, both to herself and her friend, "honest without resentment" (235). She can profit from her experience as the far more knowledgeable Mary Crawford never can.

The mortification becomes a fuller part of the learning when it comes to a conclusion, when it is the moment of final vision, the sort of epiphany announced by Reginald De Courcy at the end of *Lady Susan:* "The spell is removed. I see you as you are. Since we parted yesterday, I have received from indisputable authority, such an history of you as must bring the most mortifying conviction of the Imposition I have been under" (MW 304). There has not been much of a process here, Reginald being a silly stick, and the change occurring through the receipt of authoritative information about somebody else. Emma comes to a similar conviction, similar in words, that is, when she perceives that "she had been imposed on by others in a most mortifying degree"; but the difference is in the clause that follows directly— "that she had been imposing on herself in a degree yet more mortifying" (E 412)—and hers is a much more interesting history. Hers is a history of self-understanding and the mortifications have been an essential and continuing part of the process by which that understanding has been achieved. She has been an easy fool of others because she has been her own fool and the understanding of self and the understanding of others come to her as parts of the same experience. For her, when the spell is removed, the perception is a revision of what she is, head and heart, and of what she has valued—most notably what she has judged and felt to be worthy of love. What Emma sees for the first time, in that surprise and humiliation, is herself and the man she loves; then the knowledge of herself makes her ashamed of every sensation but one, "her affection for Mr.

Knightley" (412). The mortification is the necessary condition of the affection; the beginning of the new and larger life asks the painful end of the old and blinded self. Which returns us to *Pride and Prejudice*.

Mortification, in Jane Austen's language, no longer has a religious force. She can use it in that sense only in jest—Jane Fairfax, for example, thinking of herself as a devoted novitiate resolved at one-and-twenty to complete the sacrifice and retire from all the pleasures of life to penance and mortification forever (E 165). But it can be, we know, much stronger than a social term for an embarrassment; it can still carry a moral, renovative, force. Elizabeth and Darcy change one another because each hurts the pride and self-importance of the other, humbling, humiliating, forcing a self-recognition that requires a giving up of part of the character for which each has always felt self-esteem and a taking on of a new character. That each is capable of the loss and the renewal by mortification is what makes the love valuable. The inception, the turning point, and then the resolution of the changing relationship of Elizabeth and Darcy are, each of them, marked by mortifications: the first rousing effect each has on the other; the unsuccessful proposal and the letter that follows; and the elopement of Lydia, the event necessary for a fitting successful proposal. Each signalizes a challenge that calls forth a revealing response either of self-protective failure or of self-conquest.

The process begins immediately upon the first occasion of their being together, when Darcy looks for a moment at Elizabeth, till catching her eye, then withdraws his own and coldly refuses to dance with her because she is not handsome enough to tempt *"me"*: Elizabeth could easily forgive *his* pride, "if he had not mortified *mine*" (20). Without his intending it, and without her knowing it, he has indicated the sort of lesson Elizabeth must learn. Pride relates to our opinion of ourselves, Mary Bennet says, and it is that pride which now begins to be and will be more properly and more severely mortified. It is he, however, his withdrawn eye, which is most in need of education at this point, and the very next thing we hear of him is that she becomes an object of some interest in his eye; having scarcely allowed her to be pretty and looking at her, when they meet again, only to criticize, and making clear to himself and his friends that she has hardly a good feature in her face, he then finds the intelligence and beauty of her eyes. "To this discovery succeeded some others equally mortifying" (23). Though he has detected with critical eye more than one failure in the perfect symmetry of her form, he is now forced to acknowledge that it is light and pleasing; though he has asserted that her manners are not fashionable he is now caught by their easy playfulness. The return upon himself is just, as she, unknowingly, is catching and forcing him to admit that he has been mistaken. The first important effect each has on the other is a mortification, a lowering of self-opinion. But neither has yet been able to benefit from the effect; the effect has not been strong enough, in good part because neither is in a moral position to make the other feel the effect.

The turning point of their developing relation is Darcy's proposal to Elizabeth and his rejection. He has no right to propose. Elizabeth is quite right to reject him; he would not be a good husband. He has not, even in proposing, behaved in a gentlemanlike manner and is startled to be told that truth, and more than startled: "You could not have made me the offer of your hand in any possible way that would have tempted me to accept it"; this he must hear from the woman whose pride he mortified by saying she was not handsome enough to tempt *him*. He looks at her with "mingled incredulity and mortification" (192–93). She goes on and begins to remove the incredulity by describing how from the first moment of their acquaintance his deficiencies of manner impressed her with that fullest belief in his arrogance, conceit, and selfish disdain of the feelings of others that formed the groundwork on which succeeding events have built so immovable a dislike. Her accusations are ill founded, formed on mistaken premises, but, as he later says, his behavior to her merited the severest reproach and the mortification remains. It is from this point that Darcy's life changes importantly. It takes time. The recollection of what he said, his conduct, his manners, his expression, is for many months inexpressibly painful. Her reproof, that he had not behaved in a gentlemanlike manner—the words remain with him—had been a torture, and it was some time before he was reasonable enough to allow their justice. To a man of principle the pain of realizing the pride and selfishness of a lifetime is a hard lesson and he owes much to her who taught him. "By you, I was properly humbled" (367–69).

What we see of Darcy, of course, is mainly the result of what has happened, not the many months of pain; we see him through Elizabeth's eyes and share with her the surprise of what has happened and understand it in retrospect as it moves her. As Elizabeth rejects Darcy, producing the mortification that changes his life, our interest, as always, is in what will happen to her, and what happens to her, painfully and fortunately, is the letter from him producing the mortification that changes her life. It comes as a particularly powerful blow to her because it makes her know the meaning of feelings she has experienced repeatedly and never understood; the causes of mortification have been at work and she has felt them without recognizing their import. They have been at work in what is closest to her, in her own family, in her friend, in the man she has found so agreeable, in herself.

Elizabeth has always been confident in knowing the truth, immediately and exactly. She has believed the history of himself that Wickham gave: there was truth in his looks. Jane finds it difficult to decide between the conflicting accounts she has heard—it is distressing—one does not know what to think.

But Elizabeth knows: "I beg your pardon;—one knows exactly what to think" (86). It is the certainty that carries her straight to that extraordinary carnival of foolishness, so wealthy in detail, the Netherfield ball. She dances herself into what is, exactly, a dance of mortification, totally misunderstood by her. The prospect of that ball, extremely agreeable to every female of her family, brings to Elizabeth the pleasurable thought of dancing a great deal with Wickham and seeing a confirmation of everything in Darcy's looks and behavior. Her spirits are so high that they carry her away and though she does not often speak unnecessarily to Mr. Collins she cannot help asking whether he is going and whether he will think it proper to join the amusement. To her surprise he is not only prepared to dance but takes the opportunity she has offered by securing her for the first two dances. She feels herself completely taken in, is her own victim. She had fully proposed being engaged by Wickham for those very dances—and to have Mr. Collins instead! her liveliness had never been worse timed (86–87). She enters the dancing room at Netherfield to look for Wickham, a doubt of his being present having never occurred to her, certain of meeting him, dressed with more than usual care and prepared in the highest spirits for completing the conquest that evening. But he is not there. She suspects that it is Darcy who has caused his exclusion, then finds that it is Wickham who has wished to avoid Darcy and is thereby assured that Darcy is no less answerable for Wickham's absence than if her first surmise had been just. Pursuing that line of justice in her disappointment she is hardly able to reply with tolerable civility to Darcy's politeness, because attention, forbearance, or patience with him is injury to Wickham, and she turns from him in ill humor. She turns to Charlotte Lucas, tells that friend all her griefs, makes a voluntary transition to the oddities of her cousin Collins, whom Charlotte has not yet seen, and points him out to the particular notice of her friend. Charlotte takes particular notice (89–90).

Three sets of dances follow. The first dances are with Mr. Collins and bring distress, as in his awkwardness and solemnity and often moving wrong without being aware of it he gives her all the shame and misery a disagreeable partner can give: they are "dances of mortification." The moment of release from him is ecstasy. Wickham is not there but she next dances with a fellow officer of his and has the refreshment of talking of Wickham and hearing that he is universally liked. Then she finds herself suddenly addressed by Darcy, "who took her so much by surprise in his application for her hand, that, without knowing what she did, she accepted him." She is then left to fret over her presence of mind while Charlotte tries to console her by saying she will find him very agreeable (90). That is the succession of her partners, of the three men who will be, or seem to be, solicitous of her hand and who present to her problems of increasing complexity. She delivers herself into the hands of each with an increasing ironic ignorance, finally accepting Darcy in spite of her determination to hate that disagreeable man. Darcy had once rejected her as a partner, mortifying *her* (italicized) pride. It was her mother's advice then that at another time she should not dance with *him* and Elizabeth believed she could safely promise *never* to dance with him (20). It was a promise she kept, when the opportunity first offered, at Sir William Lucas's; her resistance to Darcy did not injure her with the gentleman (26–27). Now, at Netherfield, she accepts him and is unhappy she has lost that assured control of a mind which, a few pages before, knows exactly what to think. We never hear of her dancing with anyone else after that, but it will be a while before she will understand the meaning of what she has done. She dances badly, in fact, taking the occasion not to learn more of Darcy's mind and character but, in a sudden fancy, to punish him. She is unable to resist the temptation of forcing the subject of Wickham on him, even blaming herself for weakness in not going on with it more than she does. There are times when she literally does not know what she is saying because her mind is wandering to Wickham and she then asks searching questions of Darcy's character that are more immediately relevant to her own blindness. Elizabeth is perfectly satisfied that she knows his character and Wickham's, and contradictory information that evening, whether from Miss Bingley or from Jane, can only confirm her; she is acutely analytic in refusing to accept what they say, and she is wholly mistaken in her conclusion. Changing the subject then to Jane's modest hopes of Bingley's regard, Elizabeth, always confident, says all in her power to heighten Jane's confidence (91–96).

Perfectly satisfied with herself she is forced by the conduct of her family into a series of confused vexations and mortifications. Mr. Collins discovers wonderfully that Mr. Darcy is a nephew of Lady Catherine, insists on introducing himself, and though Elizabeth tries hard to dissuade him, determines to follow his own inclination; it "vexed" her to see him expose himself to such a man. She is then deeply "vexed" to find that her mother is talking openly of her expectation of Jane's marriage to Bingley; Elizabeth tries to check Mrs. Bennet or make her less audible, for to her "inexpressible vexation" she perceives that Darcy is overhearing; but nothing she says has any influence: "Elizabeth blushed and blushed again with shame and vexation." With a brief interval of tranquillity she then has the "mortification" of seeing Mary oblige the company by exhibiting herself in a song (98–100). Elizabeth suffers most painful sensations and agonies, until at her look of entreaty her father interferes, in a speech that makes her still more sorry. Mr. Collins takes the opportunity to make a worse fool of himself before Darcy, which amuses Mr. Bennet and draws a serious commendation from Mrs. Bennet. To Elizabeth it appears that had the family made an agreement to expose themselves as much as possible they could not have played their parts with finer success (101); and all she misses is her own even finer part.

The greatest relief in all this she owes to her friend Charlotte, who often good-naturedly engages Mr. Collins's conversation to herself. Darcy never comes near enough to speak again and feeling it to be the probable consequence of her allusions to Wickham Elizabeth rejoices in it. It has been an evening of wonderfully compounded errors. Mrs. Bennet, like Elizabeth, is "perfectly satisfied" (103).

But from that point of satisfaction the series of vexations and mortifications, unprofitable because misunderstood, begins to work upon her. Mr. Collins's proposal the next day is vexing and embarrassing, but Elizabeth can overcome that problem; the private acknowledgment of Wickham, that his regret and vexation at having been absent was in fact a self-imposed necessity to avoid Darcy, meets with her approval; the possibility, in Bingley's sudden and unexpected departure, that he may never return to Jane, she treats with contempt. The first serious surprise to her is the revelation that Charlotte's continued kindness in keeping Mr. Collins in good humor, for which Elizabeth is more obliged than she can express, is a kindness that extends further than Elizabeth has any conception of. Elizabeth could not have supposed it possible that her friend could have sacrificed every better feeling to worldly advantage. "Charlotte the wife of Mr. Collins, was a most humiliating picture!" (125). The humiliation is hers. It then becomes clear that Bingley will not return and that Jane's hope is entirely over. The perfectly satisfied Elizabeth finds herself becoming dissatisfied, not with herself but with the world; every day confirms her belief of the inconsistency of all human characters and of the little dependence that can be placed on the appearance of either merit or sense; Bingley is one instance and Charlotte is the other. Nor will she allow Jane to defend Charlotte or for the sake of one individual change the meaning of principle and integrity, confuse selfishness with prudence. Finally the sole survivor of her apparent satisfactions at the Netherfield ball disappears, as Wickham's

apparent partiality subsides and he becomes the admirer of someone else, someone whose most remarkable charm is the sudden
acquisition of ten thousand pounds. But Elizabeth, so dissatisfied
with the inconsistency of human character, less clear-sighted in
this case than in Charlotte's, finds his wish of independence entirely natural. If she did not think so, if she did not think she
would be his only choice if fortune permitted, that fortune denied him by that abominable Mr. Darcy, she would be forced
to think differently of herself. She is not young in the ways of
the world, she says, and she is "open to the mortifying conviction" that handsome young men must have something to live on
(150). In her subsequent conversation about Wickham, with
Mrs. Gardiner (153–54), she seems to have lost sight of the
difference in matrimonial affairs between the mercenary and the
prudent motive, a difference so clear to her in Charlotte's affair.
Then follows a series of observations concluding in the exclamation that she is sick of all men, that she is thankful to be visiting the home of Mr. Collins in Kent, because he has not one
agreeable quality, because stupid men are the only ones worth
knowing after all. Mrs. Gardiner's warning to take care, that
her speech savors strongly of disappointment, is serious. The
vexations and the mortifications, with their separate meanings,
have all collapsed into one, into a disappointed condemnation
of others for their contradictory conduct to her. Because she cannot turn them to an occasion of growth they begin to harm her.

The turning point is in her visit to Kent, not because she
meets again a stupid and disagreeable man but because she meets
Darcy again. She mortifies him, in what is his most valuable
moment, but not hers; she does it in the blindness and prejudice
of the mind she has brought to Kent. Her moment follows when
she receives, in return, his letter revealing to her what she must
know to convert her own badly understood mortifications into
a real mortification. Her feelings are acutely painful, difficult
of definition. Her first reaction is to disbelieve what he says, it

must be false, it cannot be true, because if it is true it will over-
throw every cherished opinion, and she puts the letter away
hastily, protesting she will not regard it, never look at it again.
The value of Elizabeth is that this will not do, the pain and
the difficulty must be borne, and in half a minute, collecting
herself as well as she could, "she again began the mortifying
perusal of all that related to Wickham," commanding herself
to examine the meaning of every sentence (205). It is the necessary first step in the understanding of the real character of Wickham and of herself; the result is the eye-opening moment, as she
grows absolutely ashamed of herself, her actions, her pride in
her own discernment and her disdain of others. "How humiliating is this discovery!—Yet, how just a humiliation!" It is the
mortification of self-discovery. "Till this moment, I never knew
myself." From this knowledge it follows that when she returns
once more to the letter, to that part of it in which her family
are mentioned "in terms of such mortifying, yet merited reproach," her sense of shame is severe, especially when she remembers the Netherfield ball. She knows now the justice of
those terms (208–9).

There is a new self-knowledge in Elizabeth. It is evident, in
a minor way, in her return to Hertfordshire, when she hears
Lydia describe the girl to whom Wickham had transferred his
admiration; such a nasty little freckled thing, Lydia calls her,
and Elizabeth is shocked to think that if she is incapable of such
coarseness of expression herself, the coarseness of sentiment is
what her own breast had formerly harbored and fancied liberal
(220). She and Darcy have given severe lessons of liberality to
each other and each is in a proper course to make use of what
has been learned. What is needed is an incident that will put
them to the test of action. It is a sad moment for Kitty when
Lydia receives her invitation to Brighton: the rapture of Lydia,
the delight of Mrs. Bennet and the mortification of Kitty are
scarcely to be described (230); but in that company it is obvious

that the effect on Kitty is not improving, and worse must follow if any good is to result to her. It comes through the more serious mortification of others when Lydia runs off with Wickham. The incident may be of excessive length and fuss for the balance of the novel, but it is a necessary weight for the two main characters, who must now bear the effects of their past, the old self, and respond with the liberal conquest of the new self. The alteration in Darcy's and in Elizabeth's understanding, consequent upon their mutual mortifications, has been large; but it is Lydia's elopement that brings the concluding mortifications and the deserved happiness.

To Elizabeth the elopement is "humiliation" and misery (278). It justifies Darcy in the two chief causes of offense she had laid to his charge—his offenses against Wickham and against her family—and it brings those two forces together in such a way as to sink Elizabeth's power over him. She believes that he has now made a self-conquest, is no longer subject to his feelings for her, and the belief is exactly calculated to make her understand her own wishes, that she could have loved him. Later, after Lydia's marriage is assured, Elizabeth is heartily sorry that in her distress of the moment she had told Darcy of her fears for Lydia; the beginning could have been concealed from him: there was no one whose knowledge of her sister's frailty could have "mortified her so much" (311). But it is not from any hope for herself, because the gulf between her and Darcy is now impassable, both her objectionable family and Wickham. She is wrong, but now it is to her credit. She accepts her loss. Even when she has learned what Darcy has in fact done she must hide her feelings: it was necessary to laugh when she would rather have cried; her father had most cruelly mortified her by what he said of Mr. Darcy's indifference to her (364). Her father may be right.

What she did not know, and her ignorance is no fault in her, is that Darcy is stronger than she could have thought. He has made a self-conquest more difficult than the one she imagined, by taking a responsibility for Wickham's act, by exerting himself, by going to Wickham and arranging the marriage. It was "an exertion of goodness" she had thought too great to be probable, but it was not: "he had taken on himself all the trouble and mortification" of searching out and supplicating and bribing those he had most reason to abominate, despise, avoid. He had done it, though she still cannot realize that fully, because of "his affection for her" (326). When she finally has the opportunity she thanks him for the compassion that enabled him to take so much trouble and "bear so many mortifications" (366). And, rightly, it is then that she learns it was done not for her family but for her, and she knows the value of his affection. Their story comes to a happy ending earned by two properly humbled people who have learned to bear mortification and to rise under it with love.

There are deserved little rewards at the end in the removal of mortifications, when Elizabeth and Darcy can leave the mortifying society of her family (384), when even Mary Bennet is no longer mortified by comparisons between her sisters' beauty and her own (386). But it is most pleasant to hear in the last chapter that Miss Bingley was "very deeply mortified" by Darcy's marriage (387), for it is a treatment she long has been needing; but that as she thought it advisable to retain the right of visiting Pemberley she was wise enough to drop all "resentment" and pay off arrears of civility to Elizabeth. Even she has profited from the mortification, but, necessarily, only to the degree she is capable, a degree of meanness.

5

A Proper Lively Time with Fanny Price

Fanny Price, quiet, easily fatigued, supine, shrinking, creep-mouse, is the least "lively" of heroines. It is a deficiency all the more striking because she follows Elizabeth Bennet, that most lively, playful, sportive of heroines, and precedes Emma Wood-house; worst of all, "gentle" Fanny must compete directly with "lively" Mary Crawford. She must also refuse Henry Craw-ford—that refusal is her most important single act—and he is a gifted actor, a creator of liveliness, wittily knowing and con-trolling of the life around him, above all a master of irony. With people of naturally strong and dominant disposition all around her, Mrs. Norris, the Bertrams, the Crawfords, Fanny's disposition keeps her trembling and near fainting. While they are acting she is anxious about propriety. While they are talk-ing and doing she sits on the edges, sees all that happens at Mansfield Park, goes to her little room, keeps it all in her memory.

But what liveliness can mean is not a simple question and certainly it cannot mean anything better than the quality of the life it expresses. Elizabeth Bennet's gets her into trouble occa-

sionally, we recall, as it does when she is in such high spirits
before the Netherfield ball that she cannot help speaking to Mr.
Collins; she finds herself engaged to him for the first two dances.
She felt herself completely taken in: "her liveliness had been
never worse timed" (PP 87). The punishment is more fitting
than she realizes, in that the cause of the high spirits is a mistaken interest in Wickham, and she has been taken in by him and
by herself. So the proper timing implies much about the reality
of the liveliness. In her visit to Mr. Collins and Charlotte in
Kent she tries to anticipate how the visit will pass, the quiet
tenor of their usual employment, the vexatious interruptions
of Collins, the gaieties of intercourse with Rosings: "A lively
imagination soon settled it all" (158). She is clever and she is
right in seeing so quickly into the immediate future of her life
and the life of those around her; but it is also true that there
is no great difficulty in doing so when she has shallow minds
to deal with; she does not anticipate the really extraordinary
event that will happen in Kent. Nonetheless, like Darcy, we
are grateful to her for the real liveliness she brings us. Darcy
himself is not lively; his friend Bingley is, by way of pointing
out early the contrast with him; and the woman he comes to love
certainly is. The first description we have of Elizabeth comes
when she hears Darcy rejecting her as not handsome enough,
which leaves her with no very cordial feelings toward him. "She
told the story however with great spirit among her friends; for
she had a lively, playful disposition, which delighted in any
thing ridiculous" (12). The first time, then, that we hear of
her liveliness it is delighting in a story that includes herself in
the ridicule and we know that there is a reach and a play of life
beyond the ordinary limits. She has a superior wit, and we see
it in action; she dearly loves a laugh, but with an understanding
of proper limits, as she explains to Darcy; for she never ridicules
what is wise or good, only follies and nonsense, whims and inconsistencies (57). She loses her way when she means to be

uncommonly clever, but the misdirection of her lively talents is temporary, is something she is capable of recognizing and correcting, and her ability to see and change is the best sign of life. Hers is a liveliness that enables her to recover (183). It is a superior awareness and command of the possibilities of life.

Her marriage with Darcy is excellent because she brings to him a thing of price that has been lacking in his life and she comes to know that he brings to her complementary values. Mr. Bennet upon hearing that the marriage is likely, and not yet knowing what Darcy is, becomes grave and anxious, because he knows Elizabeth could be neither happy nor respectable unless she truly esteemed her husband. "Your lively talents would place you in the greatest danger in an unequal marriage" (PP 376). His talents have dropped him into that danger, discredit and misery. But Elizabeth knows Darcy is a truly estimable man and the sensible Mrs. Gardiner is right when she says "he wants nothing but a little more liveliness, and *that,* if he marry *prudently,* his wife may teach him" (325). It is what Elizabeth herself began to comprehend shortly before, when she thought the marriage impossible; she and Darcy are unlike but a union would be to the advantage of both: "by her ease and liveliness, his mind might have been softened, his manners improved, and from his judgment, information and knowledge of the world, she must have received benefit of greater importance" (312). That her gift to him would be a softening of his mind sounds rather ominous, but she means of course the pliancy and responsiveness of a greater life, as opposed to an unbending stiffness, selfish and overbearing. The point comes through clearly in her subsequent happiness when her spirits rise again to "playfulness" and she quizzes him on how he came to fall in love with her; her beauty he had early withstood, her behavior to him had bordered on the uncivil. Did he admire her for her impertinence? "For the liveliness of your mind, I did" (380). She insists on calling it impertinence, but follows that deliberately witty misuse of the word with the real distinction. He was sick of the false civility, deference, officious attention he had been receiving, disgusted with women like Miss Bingley, who were always speaking, looking, thinking, for his approbation alone. Elizabeth roused and interested him because, unlike them, she taught him unpleasant truths about himself and made him change for the better. The awakening brought him more fully to life and he is just in his gratitude. If he has not yet learned to be laughed at (371), we have every guarantee that she will teach him that too. Georgiana is astonished, alarmed, at her new sister's "lively, sportive" manner of talking to him, but Georgiana's mind is receiving knowledge which had never before fallen in her way (387–88).

That real liveliness of Elizabeth's is an unusual force of mind, which Darcy knows how to prize. What we meet more often in Jane Austen is a lesser, a seeming, even a deceptive, liveliness that lacks depth. Willoughby is a young man of good abilities, of "quick imagination, lively spirits, and open, affectionate manners" (SS 48). Elinor, after her final meeting with him, feels his influence heightened by circumstances that ought not in reason to have weight, "by that person of uncommon attraction, that open, affectionate, and lively manner which it was no merit to possess" (333). There is no merit because these are all matters of appearance, without moral significance, revealing nothing of the life within, and consistent, in this instance, with falsity. Mrs. Dashwood, wise after the event, does happen to be right when she says that Willoughby's liveliness was often artificial and ill-timed, because we have seen this in his earliest conversation with Marianne; and Mrs. Dashwood makes the contrast with Colonel Brandon's manners, their "gentleness," their genuine attention to other people, and their unstudied simplicity (338). But Willoughby's captivating person and ardor of mind are exactly formed to engage Marianne's heart. Like her he says what he thinks on every occasion, without attention to person or circumstances, hastily forms and gives opinions of other people, slights too easily the forms of worldly "propriety." All this seeming freedom from forms does not in fact lead to more life but to its own deadening unreality, an imaginary life. Marianne never sees Willoughby, only an image in her own fancy. She never sees Brandon, a silent man of thirty-five who has no chance when opposed by "a very lively one of five and twenty." She and Willoughby, far from being more open to life, are unjust to those unlike themselves. They are prejudiced against Brandon for being "neither lively nor young" and are resolved to undervalue his merits. They decide on his imperfections in the mass, as Elinor says to Marianne, and "on the strength of your own imagination" (48–51). Marianne's eyes may sparkle with animation and her cheek glow with the delight of such "imaginary happiness" as receiving a large fortune from somebody, but the sentimentality is obviously unlike real life. There is little play in Marianne's mind; as she says, her opinions are fixed and she does not think it likely that she should now hear or see anything to change them. Elinor speaks from experience in saying "I should hardly call her a lively girl." Marianne is earnest, eager, sometimes talking a great deal and with animation, but not often really merry. If Edward has "always set her down as a lively girl" it is because he has been guided by what Marianne has said of herself or what others have said of her, without giving himself time to deliberate and judge (92–93).

Whether a character is possessed of a real liveliness is not immediately apparent, then, not even to those who are sensible and who are close to them. A superior judgment and extended opportunities to observe under a variety of circumstances and trials may be needed to discover the reality. Those who seem most to have a liveliness and who may have a large share of it, in wit and in motion and attractiveness, may be possessors of an animation that is without understanding, strength, or endurance.

The most insistently lively characters in Jane Austen are Mary and Henry Crawford. Mary has "a lively dark eye . . . and general prettiness" (MP 44) and this formula is repeated several times: she is "pretty, lively, with a harp as elegant as herself" (65); the superficiality of this is emphasized by its repetition in Tom Bertram's praise of her, "a sweet, pretty, elegant, lively girl" (186). Tom's meaninglessness is most obvious in the "sweet," because she certainly is not that (though Fanny is). The quality of the mutual attraction has been in Mary's own initial impression of Tom: Tom has been more in London, she knows, and has "more liveliness and gallantry" than Edmund, is also the eldest and is therefore the one she will prefer (47); she is wrong. Upon the first appearance of Mary and Henry "the manners of both were lively and pleasant, and Mrs. Grant immediately gave them credit for every thing else" (42), but that tells us rather of Mrs. Grant's untrustworthiness as a judge.

Edmund is more discriminating and tries to make the proper distinctions, but he too is not only attracted to both the brother and the sister by their liveliness but misleads himself seriously in giving credit for more than is there. If what Mary says of her uncle the admiral does not suit Edmund's sense of propriety he is induced "by further smiles and liveliness" to put the matter by for the present (57). He sees the impropriety as rising from an excess of good feelings, her respect and affection for her aunt. "With such warm feelings and lively spirits," he says, it is difficult for her to do justice to one without throwing a shade on the other (63), though he has no signs of warmth. He grants her exemption from restraints of lesser minds, the "right of a lively mind," he tells Fanny, seizing whatever may contribute to its own amusement or that of others, perfectly allowable when untinctured by ill humor or roughness (64). He finds that for amusement she does indeed seize upon matters that are not allowable, the restraints of religious devotion, and he must pull himself together a bit before he can say to Mary, "Your lively mind can hardly be serious even on serious subjects" (87). But the degree of his infatuation is such that though he knows the liveliness she and Henry brought to Mansfield was a novelty in Sir Thomas Bertram's home, he thinks that Sir Thomas would enjoy her liveliness; he is even prepared to deduce from her lively hints and unguarded expressions that in her great discernment of characters she could say more if delicacy did not forbid (197–99), though it seems likely that Sir Thomas is one character she is forbidding herself. To the end, until his eyes are opened, he thinks that her fault is the high spirits of a "too lively mind" that has been misled by bad company, and he is ready to blame himself for a too harsh construction of a playful manner (421).

But Edmund's mistake is deep, because Mary's fault is not merely that she has too much of a good thing, a lively mind that exercises itself improperly, or that needs the balance of seriousness or gentleness to put it in order, but rather that she lacks real liveliness. She is even like Maria Bertram in that. Maria would like to compete with Julia in laughter, light-heartedness, high spirits and amusement—"Naturally, I believe, I am as lively as Julia, but I have more to think of now"; but the strain is apparent and the best she can do is escape the restraint of the gate at Sotherton, and smile with the good humor of success— "I and my gown are alive and well, and so good bye" (99–100). It is a false life. With better light and lively talents Mary has a similar problem, because for all Mary's seeming wit and her elegant harp Fanny has been right in doubting her resources and accomplishments. She needs a continual application of something new to keep up her spirits. It is that rather than anything real which is the origin of her intimacy with Fanny, as Fanny sees. When the others have all departed from Mansfield Park and it is a rainy day and Mary is despondent, the sound of a little bustle at the front door and the sight of Fanny dripping wet is delightful: "She was all alive again directly" (206). There is not much internal life in that liveliness, or real spirit in the high spirits, and the play does not have a deep source.

Her brother Henry, who has more opportunity of seeking out stimulus, is an even better example of the liveliness without life. He is at his best playing a round game, with his hands full of business, in "high spirits," with happy ease, "pre-eminent in all the lively turns, quick responses, and playful impudence" (240). Edmund, taken in by the brother as by the sister, thinks that Henry's temper is an excellent complement to Fanny's— "He is lively, you are serious; but so much the better"—and they will be a good match; Fanny knows it is not true and knows that Edmund is thinking of another match. Edmund sees nothing worse than a man who is "lively, and it may be a little unthinking" (348–50), but he misses the vanity of mind. Henry has little defined life of his own, has little to do, is in need of continual reanimation. If Tom Bertram has so much leisure and "such a degree of lively talents" as are exactly adapted to the novelty of the acting scheme, Henry reacts in the same way to an untasted pleasure, is "quite alive" at the idea, feels he could be anything or everything, wants to be doing something (123). His behavior in that scheme is dishonorable and unfeeling but that is never in his mind; he always looks back upon the theatricals, he says, with exquisite pleasure. "There was such an interest, such an animation, such a spirit diffused . . . We were all alive," and he was never happier (225). His lively words will change their meaning as he finds himself, unintentionally, coming closer to a better happiness, but it is true that he will never be happier. What he does not know is that his is a liveliness that becomes most interesting as it becomes, of its own necessities, self-defeating, ironic. The really interesting thing is that life is livelier than Henry realizes, lively with ironies. We can learn something of that subject by watching him. Moreover, Henry's reversals are part of a larger ironic history.

*O*NE of the effects of irony, the one relevant to our interest here, is to make words come alive in a special way and to give them extra life: while they bear one meaning which they present for more immediate comprehension they are also working effectively with another meaning, of greater importance, frequently contradictory, frequently hidden from some hearers or even the very speaker. Our pleasure in it is that we are made participant in this greater life because irony requires that the reader perceive for himself the multiplication of significance. It requires an active sharing with the author of a superior vision of reality, in which an ordinarily unspoken and unrevealed level manifests its activity. We share with the author a control of words that rises from a control of insight. If it is amusing to see this power exercised on fools, Mrs. Elton or Mr. Collins, it is a higher pleasure to see it directed not at those lesser minds, in which the difference between the surface and the underlying level, between self-awareness and an unknown truth, is easy to apprehend. The best irony involves, rather, the best minds, in the sense of those who are themselves quick to apprehend, those in whom we cannot find amusement simply because we feel ourselves naturally superior. They may be in many ways more clever and witty than ourselves, their language in common conversation better than our own. As a continuing revelation of the finest distinctions between the pretension to control and the reality, irony is a natural instrument for Jane Austen. Elizabeth Bennet and Emma Woodhouse are noted instances of her success with it. Henry Crawford is less noted but worthy of attention because he appears in a novel that seems to have little of this typical strength of its author.

Henry Crawford thinks of himself as a man who is quite his own master, and a manipulator of others, quite in control of his own emotions and able to control the emotions of others, an ironist in fact. He amuses himself with women and has every qualification of the accomplished actor's voice and manner needed for success. But he is not what he thinks he is, and cannot in fact do what he likes, with himself or with women. We see him practicing with varying degrees of intention on three women, the Miss Bertrams and Fanny Price, and in each instance he fails, never gets the response he wants. Julia is the first and least important example, but an excellent indicator of the failure he meets with every time. He has manged well to hold both sisters in expectation by adroit varying of attention and word, but there comes a point—it is in the casting of the play, where so many elements of the early action are drawn together—that he must make a choice. Only one can be Agatha, and with a compliment and an allusion to friendly intimacies, he tries to ease out Julia. He does it pleasantly and courteously, does all that manner can do, but at this point it is the matter that is important and Julia, by seeing Maria's smile of triumph, is aware of the trick. Henry tries again, his voice is influential, Julia wavers, but he cannot control all elements and once again it is Maria's countenance that decides the matter; Julia is indignant and rounds on him: "Henry Crawford looked rather foolish, and as if he did not know what to say" (136). It is the foolish role he will play again on more weighty occasions.

When he sets into action his plan to make a small hole in Fanny's heart he is not only unsuccessful in gaining his effect upon her, but finds that he has a deeper problem than he could have foreseen, a hole in his own heart. He plans to pursue Fanny to amuse himself, on the days that he does not hunt, and he will do so, he says, because he must take care of his mind too, not live a life all of recreation and indulgence without the wholesome alloy of labor: "I do not like to eat the bread of idleness" (229). He speaks deliberately, as on other occasions, with a witty use of the apt quotation, in the language of moral and even religious principle, deliberately mocking by reversing the meanings of words. His plan is not innocent, but Fanny is protected from him in ways of which he is ignorant. The greater danger, and potential good—he knows nothing of either—is for the care of his own mind and heart.

The traditional moral failure of idleness, a wrong in itself and a cause of other wrongs, is of particular interest to Jane Austen as it signifies a mind utterly without direction, empty, making no use of time. By default it does harm, allows itself to be used by others, or, most importantly, becomes the victim of the false busyness that inevitably fills the vanity of its mind. Mrs. Allen at Bath and Catherine Morland at Northanger Abbey are mild examples. Lydia Bennet, "Vain, ignorant, idle, and absolutely uncontrouled" is a very serious one (PP 231, 213, 283). *Sense and Sensibility,* with its emphasis on exertion, has a variety of idle characters: in Lady Middleton; in Mr. Palmer; in Marianne, when she augments and fixes her sorrow by seeking silence, solitude, and idleness (104)—just what Burton and Dr. Johnson warned against; and especially in Edward Ferrars and Willoughby. Edward is aware that an upbringing which has left him without business, without employment, idle, has been a misfortune (102–3). The worst consequence was the foolish idle inclination for Lucy Steele; having no employment, being completely idle, he had nothing in the world to do but fancy himself in love (362). He is an unusual young man, and a very lucky one, to overcome so serious a handicap. Willoughby is a lesser man exposed to greater temptation; at her last meeting with him Elinor's thoughts are fixed on "the irreparable injury which too early an independence and its consequent habits of idleness, dissipation, and luxury" had made in the mind, character, and happiness of a man of so many natural advantages (331). The consequence has been a coldness and hardness of heart that, to serve its selfishness, brings evil to others.

Henry Crawford's history began in the same disastrous circum-

stances as Willoughby's, ruined by early independence, with
the further misfortune of the bad domestic example of the Admiral, and his downfall is completed when he has indulged
himself in the freaks of a cold-blooded vanity a little too long
(MP 467). It was in "the indulgence of his idle vanity," without reflecting on its tendency, that he had begun to trifle with
the Miss Bertrams (114–15). The free indulgence that idleness gives becomes its own trap, because it is in fact an abandon-
ment of the direction of one's own mind and life. Henry enters
easily upon the conquest of Fanny because, to repeat his own
ironic words, he must take care of his mind, not live wholly in
indulgence, not eat the bread of idleness. Mary, to whom he
says this, understands him perfectly, at his own level of course,
and sees that there is a simple reversal of words and that in
fact the whole idea proceeds from nothing but his own "idleness and folly" (229–30). But Henry's light phrase is taken
from Proverbs (31:27), where it is said of the virtuous woman,
the good wife, "She looketh well to the ways of her household,
and eateth not the bread of idleness." The comic misapplica-
tion of scripture is clever, as he intends it, though our amusement is no doubt qualified by the kind of idle indulgence he
is planning; it is more than a folly, as Mary calls it here, the
same word she uses for his later sin. The full amusement, however, is one that neither Henry nor Mary can share with us,
because that virtuous woman of his proverb, who takes care of
her household, is going to become his desired good wife. He is
thoroughly fooled. For one thing, Fanny knows more of him
than he realizes; she knows, from his past conduct with her
cousins, that he is taking what seems "very idle notice" of her,
and she hasn't the vanity that would make her expect more
from him (353). For another, he finds that she interests him
more than he had foreseen. "His stay became indefinite" (236).
The hole is in his own heart and Henry, on the days when he does
not hunt, has been caught in his own design: "Yes, Mary . . .

I am fairly caught. You know with what idle designs I began—
but this is the end of them" (292). There is twist upon twist
here, because being caught in this way is the best thing that
ever happened to Henry. Indulging himself in cold-blooded
vanity has, once, not by his idle design but by an opening "un-
designed and unmerited" (467) led him into the way of happiness. He is then confident of success in securing a return of his
love and if there is a little difficulty to overcome he gains spirits
from it. "The situation was new and animating" (327). But,
caught himself, he will not catch her. He cannot get the response
he wants.

Henry has only one success, with Maria Bertram, at last, and
then he is extraordinarily effective. But he is successful only in
the ironic sense that he gets a stronger response than he wants;
and that one passionate return from a woman is what ruins him.
Henry has been introduced to us by Mary as the most horrible
flirt that can be imagined. He denies it, professing high regard
for matrimony, considering the blessing of a wife "as most
justly described in those discreet lines of the poet, 'Heaven's
last best gift.' " Mary points out his dwelling on one word and
his smile and we have the indicators of his clever irony. What he
does not yet know is the final and bitter irony of that line, for
the blessing of a wife will be, in another sense, the last gift for
him, one he comes to desire and never receives. The Admiral's
lessons have quite spoiled him, Mary added, and so they have,
because like the Admiral Henry takes a mistress, and it spoils
his happiness (43). Having quoted his *Paradise Lost* this most
agreeable young man begins to delight the Miss Bertrams. "Mr.
Crawford did not mean to be in any danger." When Mrs. Grant
tries to warn him off Maria because Maria is engaged, his answer is that he likes her all the better for it because "All is safe
with a lady engaged; no harm can be done." If the logic of his
irony is good, and since he acts by it he must believe it, then
with a lady married, as Maria is at the end, the security must

be even greater. It doesn't quite work. What really worries Mrs. Grant is that Maria is only interested in the great match and doesn't care for the man she is engaged to, as Henry perceives immediately; but, still the ironist, he refuses to subscribe to that opinion: "I think too well of Miss Bertram to suppose she would ever give her hand without her heart" (44–46). He will prove more right than he can possibly suppose. At that moment of consternation at the beginning of Volume II, when Sir Thomas returns to interrupt the theatricals, Henry-Frederick is listening to Maria-Agatha, "pressing her hand to his heart," and Julia notices that in spite of the shocking news she has brought, Henry retains her sister's hand. To Julia's heart it is a wound but to Maria it is the sweetest support: "Henry Crawford's retaining her hand at such a moment" is hailed by her as an earnest of the most serious determination (175–76). She remembers that moment when he leaves her to Mr. Rushworth only one chapter later: "The hand and the heart were alike motionless and passive now!" He was gone—"he had touched her hand for the last time" (193). But that is not quite true. For at the end of Volume III when Henry tries to reestablish that same flirtation that had always bounded his views, he finds he has put himself in the power of feelings on her side "more strong than he had supposed . . . There was no withdrawing attentions . . . He was entangled" (468). Maria did not give her hand without her heart, exactly as he had said at first. "He will be taken in at last," Mary had predicted when he offered that line; and she too was right.

So the nice equivocation of meaning and manner never fails Henry, except in what is most essential to him, the control of his own life. He did not like to see Maria so near the altar, he had told her at Sotherton, and she, with an affected laugh, asked if he would give her away. " 'I am afraid I should do it very awkwardly,' was his reply, with a look of meaning" (88). The meaning will have another look when he eventually finds himself trying to do it very awkwardly. But it was on the same day at Sotherton that he then had taught her how to avoid the Rushworth gates and get out and away with him—a lesson she had learned too well. After the successful day at Sotherton and just before the theatricals began, he was able to make his manners to each of the Miss Bertrams so animated and agreeable as to lose no ground with either, and to stop just short of the consistence and warmth that might excite general notice. But it is during the theatricals that he finds it impossible to maintain these limits and hold his ground with Julia, and it is at the end of the novel that he can no longer stop short with Maria: it is her feelings and imprudence that force him to act and he goes off with her at last "because he could not help it" (468). General notice is then excited.

Henry concludes by doing what he could not help because for all his fondness for change and moving about and playing and doing and overcoming difficulties, he has an inferior spirit that needs to be acted upon. He never really does anything that requires much doing, has a great show of energy without the substance, never rises much above the level of the "bustle" that made him alive and happy during the acting scheme (225). That kind of bustle was the same pleasure Mrs. Norris had found in the same scheme (129). We have met the word already in Mary's language, as she elevates the professional attractions of the navy and army, in contempt of the church; the navy and army have everything in their favor: "heroism, danger, bustle, fashion" (109). The reality of the heroism is qualified out of existence by the terms that accompany it. We see Henry responding to a genuine "glory of heroism" when he hears William Price's recitals of his life at sea, a glory of usefulness, exertion, endurance, which makes Henry feel the contrast of his own selfish indulgence; but the wish that he were different is, in his style, eager rather than lasting (236), because to attain the glory of a William Price would require a reality of seeing and doing and suffering. The scope and morality of Henry's active spirit is in such a determination as he makes "to have the glory" (326) as well as the felicity of forcing Fanny to love him. His love for Fanny takes Henry as close as he ever gets to heroic action but he never gets much beyond the unreality Mary reports: "He is quite the hero of an old romance, and glories in his chains" (360). The last and lovely, awful, irony is in his conclusion, when he goes to that house of "lively, agreeable manners" to see Maria again (450), finds that he is "mortified" by the coldness of a woman whose smile had once been so wholly at his command, "must exert himself" and, "by animated perseverance," regains her love and more; he is caught up in exactly the sort of bustle and overcoming so dear to him and which he is so good at, but this time "when all the bustle of the intrigue was over" it is he who is conquered and his regret is infinite (468).

THE ironic reversals of Henry's career are the most publicly spectacular of the novel but they are part of a pattern in which all the major characters participate. *Mansfield Park* is a novel in which many characters are engaged in trying to establish influence over the minds and lives of others, often in a contest or struggle for control, for good reasons or for bad, successfully or unsuccessfully; usually the reasons are not good and the effort is not successful; more often than not there is an unexpected reversal. Henry's lively efforts with Julia, Maria, and Fanny lead him to the point where he is made foolish by Julia, is caught by Fanny, and destroyed by Maria. Mary, like the sisters, has designs on a man which she is unable to accomplish; hers are more importantly ambitious because they require that she win over Edmund's mind, change his career, his whole way of thinking and living. While she is working at this Edmund thinks he is going to have a decisive influence in teaching her to recover from the effects of her earlier habits, to think with more propriety. Each has a partial success in changing the other, which means of course that each has a partial failure, and then there is a mutual utter defeat. Sir Thomas, for all his severity, his cost and his care, in the shaping of the minds of his daughters, fails wretchedly. He tries by all his influence to bend Fanny to the acceptance of Henry Crawford's hand and he fails there too. Mrs. Norris takes upon herself the direction of the lives of all those she comes near, dominates Mansfield Park, and is a disastrous failure at every point. Fanny, the poor dependent, on whom so many try to impose themselves, takes upon herself the direction of no one; it is a new experience for her, and a preliminary to the climax, that in her visit to Portsmouth she finds herself teaching her younger sister Susan. Fanny, unlike Mrs. Norris, directs no one but becomes an important influence on the lives of so many of those who try to direct her and then find themselves dependent on her—especially Henry, Edmund, and Sir Thomas. Upon her return to Mansfield Park she finds Mrs. Norris an altered creature, stupefied; Mrs. Norris has Lady Bertram, Tom, and all the house under her care, which would once have been a grand advantage to her, but it is now entirely thrown away; she is unable to direct or dictate or even to fancy herself useful. When really touched by affliction her active powers had been all benumbed; she cannot support Tom or Lady Bertram, nor they each other, and all are solitary, helpless, forlorn. It is Fanny who must take the direction and reestablish the life of Mansfield Park. She has been well prepared for the task because all she has been able to direct effectively until then has been herself. It has been a struggle for her.

Fanny is not exempted from the irony directed at other characters. She is weak too. Her feelings for the poor mare, being ridden by Mary Crawford instead of herself, are not disinterested (68). Her tender apostrophes and tender ejaculations are not always to the point or are contradicted by an immediate fact (111, 208). She can treasure a scrap of paper as enthusiastically as Harriet Smith (265). The physical weakness, the quick fatigue and the over-timidity, are not given to us for admiration. They are defects she must bear as best she can—she never trades upon them—or overcome as best she can by self-knowledge and exertion. After her initial astonishment and alarm at sister Susan's Portsmouth manners it takes at least a fortnight before she begins to understand a disposition totally different from her own. Susan is trying to set things right in her home, Fanny sees, is acting on the same truths and pursuing the same system she herself acknowledges but which her own supine and yielding temper would have shrunk from asserting. Susan tries to be useful where Fanny could only have gone away and cried (395). When Susan goes to Mansfield Park her more fearless disposition and happier nerves make everything easy to her there (472). Fanny hasn't the natural strengths of the disposition that makes things easy for her. Mary Crawford is active and fearless and strongly made and nothing ever fatigues her but doing what she does not like; this merit in being gifted by nature with strength and courage can be fully appreciated by the Miss Bertrams, whose merits are the same, who see energy of character and quality of mind in her good horsemanship (66, 68, 69). But it is Fanny who has the strength of character, and that comes by another process, for character is not a gift of nature and, so far as a life has a character, life is not a gift of nature but something made, a long and responsible history of disposition, education and habit.

The natural qualities of Mary Crawford and the Miss Bertrams have never been properly taught; their dispositions have never been educated. Disposition is the material, the natural inclination and temper of mind, from which character is shaped (though the word can be used also to indicate the result of the shaping process). "I am inclined to think very well of her disposition," Mr. Knightley says of Harriet. "Her character depends upon those she is with; but in good hands she will turn out a valuable woman." That is why he thinks she should accept Robert

Martin, and a reason why he is angry with Emma's interference (E 58, 61). The natural disposition will be different in different individuals, and one of the problems of education is to understand the disposition, but whatever it may be it requires an education to correct its faults and bring out its best. It is false to argue that our dispositions are not in our power, says Mrs. Chapone, in her letter "On the Government of the Temper"; that is the delusion of those who will not take the trouble to correct themselves, who think that not having an amiable disposition is their unhappiness rather than their fault. It is true that "we are not all equally happy in our dispositions" but human virtue consists in cultivating good inclinations and subduing the evil; if one is born with a bad temper it can be made good "by education, reason, and principle." (*Letters on the Improvement of the Mind, Addressed to a Young Lady,* 1773, and many later editions, 2: 9–10.) "There is, I believe, in every disposition a tendency to some particular evil, a natural defect, which not even the best education can overcome," says Mr. Darcy (PP 58). But this is his early attempt to defend himself and his temper of mind. The point is not whether his abstract proposition is right or wrong, but whether his education has done enough to overcome his particular natural defect, and, as he understands later, it had not; as a child he had not been taught to correct his temper (369). The contrast of Portsmouth and Mansfield makes Fanny aware of how different circumstances can affect dispositions essentially similar. Her mother's disposition is naturally indolent, like Lady Bertram's, and a situation like Lady Bertram's would have been more suited to her capacity than the exertions and self-denials demanded by her marriage (MP 390). But the point is that Mrs. Price had been imprudent to make a marriage which placed her in a situation unsuited to her disposition and that then she had never acted to face the necessities.

"I hope she will prove a well-disposed girl," Mrs. Norris

had said in Chapter I in anticipation of Fanny's arrival from Portsmouth. "Should her disposition be really bad," Sir Thomas answered, "we must not, for our children's sake, continue her in the family." But he trusts there will be no danger to his daughters and that it is Fanny who will learn from the association with them. "It will be an education for the child," Mrs. Norris agrees, "only being with her cousins" (10). When she arrives Sir Thomas and Mrs. Norris pretty soon decide between them that though she is far from clever she shows a "tractable disposition" and seems likely to give them little trouble (18), which is satisfactory for them. But Sir Thomas and Mrs. Norris know nothing of disposition or of education beyond what meets their own immediate satisfaction. On the same page we begin to see what Mrs. Norris has been doing to form the minds of her nieces. With all their promising talents and early information those girls are entirely deficient in the less common acquirements of self-knowledge, generosity, and humility. "In every thing but disposition, they were admirably taught" (19). Sir Thomas does not know what is wanting in them; and Lady Bertram pays not the smallest attention to the education of her daughters. In the foolish marriage of Maria Sir Thomas has judgment enough for grave doubts, but not enough knowledge of Maria to know how unfortunate it must prove to be; he is happy to secure a marriage which will bring him such an addition of respectability and influence, and "very happy to think any thing of his daughter's disposition that was most favorable for the purpose" (201). On that wedding day Mrs. Norris is so joyous and triumphant that no one would have supposed that she "could have the smallest insight into the disposition of the niece who had been brought up under her eye" (203).

The eventual anguish that arises from Sir Thomas's conviction of his errors in the education of his daughters is never entirely done away with. He had given them to the excessive indulgence and flattery of Mrs. Norris and by trying to counter-

act her influence by his own severity he had increased the evil
by repressing their spirits in his presence and making their "real
disposition" unknown to him (463). But that had not been the
most direful mistake in his plan of education. He had never educated those dispositions. The essential point about the disposition
is that though it varies from one person to another, and though
some are more gifted by nature than others, there is a center of
life to which all must be taught to submit themselves if they
are to have life, something of greater strength and endurance
than the self and the selfish desires. When Mrs. Chapone spoke
of governing the disposition, temper, and inclination by education, reason, and "principle," she meant of course religious
principle; her first letter is "On the First Principles of Religion";
and "the cultivation of an amiable disposition is a great part
of your religious duty" (2: 3). That center of life is defined
briefly at the moment of anguish as Sir Thomas traces it back:
from principle, the "active principle" that had been wanting
within his daughters; to the duty that is the source of the principle, for "they had never been properly taught to govern their
inclinations and tempers, by that sense of duty which can alone
suffice"; to the religion that is the source of the duty, the "daily
practice" of "religion" that had never been required of them.
Their education had been directed to produce an external show
of life but not to have a moral effect on the mind. He had meant
them to be good but his care had been directed to the understanding and manners, "not the disposition," and they had not
been taught the necessity of self-denial and humility (463).

It is only briefly and only at moments like this, as we have
seen in *Sense and Sensibility,* when the ruin of an entire life is
suddenly realized, that we are given explicitly what is otherwise the assumed underlying reality of social and moral life.
There can be no stability of life, no certainty of conduct, without
principles of action, a matter of continual importance to Dr.
Johnson as to Jane Austen. Even compassion, if it be no more

than a sensation, will only produce effects desultory and transient and will never settle into a "principle of action" (*Idler* no. 4). Henry Crawford can do a good deed and be moved by a good impulse but there is "no principle to supply as a duty what the heart was deficient in" (329). Mary Crawford can be very kind in comforting Fanny when Mrs. Norris is nasty, because she has "really good feelings" by which she is "almost" purely governed (147); hers are not "faults of temper," but there is no dependence on her action in more serious moments because hers are "faults of principle," the vitiated mind (456). And the final guarantee of principle, necessary for self-denial and humility, must be the religion by which we habitually regulate the self. The great art of piety, as Johnson calls it, the end for which all the rites of religion seem to be instituted, is the perpetual renovation of the motives to virtue by a voluntary employment of the mind in contemplating the excellence, importance, and necessity of virtue; the more frequent and willing this practice of the mind the more forcible and permanent the influence of those motives, until in time they become the reigning ideas, "the standing principles of action," the test by which the judgment rejects or approves; thus we come to the conquest of ourselves (*Rambler* no. 7). Such regular rites do not at all appeal to Mary; in her words, everybody likes to go their own way, choose their own time and manner of devotion. Her lively mind can hardly be serious even on serious subjects, nor will it struggle against itself. Edmund cannot make her understand how clergymen influence the manners, in the sense of conduct, which are "the result of good principles; the effect, in short, of those doctrines which it is their duty to teach and recommend" (MP 86–88, 93). Darcy, unlike Mary Crawford, has faults of temper, faults his defective education has not corrected in his disposition; but he has been a selfish being in practice and, unlike her, not in principle. He was given "good principles, but left to follow them in pride and conceit," until Elizabeth properly humbled him (PP 369). Elizabeth had already recognized that distinction and had recognized the source of the principles. Proud and repulsive as his manners were she had never seen anything that betrayed him to be "unprincipled or unjust," anything that spoke him of "irreligious or immoral habits" (207): the parallel of the pairs is carefully drawn. What we normally see in the action of common life in the novels is the social and moral expression of that ultimate reality. For example, a few pages after Sir Thomas Bertram defines the source of his mistake we see the result of Maria's adultery: the social disgrace is less for Henry Crawford than for Maria, because in this world the penalty is less equal than could be wished; there may be a juster punishment "hereafter" but the novel does not presume to look forward to that; it is more interested in defining the moral and personal loss that a man of sense like Henry Crawford will have, to the degree that he is capable of it (MP 468–69). He had determined to marry Fanny Price because he had "too much sense not to feel the worth of good principles in a wife, though he was too little accustomed to serious reflection to know them by their proper name." It is only social and moral language he has, but when he talks of her regularity of conduct, the honor and decorum that warrants fullest dependence on her faith and integrity, he expresses what is inspired by the knowledge of her being "well principled and religious" (294). When the bustle of his last intrigue is over he has learned, by force of contrast with Maria, to place a yet higher value on Fanny's sweetness of temper, the purity of her mind, and "the excellence of her principles" (468).

It is in the moral and social conduct of Fanny that the action of the educated disposition is most fully tested. Fanny has been "properly taught" to govern her inclinations and temper and Fanny knows what propriety is. She has a "propriety of mind" (223). She does not have the gifts or the strength of Mary

Crawford or her cousins, she is timid, anxious, doubting, she has "a disposition which not even innocence could keep from suffering," she is near to fainting, she is in excessive trembling (176). But she struggles and endures as the others cannot. It is she who receives and hands on the proper teaching and alone maintains its life when all others seem to have lost it. Fanny at Portsmouth fears that Susan's disposition must be far from amiable, after a fortnight begins to understand a disposition so totally different from her own, and then by doing something for Susan comes to understand the worth of that disposition. Her wonder then is not that Susan should have acted badly at times but that brought up in negligence and error she should have formed "such proper opinions of what ought to be"—she who had had no cousin Edmund to "direct her thoughts or fix her principles"; Fanny will now help to teach her, as she herself had been taught, to improve (391, 395, 397–98). It was from Edmund that Fanny has learned so much, but when Edmund wanders in his understanding of disposition and education Fanny must do better than her teacher. Fanny knows that she and Henry Crawford have dispositions so totally dissimilar as to make mutual affection incompatible; they are unfitted for each other, she says, by nature, education, and habit (327), which is an exhaustive classification. Edmund is infatuated, thinking of his own match with Mary, when he reverses Fanny's understanding of disposition and affection and says that when she and Henry are united by mutual affection it will appear that their dispositions are exactly fitted to make them blessed in each other (335). He tries to convince Fanny that the dissimilarities of temper and disposition—"He is lively, you are serious"—is so much the better (348). Fanny knows otherwise. Henry never understands his own disposition (438). Similarly, Edmund is early pained by Mary's manner. He knows—so he says—that her disposition is as sweet and faultless as Fanny's, but the influence of her former companions makes her seem wrong: she does not think evil but speaks it, in playfulness. " 'The effect of education,' said Fanny gently" (269).

If Fanny has had a better education than the Crawfords and the Miss Bertrams, that does not make her "proper" life easier for her. If the others have been unfortunate in their educations, that does not relieve them of responsibility for their lives. The knowledge and the opportunity for proper action is always there but they do not struggle against habit, or they make only a short struggle. Fanny's way to propriety is not clear before her, it requires a continual effort to maintain itself against the pressures of others and against her own weaknesses, and her ability to endure is not assured.

$\mathcal{I}$F it is easier for us to mock propriety than to understand it, to see it as a foolish or pretentious or dangerously restrictive formula, it is well to know that Jane Austen was making fun of it, and seeing it also as a not so funny hypocrisy, from the time of her earliest works. As with every value, there are several false varieties and the word appears very frequently indeed in its false senses. There are the mere "rules of Propriety" that are so absurdly paralyzing on the first page of "Volume the First" (MW 4); or the more threatening invocation of the word to coerce and dominate others, as it is used by the aunt in "Catharine" and by her successor, Lady Catherine de Bourgh. There is a propriety that is only the foolish fashionableness of Mrs. Elton, and the insipidity of Lady Middleton; or there is the more clever and unscrupulous exploitation of propriety by Frank Churchill and, more darkly in *Mansfield Park,* by Maria Bertram, to gain unacknowledged desires. The common element of all these versions is the silly substitution of an external form for the moral reality, or the more deliberate but still rather simple separation of the two. There is a falsification of what should be defined. But a real propriety is a true definition, in which the difficult fact and the form it ought to have are united. It is then a high sense of the shape of life. It is then an attainment of spirit and not at all easy. Marianne Dashwood may think that if there is any real impropriety she would feel it, but it is in fact only her own pleasure she is consulting (SS 68); a real propriety requires a much larger vision and comprehension of many more complex parts and an understanding adjustment of their relationships. Sir Joshua Reynolds, for example, in a difficult rhetorical situation, relative to a mixed audience and to the different kinds of advice appropriate to the several levels of his art, recognizes a problem in propriety: "It is not easy to speak with propriety to so many students of different ages and different degrees of advancement" (*Discourses,* III). In a moral situation the problems multiply as one's own integrity becomes involved, so that "an attention to propriety" follows "a habit of self-command" and "a consideration of what is your duty" (as Emma can say, if not exemplify, E 268). A moral problem may require a "delicacy" to perceive both the quality of the smallest parts that compose the whole and the manner in which they affect one another. The delicacy that is a weakness, the false delicacy that had been a subject of parody in the late eighteenth century, as it is in Jane Austen (e.g., MW 84, 100; NA 132), is the accompaniment of the false sensibility that puts its willing possessor at the mercy of external or uncontrollable forces; it thereby renders him incapable of thought or action. Fanny, in her physical delicacy, has an unfortunate weakness and one that she must bear. But her delicacy of mind is a strength. A genuine delicacy is a strong form of propriety necessary for making the finest distinctions, especially in the feelings of others, and for determining the appropriate response.

When there are so many ways of losing the path, and so many forces can divert, choosing exactly the right line of conduct becomes a severe and revealing test. How difficult it can be is painfully exhibited in the major episode that leads to the climax of Volume I. The question of the propriety of the theatricals in *Mansfield Park* is frequently disturbing to readers, because it seems strange that what is, for them, such a small matter and an amusement so little threatening as play-acting at home should be taken with such solemnity and seen as such an obviously wrong thing. But the point is rather that the private theatricals at Mansfield Park are not obviously wrong. If they were they would not serve their major purpose as an episode in the novel, which is to present almost all the characters with an occasion in common, when they must make proper choices, with varying degrees of awareness, from a variety of personal circumstances, at an unusual time.

If the circumstances were ordinary and the proper conduct were evident or an authoritative voice were there to point out what should or should not be done, then Mrs. Norris would be quick to interrupt. Mrs. Norris has a quick and complete sense of propriety, she thinks. At the very beginning of the novel when she proposes that Mrs. Price's nine-year old daughter be sent for, but Sir Thomas sees that there will be consequences for the child that must be considered, Mrs. Norris interrupts him with a reply to all his objections, stated or unstated: she perfectly comprehends him, she says, and she does justice to the "generosity and delicacy" of Sir Thomas's motives and she entirely agrees with him "as to the propriety" of doing what must be done for the child (6). There will be some difficulty, Sir Thomas knows, as to "the distinction proper to be made" between his daughters and their cousin, since there must not be arrogance on the one side or depression on the other, but there cannot be equality in rank, fortune, rights, and expectations. "It is a point of great delicacy and you must assist us in our endeavours to choose exactly the right line of conduct." Mrs. Norris is quite at his service, perfectly agrees that it will be most difficult, and will, with Sir Thomas, manage it easily (10–11). When he must leave his family for Antigua and is concerned for the direction of his daughters at their present interesting time of life, he has no fears because he has confidence in Mrs. Norris's watchful attention (and in Edmund's judgment). But Mrs. Norris with all her watchful attention sees nothing wrong in the theatrical amusement and when, upon his return, he expresses his surprise in her acquiescence, she is a little confounded, as nearly silenced as ever in her life, ashamed to confess "having never seen any of the impropriety which was so glaring to Sir Thomas" (188).

The kinds of arguments offered by Edmund, who must be the chief spokesman against the scheme, show the sort of problem it presents. In a general light private theatricals are open to some objection, he says, "but as *we* are circumstanced" they would be more than injudicious. It would show great want of feeling for Sir Thomas, who is absent and in some degree of danger, and it would be imprudent with regard to Maria's situation (125). It is not that Sir Thomas is opposed to theatricals of any sort, any more than Edmund is (or Jane Austen). The question is one of these people in these circumstances. There is a whole series of objections, increasing in specificity and force, which Edmund raises as he sees the plans becoming more and more serious, but there is no sign that the most general, with which he begins, in the hope that they will be sufficient, are universal rules. On the contrary, at each stage his objections are qualified by someone and he must come to the next level of specificity. When he expresses his first alarm, by mock extravagant encouragement, Julia's retort is that no one loves a play better than he. He then must distinguish between real hardened acting and gentlemen and ladies struggling with the disadvantages of decorum. When this is ineffective he comes to the question of his father and Maria. Sir Thomas's degree of danger is real, not only from the normal hazards of the tropics but because of the war at sea. Tom, trying to turn that objection to a motive—the play will amuse their mother in her anxiety—sees for himself the absurdity of his attempt; no one is less anxious than their gently dozing mother. Tom then tries another, more specious line: Edmund is wrong in thinking Sir Thomas would disapprove, because Sir Thomas always encouraged their acting and reciting when they were boys. Edmund then must make the distinction between what Sir Thomas would approve in his boys when they were young and in his daughters when they are grown up, because Sir Thomas's sense of decorum, he says, is strict. Failing in that appeal Edmund then tries to limit the scale of the production, because to build a theater will be taking liberties with Sir Thomas's house and if Tom will not see that it is wrong as an innovation then he should see that it will be wrong as an expense. Step by step Edmund comes to more and more particular distinctions, relative to this family, with this father, at this time (124–27).

When the choice of play is made, that adds another level of impropriety. Fanny, who is the first to realize this, would like to see something acted, for she had never seen even half a play. So here too the objection is directed to the circumstances; she would like to see the acting but everything of higher consequence is against it. Fanny, more than anyone, understands what is happening because she knows the cross-purposes among the prospective actors, as Edmund does not, and therefore sees, as he does not, even more specific reasons why there is a moral problem; the proposal is bringing forth the selfishness of each actor (131). When the choice settles on *Lovers' Vows* she reads it eagerly but is astonished "that it could be chosen in the present instance," in a private theater, the characters of Amelia and Agatha appearing to her in their different ways "totally improper for home representation," and she can hardly suppose that her cousins can be aware of what they are engaging in (137).

One of the main objections Edmund has seen immediately is that the scheme would be imprudent with regard to Maria, "whose situation is a very delicate one, considering every thing,

extremely delicate" (125). Maria is engaged and hers is an engagement, moreover, that still is awaiting the return and approval of her father, who is absent at a great distance; her situation requires a more than ordinarily careful conduct. Julia
understands this, but only to the end of furthering her own desires. She admits that Maria's situation may require "particular
caution and delicacy," but she herself is therefore quite at liberty.
Maria, to gain her desires, reverses the meaning of her engagement, using it as Henry Crawford had already used it, to raise
her above restraint, with less occasion than Julia to consult either
mother or father (128–29). Maria is not, here or elsewhere, an
unseeing fool. After Edmund hears that the play chosen is
Lovers' Vows and that almost every part is cast, he looks at her
and asks, "But what do you do for women?" Maria blushes in
spite of herself. As they argue she denies his judgment that it
is exceedingly unfit for private representation, but the fact is
that she has already recognized the force of his question. For us as
readers the important thing is not whether *Lovers' Vows* is or
is not a proper play but that Maria thinks it is not, will not let
that thought balk her, and finds specious arguments. The point
is emphasized by one of her arguments, directed *ad hominem*
at Edmund, that she is not the only young woman who thinks
the play is very fit for private representation. It is well directed
because Edmund himself later gives in and becomes an actor,
against his own best judgment. The size of his own later blunder,
for foolish reasons similar to Maria's, is prepared for by his
insistence here that it is her place to put others right and "shew
them what true delicacy is," that in all points of decorum her
conduct must be the law for others. "Do not act any thing improper, my dear," Lady Bertram says; "Sir Thomas would not
like it." And she has said exactly the right thing, but merely
as words, not knowing what she is saying, not alive enough to
care, more interested in having her dinner. Nor is Mrs. Norris
any more useful than her sister at the moment. Such opposition

as she has made to the acting has been soon talked down and she is delighted to make the scheme an occasion of immediate petty advantage to herself and her sense of her own importance. Her attention is directed to small matters but not to the fine distinctions of propriety, to making little economies in the preparations for the play and looking about to catch a servant's boy with two bits of board, but not to the substance of the play itself: that she has never read, but she tells Edmund his objections are over-precise. Whatever small chance of success Edmund had in convincing Maria is killed by Mrs. Norris. As Mr. Rushworth is to act too, she says, there can be no harm, again missing the point (139–41). Mrs. Norris and her favorite niece are in agreement on the matter of propriety.

In Mrs. Norris's own words, her "dear Maria has such a strict sense of propriety, so much of that true delicacy which one seldom meets with now-a-days" (117). This she had told Mrs. Rushworth just before the play-acting was suggested, during the little ball at Mansfield. What she never sees is how Maria has used and, at the very moment, is using that strict sense of propriety and the observance of common forms for purposes of particularity, for engaging Henry Crawford's attention as she dances with Mr. Rushworth. The entire history of Maria and Mr. Rushworth, which begins with the zealous promotion of Mrs. Norris, has been a very proper one. Maria has found it her "evident duty" in her twenty-first year to marry an even larger income than her father's; and so she dances with the man "at a proper number of balls" (38–39); and thus the history continues to the moment when Mrs. Rushworth removes herself from Sotherton to Bath "with true dowager propriety" and the ceremony takes place. "It was a very proper wedding." The bride was elegantly dressed, the bridesmaids were duly inferior, there were the signs of emotion as her mother stood with salts in her hand, expecting to be agitated, and her aunt tried to cry (202–3). Maria is very nearly mistress of the art of propriety as the proper show. She controls the surface. In the ride to Sotherton, spoiled for her by Julia's superior position beside Mr. Crawford, the continual prospect of their pleasure was a perpetual source of irritation "which her own sense of propriety could but just smooth over" (81). The feelings that work uneasily beneath that smoothing over are hidden to almost everyone: to Mrs. Norris; to her father, to whom her strong passions were made known only in their sad result (464); to her brother Edmund, who thinks she has given proof that her feelings are not strong (116); to Henry Crawford, who found to his final regret that he had put himself into the power of feelings on her side more strong than he had supposed (468); and to herself, who did not understand their power and was destroyed by them. In the choice of the play Maria is aware to the degree of knowing the impropriety, but not to the degree of resisting it.

As the acting scheme continues it gets worse and worse, as Edmund says even as he slips into it. Fanny, pressed to take a role, and declining, begins to doubt herself and feel undecided as to what she ought to do. Once again the whole force of the episode is that it raises questions which are not simple, least so for those who are most aware of the problem of propriety. She owes much to the cousins to whom she is refusing what they warmly ask of her. She asks herself if it is not ill nature in her, selfishness, a fear of exposing herself. Is Edmund's judgment, that Sir Thomas would disapprove of the whole scheme, enough to justify her denial in spite of the other claims? Because the fears of her own retiring nature would make acting so horrible to her she is inclined to suspect the truth and purity of her own scruples. She grows bewildered. She is making an attempt "to find her way to her duty." In the midst of this, Edmund, whose judgment has been firm, whose judgment she has just been questioning only because he has been a single weight against the others, comes to her for advice. The choice of the play was bad, he says; now, to complete the business, a young man very slightly known to any of them is to be asked into their home. This is one more step in the successively important improprieties. "This is the end of all the privacy and propriety which was talked about at first." The excessive intimacy, the more than intimacy— the particularity—that will result is highly objectionable (152– 54). To feel that Edmund is being rather priggish here is to lose sight of what has happened and is happening. There had been no disagreement between him and the others on the importance of the privacy to the propriety of the scheme. It was to be, Tom had insisted, nothing but a little amusement among themselves, with no audience and no publicity, just as his next assurance had been that the choice of play would be perfectly unexceptionable (125–26). Furthermore, Mary Crawford, who has been happy to take part in the acting, says openly that this admission of a stranger is unpleasant to her. In the play she will have to make love to him and, she tells Fanny, she will shorten some of his speeches and a great many of her own before they rehearse: the acting scheme will be very disagreeable now and by no means what Mary expected (148–49). This is the moment at which Edmund's judgment fails and, to prevent this next overstepping of the original plan, he decides to take the part himself. It will be, on the face of it, inconsistent, absurd, he knows, but he has heard what Miss Crawford said to Fanny and he feels for Miss Crawford. He has begun by arguing against the acting scheme in every way, and when it is past he will say "Nothing could be more improper than the whole business" (350); but, for all his opposition, this weakness in him has been potential from the beginning, when Mary's ready willingness to take part had, by the ingenuity of his love, turned his mind to dwell more on how obliging she was than on anything else (129). His present delusion appears further in his hopes that if he does enter the folly he will be in a better position to restrain it. He has come for Fanny's advice, but he does not want it. Without her approbation he is uncomfortable and knows that if she is against him he ought to distrust himself, but the strength of Mary's attraction outweighs everything.

Fanny is now the sole survivor, but the effect upon her is deeply disturbing, at first even a misery that makes her indifferent to what will happen. Though she has done nothing wrong herself, her heart and judgment are equally against the decision of the self-deceived Edmund, and his subsequent happiness in Mary's company makes her wretched. She is full of jealousy and agitation. The effect of the increasing deterioration of proprieties, then, is that no one escapes, and Fanny, having done nothing wrong, is drawn into the same whirl of unworthy emotions as the others. Excluded from the gaiety and busy employment of the others, alone, sad, insignificant, seeing Mrs. Grant promoted to consequence and honor because Mrs. Grant accepted the character she herself refused, Fanny is in some danger of envying her. What distinguishes Fanny here, and throughout, is that she is capable of thought and recovery, and in this instance reflection brings better feelings, showing her that even if she could have received the greatest respect she could never have been easy. It would have been to join a scheme which, considering only her uncle, she must condemn altogether (159–60).

She does not, even now, condemn theatricals in themselves; the others are vexed and discontented, each for his own reasons of conflict, but she derives as much innocent enjoyment from the play as any of them and it is a pleasure to her to attend the rehearsals (164–65). And her feelings about the feminine roles of the play do not arise from her own peculiarities; Mary Crawford shares them, at least to the extent of feeling the need to harden herself a little, as she says, before she can rehearse with Edmund: she hasn't really looked at the part before, did not think much of it at first, but is now examining *that* speech, and *that,* and *that* (168). We may recall Edmund's original point about real hardened acting and note in passing that one of the objections to ladies and gentlemen acting at Mansfield

Park is not a Platonic fear of assuming a role but, rather, their amateur inability to keep their private lives from taking over their assumed roles; they don't really act. The now personal application of the part may indeed increase its attraction for Mary, but Fanny's judgment of the impropriety is corroborated. Fanny herself is again caught up in the agitation of her own emotions as she sees Mary and Edmund rehearsing and knows that she ought to stay away. The climax comes that evening when Mrs. Grant is absent and Fanny is surrounded by supplications, everybody asking that she take the part in rehearsal: this time Edmund is among the everybody. Fanny "had known it was her duty to keep away. She was properly punished" (171–72). The others persevere, Edmund repeats his wish, with fond dependence on her good nature, she must yield, and the impropriety has run its full course, exempting no one. At that moment Sir Thomas returns, a dramatic and deserved little rescue for Fanny.

In the return of Sir Thomas the episode is concluded as it has begun and continued, with responses at various levels of awareness of what has been happening. Yates and Rushworth are obtuse, each in his own way, but every other heart sinks under some degree of self-condemnation or "undefined alarm" (175), another sign that the important thing is that the participants all do acknowledge something improper has been going on. For the Crawfords, more sensible than Yates, the matter is resolved by their soon agreeing on "the propriety of their walking quietly home" (177). But the others must stay. Lady Bertram, unusually animated by the return of her husband but, as usual, not alive to what is happening, is the one who tells Sir Thomas that they have been "all alive with acting." His reaction is not condemnation but curiosity. "Indeed! and what have you been acting?" (181). It is not until he discovers more of the particulars of the scheme that he can judge it. Tom answers him by reducing the scale of the theatricals—something they have been doing just within the last week, a few scenes, a mere trifle. Had it been only that it would have been of less or of no importance, and Sir Thomas asks nothing more. The greater magnitude of what has in fact happened is unconsciously hinted at as Tom goes on in his attempt to distract Sir Thomas by turning the talk to shooting; he and Edmund might have killed six times as many birds as they did "but we respect your pheasants, sir, I assure you, as much as you could desire." Their serious lack of respect for his home, however, is now revealed when Sir Thomas, saying that he cannot be any longer in the house without just looking into "his own dear room," finds what changes have been made. The comic meeting of Sir Thomas and Mr. Yates, given to us through the eyes of Tom, effectively reduces Sir Thomas to a father finding himself bewildered in his own house, himself caught in the action, making part of a ridiculous exhibition in the midst of theatrical nonsense. The seriousness of what has happened grows slowly in his realization, as it grew in coming into being. The other value of showing this to us through Tom's eyes is that we see Tom understanding his father's thoughts and beginning to see more clearly than ever he had before that there might be some ground of offense. His father looks around and wonders what has been done to his home and his room. It is only much later that Tom sees other, moral, reasons of offense. Sir Thomas's gravity increases; he has been taken by surprise, "as I had not the smallest suspicion of your acting having assumed so serious a character." Tom makes a light attempt to explain the growth of the infection, as he now calls it, by saying that after Yates had brought it into the house it had spread faster because Sir Thomas had encouraged that sort of thing in them formerly (182–84). It is an attempt to shift responsibility, but it is plausible. There are many better plausible reasons that can explain. Even Edmund offers his, but now with an honest acknowledgment of his lack of judgment and deserved blame. Only Fanny, as he says, has judged rightly and been consistent, because she never ceased to think of what was due Sir Thomas.

The final judgment of what has happened is made by his father: "Sir Thomas saw all the impropriety of such a scheme among such a party, and at such a time" (187). The impropriety is not in any one of the elements but in the qualification of each part and the composition of the whole: exactly what was being done, by whom, and when.

But having seen all that, Sir Thomas then reinforces the point for us by his own blindness. It has been disagreeable for him and he wants to forget how much he had been forgotten himself; after restoring the house to "its proper state" (187), he says no more to his children, being more willing to believe they feel their error than to run the risk of investigation. Wiping away every outward memento, sweeping away the preparation, dismissing the workmen, and burning every copy of the play that meets his eye will, he hopes, be sufficient (191). In getting rid of Mr. Yates, the stranger, who he thinks has been the disturber of his home, he hopes he is rid of the worst and last object. He restores an external smoothness, calls for music, which conceals from him the want of real harmony. But we know already how much he does not see or hear and the last bit of action belongs to Mrs. Norris, who now has seen some of the impropriety but is able to foil him by her evasions and her flattery, and, ironically, by her promotion of Mr. Rushworth as his son-to-be: the theatricals end with Mrs. Norris continuing to remove an article from Sir Thomas's sight that might have distressed him, the curtain which she takes to her cottage, where she happened to be particularly in want of green baize (194–95).

*I*T is always Fanny who sees the entire process, who sees what others are doing when they themselves do not understand their own actions, sees the whole drama of their interaction. Her propriety has a large source and is a comprehensive virtue. She sees, above all, the whole extent of time in which the action occurs. Sir Thomas has been forgotten but Fanny never forgets what is due Sir Thomas; he wants to forget what has happened but Fanny's memory is, luckily for all, better than his. At her first arrival in Mansfield Park her young cousins think her so very ignorant because she does not know the chronological order of the kings of England, which they have long since been able to repeat, with similar information, but Mrs. Norris explains that this is because they are blessed with wonderful memories and their poor cousin has probably none at all (19). In everything but disposition they were admirably taught, as we are told on the same page. There is a vast deal of difference in memories, Mrs. Norris points out, and this is certainly true, though it is Fanny whose memory will be so fine, morally significant.

"It is indeed the faculty of remembrance, which may be said to place us in the class of moral agents," Dr. Johnson said, for without it we could act only from immediate impulse, not from the direction of internal motives of choice, would be pushed forward by an invincible fatality, without power or reason to prefer one thing to another except for what happens to be present (*Rambler* no. 41). Mr. Rushworth with his two-and-forty speeches he can never remember seems to be below the level at which a moral life is possible, and the lively Henry Crawford may tell Fanny it can never be forgotten how kind and patient she was in trying to give Rushworth a brain nature had denied him. But what Johnson points us to, more importantly, is a fair account of how very limited is the moral life of the minds of both Henry and his sister.

Neither Henry nor Mary has a memory or much conception of anything beyond a small present. He is quick, he completed all improvements on his estate within three months of coming to age and has left himself with nothing more to do there, or so he thinks; he has been a devourer of his own happiness, as he says (61), and as he will be at the very end. The long history and slow growth of a home is for him reduced to the short interval that makes for his own immediate gratification. Going to Sotherton, to give advice on improvements there, he plays with Maria's feelings by saying that he will never again see Sotherton with as much pleasure, that another summer will hardly improve it for him. "My feelings are not quite so evanescent, nor my memory of the past under such easy dominion as one finds to be the case with men of the world." But in the very next speech, when she changes the subject by recalling that during the drive to Sotherton that morning he and Julia were laughing the whole way, he replies: "Were we? Yes, I believe we were; but I have not the least recollection at what" (98–99). He has in fact no memory, he has no forethought, "he would not look beyond the present moment" (115). The fortnight seems to be the unit by which he lives (114–15, 229). In his subsequent return to Mansfield, after Maria's marriage, Maria is much in Fanny's thoughts when she sees him, "but no embarrassing remembrance affected *his* spirits." He is again on the same ground where all had passed before and he is apparently as willing to stay and be happy without the Miss Bertrams as if he had never known Mansfield in any other state (224). Memory is at his disposal, to claim for his purposes, to remake the past as he chooses. If William wants to know whether Fanny dances well, Henry engages to answer every inquiry: it is true that he once saw her dance and equally true that he would now have answered for her performance, "but in fact he could not for the life of him recall what her dancing had been, and rather took it for granted that she had been present than remembered any thing about her" (251). The life of him, this lively man, has no lasting power. It is the crucial test he proposes when he understands that Fanny thinks him unsteady, "easily swayed by the whim of the moment," easily tempted, easily put aside, that he will endeavor to convince her not by telling her that his affections are steady but by his continuing conduct: "distance, time shall speak for me" (343). He is so far amenable to Fanny's influence that in performing his duty as a landlord, and in discovering there were improvements to be made in the estate, not for himself but for his tenants, "he had secured agreeable recollections for his own mind" (404). For the first time Henry is acting beyond the present, preparing for the possibility of memory. Had he done as he intended, and as he knew he ought, and returned to Everingham, he might have looked forward to a happier destiny, but the triumph of immediate pleasure was too strong and that was the end of Henry.

But the test that Henry proposes for himself, and by which he fails and ruins his love and life, is the test by which Fanny has long lived. We see it in the love between her and William, a necessary part of the novel because he offers our only opportunity to see Fanny in an unchecked, equal, fearless exchange of emotion. That love of a brother and sister so long separated is based in the shared evil and good of their earliest years, the former united pains and pleasures that can be retraced with "fondest recollection." The strength of those first associations and habits have been for these two, as they should be, never entirely outlived, a sentiment still prime and fresh, "feeling the influence of time and absence only in its increase." There is a "lively" admiration in William as he talks with her. Henry has moral taste enough to value what he sees; it removes for him any doubt he may have of the capabilities of her heart and of her genuine feeling, makes him realize that it would be something to be loved by such a girl; it is the point at which he finds himself more interested than he had foreseen; a fortnight will not be enough (234–36). He has taste enough to value what he sees but he has nothing in his life that can make him under-

stand that the love and the liveliness he sees are not to be measured in fortnights but are the experiences of a life that is deep
in memory and time.

Fanny's large strength rises not only from her own memories
but from her sense of life as it is part of a long history. At
Sotherton, where all play out their characteristic roles and fore-
shadow their fates, Mary Crawford, who has seen scores of great
houses and cares for none of them, is not interested in listening
to its story; but Fanny wants to hear all that can be related of
the family in former times, its rise and grandeur, regal visits
and loyal efforts, and is delighted to connect anything with history already known or warm her imagination with scenes of the
past. She estimates the house at a higher value than its possessors,
it having less grandeur and history than she confers on it. Prayers
were always read in the chapel by the domestic chaplain within
the memory of many, but the late Mr. Rushworth left it off;
every generation has its improvements, Mary says with a smile,
but to Fanny it is a pity that the custom should have been dis-
continued. "It was a valuable part of former times. There is
something in a chapel and chaplain so much in character with a
great house, with one's ideas of what such a household should
be!" Mary, we know, laughs at the idea of a whole family as-
sembling regularly for prayers—everybody likes to go their own
way, choose their own time; her lively mind can hardly be serious even on serious subjects (85–87). At the end of the same
chapter she is measuring time and distance with her own feminine lawlessness (94–96).

At the beginning of that intimacy which Mary later estab-
lishes Fanny tries to talk with her about memory. Fanny talks
of the striking growth and beauty of the shrubbery at Mansfield
parsonage. Three years ago it was nothing but a rough hedgerow, never thought of as anything, or capable of becoming anything; now it would be difficult to say whether it is most valu-

able as a convenience or an ornament; in another three years it may be forgotten, almost forgotten, what it was before. "How wonderful, how very wonderful the operations of time, and the changes of the human mind!" (208). What she sees is no bad figure of her own life—and of the movement of the fortunes of Mansfield, of the contrast time is forever producing between the plans and decisions of mortals, for their own instruction and their neighbors' entertainment (472). She cannot know that now, so what is important now is her feeling for those operations of time and the changes of the human mind. "If any one faculty of our nature may be called *more* wonderful than the rest, I do think it is memory. There seems something more speakingly incomprehensible in the powers, the failures, the inequalities of memory, than in any other of our intelligences. The memory is sometimes so retentive, so serviceable, so obedient—at others, so bewildered and so weak—and at others again, so tyrannic, so beyond controul!—We are to be sure a miracle every way—but our powers of recollecting and of forgetting, do seem peculiarly past finding out." The quality of memory, the kind of power of recollecting and forgetting, the weakness and the control, become deeply expressive of the quality of life. Mary is untouched and inattentive, has nothing to say; there is an emptiness of life there that has no conception that the subject is of any interest. It is difficult for Mary to get outside of herself; when Fanny tries to interest her by talk of the variety of nature it is to herself that Mary must return. But there is a hopeful possibility in Mary's wonder at her own presence in Mansfield; if anybody had told her a year ago that this would be her home, that she should be spending month after month here, she should not have believed them; but she has been here nearly five months, the quietest five months she ever passed (208–10). Mansfield has an effect on Mary, surprises her with the passage of slow time with which it builds the events of such a life as she has never known. She loses that momentary effect by shaking it off "with renewed animation," in her old style, but it returns.

It returns to her most sensitively in their last meeting, when she visits Fanny in the former schoolroom at Mansfield that has become Fanny's because no one else wanted it. That is a particularly appropriate place, beyond Mary's knowledge of it, because it contains so many memories for Fanny. We have heard of the East room during the theatricals, after Mary has tried to comfort Fanny in reply to Mrs. Norris's attack: it is not, however, in Mary's power to talk Fanny into any real forgetfulness of what has passed and Fanny has recourse to her room to walk about and think. It is a place which gradually, over the years, in its plants, books, worn furniture, little pictures with family and childhood associations, has become a place of comfort for Fanny: "she could scarcely see an object in that room which had not an interesting remembrance connected with it." There has sometimes been much of suffering to her and of injustice, as at the present moment, but consolation has always followed, especially through Edmund's active support and friendship—"and the whole was now so blended together, so harmonized by distance, that every former affliction had its charm. The room was most dear to her . . ." (151–52). She is about to be thrust into a deeper misery, because Edmund now appears not to bring support but the news that he himself will be acting, has in fact become inconsistent and self-deceiving; this too will have to be absorbed. It is not long after that Mary comes to the room to seek Fanny's help in rehearsing her part, followed unexpectedly by Edmund on the very same business, which gives those two great pleasure while Fanny must bear the brunt (168–70): this is at the end of Volume I. It is always Fanny who must bear the burden of the total history, a task for which others depend on her, usually without knowing how much they ask. In that style Volume III begins. Sir Thomas, coming to the East room, discovers to his surprise that no fire has ever been allowed there, by Mrs. Norris's orders. A wrong has been done, he sees, but it was a mistaken good intention on Mrs. Norris's part, an excess of her good principle that young people should be brought up without unnecessary indulgence, and any distinction she has made between Fanny and her cousins has been kindly meant as a preparation for the more mediocre condition that seemed to be Fanny's lot. He knows, however, that Fanny will not harbor resentment against Mrs. Norris, that Fanny has an understanding which will prevent her from receiving things only in part and judging partially by the event. "You will take in the whole of the past, you will consider times, persons, and probabilities . . ." (313). He is ignorant about Mrs. Norris; and he has come to the East room only to bring his own greater share of wretchedness to Fanny by trying to force upon her Henry Crawford, about whom too he is ignorant, as Fanny is not: when she will not submit Sir Thomas reproaches her dreadfully with ingratitude. But he is right about Fanny's taking in the whole of the past, a longer past than he knows, as the future of his home is safer in her hands than he knows. She then sits in the East room, now with the fire Sir Thomas has ordered, to make her think herself ungrateful, "wondering at the past and present, wondering at what was yet to come" (329).

It is in that room that Fanny and Mary meet for the last time (357–65) as Mary insists on a private talk in order to scold Fanny into the acceptance of Henry's proposal. Finding herself again in the East room produces a strong effect on Mary's mind and suddenly changes her ideas and delays her intent. There is an "instant animation." She was in that room before, once only. "Do you remember it?" It is a foolish question to be asking someone like Fanny, but for Mary a memory is a novel experience, and the details of the delightful rehearsal scene come back to her. "I shall never forget it . . . Oh! why will such things ever pass away?" For Fanny the memory has a different meaning but happily for her Mary wants no answer. "Her mind was entirely self-engrossed. She was in a reverie of sweet re-membrances." The animation and the sweet remembrances are self-centered on the exquisite happiness of the week of the theatricals, in which she gained her ascendancy over Edmund, making his sturdy spirit to bend, as she recalls; it was the un-welcome Sir Thomas who destroyed it all. That much of the live-liness and memory is the recognizable Mary who has not changed very much, but the memory is important to her now because it was the beginning of what has happened to her at Mansfield. She may have hated Sir Thomas for many a week but she does him justice now and he is just what the head of such a family should be; and if we know that is not a full justice it is closer to it than Mary has ever been. She has come to have a sense of a family and what it should be. "Nay, in sober sadness, I believe I now love you all." She says so and says it with a degree of tenderness and consciousness which Fanny had never seen in her before. The scene then fluctuates as Mary tries to recover from her little fit, as she calls it, with a playful smile that takes her away from the better direction she has been following. (Edmund will see that smile once again.) She then returns to her love for Fanny, her feelings for Mansfield, the trust and confidence there which she has never known elsewhere, again to her remembrance of the East room. But the last and longer portion of her talk is her attempt to bring Fanny to accept Henry, by stories of her friends and by devices that will never convince. Fanny even learns that the necklace Mary once presented to her "to be a family remembrancer" (259) was in fact Henry's doing entirely; Mary even insists that Fanny received it consciously just as it was meant: "I remember it perfectly." Mary's memory is less than perfect. This last scene at Mansfield, where she is touched by the memory that brings her closest to an understanding of the meaning of a real family remembrance, of the worth of life at Mansfield Park, is the best she can do. Having left Mansfield she cannot persevere at that level. Fanny at Portsmouth hears nothing from her: her attachment to Edmund, the most respectable part of her character, her friendship for Fanny, which had been blameless—"where was either sentiment now?" (433). It is only the selfish motives, roused by subsequent events, that are able to bring back some sign of life, false life, to those feelings which cannot meet the test of time and absence: the happy possibility that Tom may die and Edmund become Sir Edmund; the unhappy rumor about Henry—"a moment's etourderie" she calls it (437)—which may spoil all plans. That sense of a family and what it should be is lost.

Fanny herself now at Portsmouth is learning more of what a family should be. The absence, the distance and time, from Mansfield Park make her see it with an increase of feeling for its values. It is no good our being offended with what is said of the vulgarity of the people or of the smallness of the rooms at Portsmouth. Mrs. Jennings can be fat and vulgar and Captain Harville and his family can live in astonishingly small rooms without losing our esteem; and Lady Catherine de Bourgh and Sir Walter Elliot can have all the splendors of their pedigrees and their estates about them without gaining esteem, or without being well-bred for that matter. But the family at Portsmouth is a chaos of "noise, disorder and impropriety," with nobody in their right place and nothing done as it ought to be (388–89). There is not a better life at Portsmouth, more color or warmer feelings in its roughness and its discomforts, but a lesser life. Fanny had gone there to heal her pains, looking to be in the center of a circle of love, to feel affection without fear or restraint (370), for it would have solved much for her to be given all that. But Jane Austen has no sentimental gifts for her. Sir Thomas had sent her to Portsmouth to make her sick of it, to make her abstain from the elegancies and luxuries of Mansfield Park and incline her to a juster estimate of the value of the home of greater permanence and equal comfort offered by

Henry Crawford (369). Fanny sees more than Sir Thomas does. She values Mansfield Park more highly than he does, appreciates it not for its luxuries but for its propriety, order, and peace that make life possible (383, 391). She knows the pains of Mansfield Park better than anyone, she has always known the disharmonies there he has not heard when he calls for music, she knows the disorders there he has not yet seen. Furthermore it is Fanny who, by holding out against him, produces the crisis that seems to destroy life at Mansfield Park. But it is of course that act that really saves Mansfield Park and it is Fanny who then returns to pick up the pieces, to reestablish the life there on a stronger basis, and to confirm it by marrying Edmund.

Mansfield Park is not what a family should be any more than Sotherton is what a great house should be. But to Fanny the idea created by scenes of the past and by the memory that takes in the whole and harmonizes its sufferings and injustices, is a source of life. It is she who makes it possible for Mansfield to sustain its life, in spite of its serious failures, by taking from it the best it has offered and by making it live in accord with its best life.

6

The Imagination of Emma Woodhouse

Emma Woodhouse is an "imaginist" (E 335); that is a nonce word, invented for her, according to the *OED*. There is that special charm in Emma, who always deserves the best treatment because she never puts up with any other, which demands a word of her own. A word made for her, and this very one, is surely the best treatment deserved by the Emma whose imagination creates a world of its own. It is a world made to a boundless perfection by desire, for in that dominion conferred by the imagination there are no limits upon life, either upon what can be known or what can be done. Emma's perfection is limited only by her imagination. But the truth is that her extraordinarily active imagination is surprisingly limited. It gives her none of that controlling power she is certain she wields over the finest details of life, not in action and not in understanding. That command of propriety and delicacy, her high value for elegance, and her mind at ease in its own world are the very things it takes from her. It is a humbling experience to discover that the real beauty of the world is not something to be made by the imagination but resides in the simple truth, and to find that the truth is so much more moving, so much more difficult to see, altogether a larger achievement of spirit. With Mr. Knightley we are happy she is capable of the mortification, because Emma is too good to be no better than perfect.

*I*F Jane Austen had a special liking for Emma, one reason is that her own special subject, early and late, was the eighteenth-century problems and pleasures of imagination. It is not only in the juvenilia and the early novels, where we would expect familiar eighteenth-century materials, that we find girls of quick imagination and less judgment, Catharine Percival or Catherine Morland or Marianne Dashwood. Mr. Parker of *Sanditon,* we are told very soon, has "more Imagination than Judgement" (MW 372) and in meeting his sisters we see that we are in "a family of Imagination & quick feelings"; he finds his vent as a Projector and they in their fancy of suffering ill health (412, 385). Sir Edward Denham of the same story has read more sentimental novels than agreed with him; his "fancy" has been caught by all the impassioned and most exceptionable parts and with "a perversity of Judgement," which must be attributed to his not having a very strong head, he is interested and inflamed to emulate the villains of the novels (404). How Jane Austen would have managed these varied imaginations, playing them against Charlotte Heywood and Sidney Parker and Clara Brereton, who see through them, would have been a major part of the development. In this respect, at least, *Sanditon* offers us quite familiar material and language, and in its use of terms like "Projector" (and "enthusiast") for the particular form of Mr. Parker's aberrant imagination its language has an early eighteenth-century sound. Readers of Swift as well as Johnson, and of a hundred lesser observers of possessed humanity, would have recognized its validity.

The contrasting of "imagination" or "fancy" or "wit" with "judgment" or "understanding" or "reason"—all the terms are used and all are important in *Emma*—is a commonplace in the writers of the eighteenth century; it was in language philosophical, moral, and literary, and it was part of the language of common life. For our present purpose the multiple variations of the eighteenth-century history are of less importance than the broad oppositions. The judgment makes careful distinctions, usually working with patience and with study, separating facts from errors, discerning just relations and distinguishing proprieties. It is interested in determining truth. The imagination, less concerned with real differences, ranges widely and moves quickly, sees similarities or makes its own agreeable combinations and unities, guided by its feelings. It is interested in finding pleasure. Imagination has a larger part in poetry than in other pursuits; poetry is the art of uniting "pleasure" with "truth" by calling "imagination" to the help of "reason," Dr. Johnson said (*Lives of the English Poets,* ed. Hill, 1: 170). The poet needs the proper balance: he needs the spirit and liveliness of imagination and he needs the judgment that controls what would otherwise be the unnatural and wandering tendencies of imagination, its disregard for the nature of things. The serious dangers of the unguarded imagination are in common life, where its extravagances can take possession not of a poem, not of a romance, but a mind. That was a problem Johnson knew, bitterly, in himself. He prayed and struggled against the strength of his own imagination, wicked, depraved, sinful, corrupt, and tyrannous over him (*Prayers and Meditations*). In his published work, in *Rasselas* especially, he writes as powerfully as any man ever has on that hunger of imagination which preys incessantly upon life (chap. 32), on the general human problem of "The Dangerous Prevalence of Imagination" (the title of chap. 44). Imagination is a formidable and obstinate disease of the intellect; when radicated by time its remedy is one of the hardest tasks of reason and virtue (*Rambler* no. 89). It was a disease that he studied, especially in himself (Mrs. Piozzi, *Anecdotes,* 4th ed., 1784, p. 52), with fearful cause. Madness is occasioned by too much indulgence of imagination (Boswell's *Life,* ed. Hill, 4: 208). If Emma's story is nothing so somber as this, is a glorious comedy, it is her good fortune, because her story would not be quite so comic if Emma were not yet twenty-one and her fault of mind not yet a disease radicated by time. Nor would it move with such security to its happy remedy if she had not that clear-your-mind and rather Johnsonian figure of Mr. Knightley watching and correcting its course. Even so, and with the many other forces within and without her that ensure her safety, what her imagination leads her to is a most serious set of consequences for others and for herself.

The danger of a prevailing imagination, what makes it central for Johnson and Jane Austen, in their very different ways, is that imagination reshapes the world, and the self, to the desires of the mind. Imagination submits the shows of things to the desires of the mind, not as the poet but as the Quixote who loses the distinction between the real and the fanciful. Turning from the difficult work of seeing and understanding what is before it and within it, and the exertion of acting upon that knowledge, the mind bends the world to its own wants. It breaks bounds, emancipates itself from space and time, raises itself above the limiting human conditions, assumes higher powers, subjects things to its own will, makes all perfect. It makes its romance, sometimes of a pleasurable alarm, usually of pleasurable self-importance, whatever it craves. The desperation that had seized Marianne Dashwood at sixteen and a half, that she would never see a man who could "satisfy her ideas of perfection," had been rash and unjustifiable: "Willoughby was all that her fancy had delineated in that unhappy hour and in every brighter period" (SS 49). And when Colonel Brandon replaces him Brandon is embellished by Mrs. Dashwood's "active fancy, which fashioned every thing delightful to her, as it chose" (336).

"That very dear part of Emma, her fancy" (E 214), is dear to her because it gives her so much pleasure in making up her own truth. Harriet, who has no penetration, cannot tell who her parents are, so that "Emma was obliged to fancy what she liked" (27); but fancying what she likes is just the obligation Emma loves to assume. She has views of improving her little friend's mind but they come to nothing because it is easier to chat than to study, "much pleasanter to let her imagination range and work at Harriet's fortune, than to be labouring to enlarge her comprehension or exercise it on sober facts"; the only mental provision, appropriately, is the collection of riddles (69) and the obfuscation of facts that follows. It was as Mr. Knightley had predicted: she will never submit to anything requiring industry and patience, "and a subjection of the fancy to the understanding" (37). Facts become what the private light of the fancy wills, and when they are not there she invents them. Others are in the dark, she tells Harriet, removing Robert Martin by bringing forward the idea of Mr. Elton: "Hitherto I fancy you and I are the only people to whom his looks and manners have explained themselves." She then conjures up the entire scene of Mr. Elton and what he is doing at the moment with Harriet's picture and how he is showing it to his mother and sister and what he is saying to them and how they are responding. "How cheerful, how animated, how suspicious, how busy their imaginations all are!" Harriet smiles and her smiles grow stronger. A whole secret, and nonexistent, world has been created and conferred (56). The adventure of Harriet, Frank, and the gypsies presents a similar constructive opportunity to Emma, to "an imaginist, like herself," on fire with speculations and foresight, especially with such a groundwork of anticipation as her mind has already made. She sees the event as a very extraordinary thing, dependent on several coincidences, all making a unity in her mind—as if everything united to promise the most interesting consequences and making it impossible the occurrence should not bring Frank and Harriet together. But Emma as artist is defined by her position in this incident: with her old father and her little nephews, the only others to whom the story remains a significant pleasure. Mr. Woodhouse is comforted by his neighbors' inquiries after himself and his daughter and he has the pleasure of returning the answer that they are very indifferent; which is not exactly true, as Emma knows, because he must invent illnesses for her. The gypsies have in fact disappeared before the panic began and the whole history dwindles into unimportance, except for Emma and her nephews: "—in her imagination it maintained its ground," and they still ask every day for the story and tenaciously set her right if she varies in the slightest particular from the original recital (335–36).

We may not like Emma, and Jane Austen foresaw that possibility, but if she causes us discomfort it is because we cannot disown kinship with her. As Imlac says in establishing our kinship with the mad astronomer of *Rasselas,* there is no man whose imagination does not sometimes predominate over his reason, and under certain conditions it will begin to influence speech and action (chap. 44). Emma is rather like that lonely astronomer who thought he controlled the weather. The marriage of Miss Taylor leaves Emma in the great danger of suffering from intellectual solitude (7). Like the astronomer, having little to keep her busy or to divert her she finds pleasure in her own thoughts and conceives herself as what she is not, for who is pleased with what he is? Emma has a disposition to think a little too well of herself and, as Johnson says elsewhere, we always think ourselves better than we are and are generally desirous that others should think us still better than we think ourselves; that is what enables the flatterer to fill the imagination and make his appeal to human vanity (*Rambler* no. 104). Frank Churchill understands that. Emma's imagination amuses her desires and confers upon her a dominion, not over the heavens, but over the large and populous village of Highbury and the course of true love. She takes credit not for the sun and rain but for the match of Miss Taylor and Mr. Weston, though with no better reason.

From there her mind begins to make up scene after scene, uniting and making combinations that delight, and her action begins.

The imagination is "lively" and gives added life; it gives power over life, over others and one's self, and Emma enjoys the power of having rather too much her own way. Rasselas admits, as Imlac finishes, that he too has his daydreams of ruling in perfection. Emma, like him, has some excuse for such ranging thoughts, having lived too long at the center of a happy little enclosure, seeming to unite in herself and her home some of the best blessings of existence. She has no equals in Highbury, where the Woodhouses are first in consequence and all look up to them (7). Mr. Woodhouse can command the visits of his own little circle, in a great measure as he likes (20). In this circle there are the Westons, Mr. Knightley, and Mr. Elton, and after them there is a "second set," the Bateses and Mrs. Goddard, who introduces Harriet. Beyond this Emma has seen little, so that Harriet's talk of the Martins amuses her by such a picture of "another set of beings," such an "order of people" with whom she feels she can have nothing to do (27, 29). Noting later the easy conceit of Mrs. Elton, Emma can fairly suppose that the lady has been "the best of her own set" (272), which is a fair supposition, but there is a Mrs. Elton in every set. Mr. Woodhouse cannot suspect that Emma is not "thought perfect by every body," and, with one exception, which is not particularly agreeable to Emma, he is right (11). "Can you imagine any thing nearer perfect beauty than Emma altogether—face and figure?" Mrs. Weston asks (39). Beautiful she is, but Mrs. Weston is a fondly biased witness, concealing imperfection when she can in those for whom she is anxious (212). And if, among young men, "Mr. Elton is the standard of perfection in Highbury, both in person and mind" ("Very true," says Miss Bates), the standard is not high (174; cf. 142). Emma sees the standard well enough, but she is not prepared to give up her perfection among the women and she has less scruple and much less compunction toward what she calls, not pleasantly, the "amiable, upright, perfect Jane Fairfax" (243). Jane Fairfax is not perfect; Mr. Knightley sees that (288) without ascribing to her the very reprehensible feelings that Emma imagines. Even Mrs. Elton is prepared to see that Jane's character needs a supplement, and offers herself, very much in the spirit of imagination coming to the aid of judgment: "My liveliness and your solidity would produce perfection" (456–57). But Emma will not share her perfection. She is clever, spoiled by being the cleverest of her family—like a fairy, her father says (78), and not so absurdly because she has in fact thrown a charm over the senses of her circle (37), thinks she knows what bewitches the senses of men and satisfies their judgment (64). With her quotation from *A Midsummer Night's Dream* she undertakes the fairy-like function of supervising the course of true love and doing the job rather more smoothly. Like Puck she stands above the fools (75); she plays tricks (137), she acts a part (145), she mimics (225). Above the mortal action, so charming as she is she sees no one who charms her, no one very superior who can tempt her to love and to a change of situation: "I cannot really change for the better." She is exempt from the ordinary way of human nature, falling in love, for "it is not my way, or my nature" (84). That clever and delightfully superior Emma has the quickness and assurance of the imaginative mind (37), she has the "quick eye"—"Such an eye!" Mrs. Weston says, "and so brilliant!" (39)—that makes her sufficiently acquainted with Robert Martin as soon as she sees him (31), that discerns the consciousness of Mr. Elton when she imagines the cause of his charade and his visit (81). She has that ability to see into others, the "instinctive knowledge" which is the gift of imagination (122). Nobody else could have had any idea that Frank Churchill was in love with Jane Fairfax, Harriet says, but Miss Woodhouse perhaps might, she "who can see into everybody's heart," she may have "imagined" it (404–5). But that last expression of faith is not fully gratifying at the moment it is delivered. "My dear Harriet," she says as Harriet is revealing the substantial confusion, "I perfectly remember the substance . . ." (406). "My dear Emma," Mr. Knightley had asked with earnest kindness, "do you think you perfectly understand the degree of acquaintance between the gentleman and lady . . . ?" "Oh! yes, perfectly.—Why do you make a doubt of it?" (350).

One result is nonsense, and there is a lot of nonsense in *Emma*. It's part of the pleasure of knowing her, but then it's not all innocent either. It begins early and it has unpleasant results, in her first quarrel with Mr. Knightley, when he is indignant with Harriet's foolishness in refusing Robert Martin. Emma assumes she knows why the refusal is incomprehensible to Mr. Knightley: "A man always imagines a woman to be ready for anybody who asks her." But Mr. Knightley sweeps her off in his best Johnsonian way. "Nonsense! a man does not imagine any such thing" and as he goes on to discover what has happened it is clear that he means just what he says (60). In "common language," Thomas Reid said, "sense always implies judgment," so that a man of sense is a man of judgment and good sense is good judgment. "Nonsense is what is evidently contrary to right judgment. Common sense is that degree of judgment which is common to men with whom we can converse and transact business" ("Of Judgment," *Essays on the Intellectual Powers of Man,* Edinburgh 1785, p. 520). Faced with the results of a later miserable business Emma realizes that common sense would have directed her to converse differently with Harriet. " 'But, with common sense,' she added, 'I am afraid I have had little to do' " (402). The non-sense of her imagination is an abuse of judgment in which she has not elevated her gifted mind but madly sunk it below the level necessary for common life. "Better be without sense," Mr. Knightley says, "than misapply it as you do." To him her defense of what she has done because of her estimates of the relative gentility of Harriet and Robert Martin is "Nonsense, errant nonsense, as ever was talked!" (64–65). She is a decisive judge of the nonsense of others, of Mr. Elton (129, 134) or of Frank (205), but without recognition of her own responsibility for inducing it in the one and without understanding its intentions in the other. Frank is adroit and shameless in the use of nonsense to blind others, can make himself talk it very agreeably, and Emma is his readiest dupe. It is at Box Hill, where "Any nonsense will serve" (369) that nonsense makes Emma lose her sense. And seeing her conduct, finally, with a clearness which had never blessed her before, she is ready to give it the name of "madness" (408).

So Emma is the story of a girl of too much imagination. But there is another way of saying that.

𝒯HE great Mrs. Churchill of *Emma,* whom we never see but who is so disagreeable that she can clear her ill-fame only by dying, is in one point fully justified in death. No one had ever believed her to be seriously ill. "The event acquitted her of all the fancifulness, and all the selfishness of imaginary complaints" (387). As a matter of fact, she doesn't deserve even that small justice, because she had been carried off after a short struggle by a sudden seizure of a different nature from anything foreboded by her general state. There is a deficiency of imagination in almost every character in the book, even Mrs. Churchill, even those who acquit her and attribute to her a suffering "more than any body had ever supposed" and to Mr. Churchill such a dreadful loss that he would never get over it (388). That deficiency is pervasive because the nature of characters of various sorts is such that they cannot imagine certain kinds of possibilities. Mrs. Churchill was known to be a capricious woman when Mr. Weston had given up his son to her, "but it was not in Mr. Weston's nature to imagine" that any caprice could affect one so dear to him as Frank (17). When Mrs. John Knightley heard of Miss Taylor's marriage she so grieved for Mr. Woodhouse and Emma, because, as she says, "I could not imagine how you could possibly do without her" (93–94). Miss Bates always makes a point of reading to herself Jane's letters before reading them aloud to Mrs. Bates, for fear of there being anything in them that will be distressing, but when she read that Jane was unwell she burst out quite frightened with an exclamation. "I cannot imagine," she says later, "how I could be so off my guard!" (162). If, near the conclusion of the novel, poor Mr. Woodhouse could know the marriage that Mr. Knightley is plotting in his heart he would care less for the state of Mr. Knightley's lungs; "but without the most distant imagination" of the impending evil, without the slightest perception, totally unsuspicious, he is quite comfortable (434). He has a "favouring blindness," as it is called on an earlier and similar occasion (193). Mr. Knightley, under the happy influence of his successful love, not yet publicly known, forgets an appointment with Mr. Elton; the important Mrs. Elton, whose world is very small, feels the indignity done her husband: "I cannot imagine . . . I cannot imagine how he could do such a thing by you, of all people in the world!" (458). Reality comes to each of these characters through such a selective vision, shaped by their own capacities and needs, that much of it is simply excluded.

But what seems to be true is that a deficiency of imagination is the necessary correlate of an excess of imagination within a narrow range of concern. Mrs. John Knightley cannot imagine how an ordinary event can be possible, but when there is a report of snow at Christmas (half an inch, it turns out) she is all alarm: "The horror of being blocked up at Randalls, while her children were at Hartfield, was full in her imagination" (127). Miss Bates may not be able to imagine herself off guard (though the reader never sees her in any other condition), but she is so, in this instance, because she "fancied" a bad illness for Jane. Mr. Woodhouse cannot imagine Mr. Knightley marrying Emma because his mind is fully occupied with an imaginary anxiety that Mr. Knightley may have taken cold. Mrs. Elton cannot imagine how Mr. Knightley could have any unknown engagement more important than a meeting with her husband, but a few moments earlier she has been delighting herself in an anxious parade of mystery about Jane's engagement, "fancying herself" acquainted with secret knowledge of forthcoming marriages (453). Nor is it merely the silly, or even less intelligent, whose imagination cannot function under certain circumstances. Mrs. Weston, as an example, knows her sanguine husband is always expecting Frank to make his first appearance while she, sensibly, is more restrained; but it means more to her than it does to her husband that Frank should pay his visit: "I cannot bear to imagine any reluctance on his side" (122). It is the remark of a sensitive woman and we must like and respect her for it—Mr. Knightley appreciates what is going on in her mind (149)—but Mrs. Weston is trying to avoid seeing a truth, as she does elsewhere when affection leads her.

To say, then, of Emma that she has too much imagination is to say that she has too little imagination. There are certain things she cannot imagine. John Knightley gives her a sly and sharp hint that Mr. Elton is interested in her. She is astonished: "are you imagining me to be Mr. Elton's object?" "Such an imagination has crossed me, I own Emma; and if it never occurred to you before, you may as well take it into consideration now." It is not an idea Emma can entertain seriously and she is amused at the blunders that arise from partial knowledge and the mistakes which people of "high pretensions to judgment" are forever falling into; nor is she pleased with Mr. John Knightley "for imagining her blind and ignorant" (112). As Mr. Elton on the fateful evening moves physically closer to her, Emma cannot avoid the internal suggestion of "Can it really be as my brother imagined?" (118). Similarly, just after Emma has, by "the judicious law of her own brain" (341) determined how she will promote the match of Harriet and Frank Churchill, Mr.

Knightley begins to suspect some relationship between Frank and Jane Fairfax. "I have lately imagined," he says to Emma, "that I saw symptoms of attachment between them." She is excessively amused: "I am delighted to find that you can vouchsafe to let your imagination wander—but it will not do—very sorry to check you in your first essay—but indeed it will not do" (350). But it is of course Emma's imagination that will not do what needs doing. The Emma who sees into everybody's heart never "imagined," "never had the slightest suspicion," of Frank Churchill's having the least regard for Jane Fairfax (405).

The imagination offers a freedom to the mind, a freely ranging and lively activity, the quick eye that is not held by a limited vision, the insight into what is otherwise hidden. But the paradox of imagination, as Johnson had understood, is that it fixes its attention upon one train of ideas and gains its gratification by rejecting and excluding what it does not want. Seeing more, in its own conceit, it sees less, and having put its own shape upon the world it cannot conceive what lies beyond its preconceptions. Emma closes herself off from seeing or hearing. The same symptoms in Mr. Elton that lead John Knightley to imagine what his object may be are lost on her, "too eager and busy in her own previous conceptions and views to hear him impartially, or see him with clear vision" (110). While she is fancying what she likes for Harriet her infatuation for that girl blinds her, as the imagination becomes the victim of its own creation. She takes charge of the mind of lesser fancy, "could not feel a doubt of having given Harriet's fancy a proper direction" toward Mr. Elton (42). Harriet accepts that direction because whatever Miss Woodhouse says is always right—"but otherwise I could not have imagined it." Emma is reassuring: "Receive it on my judgment" (74). Those words return upon her in the later astonishment that Harriet could have the presumption to raise her thoughts to Mr. Knightley: "How could she dare to fancy herself the chosen of such a man . . . !" But if the inferiority of mind or situation is little felt, who but herself had taught Harriet (414)? While Emma has been teaching Harriet how to elevate her imagination, Harriet has been giving Emma's imagination not more opportunity but less. Harriet has been the very worst sort of companion Emma could have, fulfilling Mr. Knightley's prediction. "How can Emma imagine she has any thing to learn herself, while Harriet is presenting such a delightful inferiority?" (38).

By limiting reality to its own ideas the imagination loses its control not only of others but of itself and is then controlled by what possesses it. Taking up an idea and "running away" with it is a common failing, one that Mrs. Elton warns Mr. Weston against (306), though that is obviously advice she herself needs rather more; it is a fault that Miss Bates recognizes in herself (176), which gives her some self-knowledge Emma lacks. Emma may find Miss Bates ridiculous in her uncontrolled talk, but Emma is very like her: Miss Bates knows that now and then "I have let a thing escape me which I should not" (346); Emma knows she should not have betrayed her suspicion of Jane's feelings to Frank Churchill, because it is hardly right, "but it had been so strong an idea, that it would escape her." Frank is so complimentary to her penetration that she isn't certain she ought to have held her tongue (231). As with Miss Bates there is much running away in a mind that is subject to its own desires. Emma can be acute in argument, as she is when warning Mrs. Weston about running away with the idea that Mr. Knightley may be attached to Jane ("proof only shall convince me"), but it is an argument in which sound thought serves her emotion and it reveals how little knowledge she has of her own mind and heart (226). For all its power and all its desires Emma's imagination is weakest in understanding her own desires. She can describe so well what a man ought to be and how "She could fancy such a man" (320), without any recognition that she has seen and heard such a man all her life.

*E*MMA'S imagination does not give her that free dominance of life she presumes. She is confident in the mastery of the arts of life—the propriety, delicacy, elegance, ease—that ask for the mind of greater beauty of insight and of conduct. But in so many ways her imagination dulls her perceptions and it blunts her moral sensitivity. An "ingenious and animating suspicion," for example, enters her brain with regard to Jane Fairfax and Mr. Dixon (160). But a groundless suspicion had always been considered a token of a mean mind; and if Emma is not open here to the heavier censures of the moralists (e.g., *Rambler* no. 79), her suspicions are certainly "ungenerous," or even "abominable," as she later calls them when she sees how they have become a cause of distress to the delicacy of Jane's feelings (380, 421). The one suspicion she ought to entertain, for the man who pretends so flatteringly to be guided by her suspicions, whose judgment is carried by her reasonings (216–17, 219), is of course the one that never occurs to her; it does not because the imagination of the same ingenious mind has conferred on him the honor of being in love with her (206): the suspicion of their being marked for each other had taken strong possession of her mind (192).

Emma's ingenious suspicion is that Jane has formed an "improper attachment" (421). She thinks of herself as an accurate and decisive judge of propriety; but a perception of that nice adjustment of the parts that constitute the whole of any social or moral moment, in a true propriety, must be missed by an imagination that sees what it wants to see. Frank Churchill is practiced in the art of a seeming propriety, the agreeable manner that pleases. If he can fool gentle and uncomprehending people, Mr. Woodhouse or Isabella Knightley, by his "very proper," handsome, pleasing letters which are substitutes for reality (96), Emma is also prepared to accept the man who will adapt his conversation to the taste of everybody and be universally agree-

able, "just as propriety may require" (150). Mr. Knightley insists that her own good sense could not endure such a puppy
when it came to the point, but when it comes to the point Emma's
good sense not only endures but is perfectly satisfied: "nothing
could be more proper or pleasing" and Mr. Knightley has not
done him justice (196–97). There follows immediate evidence
of how Frank is prepared to ignore or use propriety to attain his
own ends (198, 199), but it is lost on Emma. He uses other
people's feelings. In the shock of the final revelation, when Emma
hears from Mrs. Weston what Frank has been doing, she thinks
him greatly to blame. Mrs. Weston's explanation, that there
have been misunderstandings between him and Jane which may
have arisen from "the impropriety of his conduct," produces an
explosion from Emma. "Impropriety! Oh! Mrs. Weston—it is
too calm a censure. Much, much beyond impropriety!" She sees
in him now "such horrible indelicacy" (397): where she thought
she had seen propriety there had been something beyond impropriety.

"Delicacy," as we have seen it in *Mansfield Park,* is a more
intensive word, indicating a moral and social discretion able
to make even finer distinctions, beyond the ordinary demands of
propriety. There is a false delicacy with pretensions to such
feminine nicety in its own feelings that it is forever overcome
and inactive, but a true delicacy is a principled concern for the
feelings of others and it is neither weak nor peculiarly feminine.
Colonel Brandon is a man of a delicacy equal to Elinor's (SS
283, 287) in consulting the feelings of others. Darcy is a proud
man but Jane Austen thought of him as a delicate man too: "I
can imagine he w^{d} have that sort of feeling—that mixture of
Love, Pride & Delicacy" (L 312). Admiral Croft is the bluntest
and most outspoken of men and the least likely to be suspected
of delicacy, but when he thinks he may have given pain unintentionally the delicacy of his good nature keeps him from saying
another word (P 262–63). And so in *Emma* one finds delicacy

where it seems least likely to appear, or at least where Emma thinks it least likely. She has assumed that the Martin family must be coarse and unpolished, then reads Robert Martin's letter and is surprised to find it so much above her expectation in several ways: it expressed good sense, warm attachment, liberality, "propriety, even delicacy of feeling." She thinks one of his sisters may have helped him, but she sees that his style is not the style of a woman, being too strong and concise; he thinks strongly and clearly and when he takes pen in hand the thought naturally finds "proper words" (50–51). Her impression is confirmed in the next volume when Harriet, having dropped the Martins, meets them accidentally and is made uncomfortable by their kindness. Emma is not comfortable herself because the young man's conduct and his sister's seemed the result of real feeling, an interesting mixture of wounded affection and "genuine delicacy" (179). She explains it away, however. The fact is, Robert Martin is delicate but Emma Woodhouse is not. She does not appreciate propriety and delicacy in others because the needs of her imagination make her own mind improper and indelicate.

After reading Mr. Martin's letter she arranges Harriet's response by the appearance of refusing to give advice and insisting that the letter had much better be all Harriet's own: "You will express yourself very properly, I am sure," she says, and "such expressions of gratitude and concern for the pain you are inflicting as propriety requires, will present themselves unbidden to *your* mind, I am persuaded" (51–52). Now this is unhappily perverse, this use of propriety as a polite exterior to cover the inflicting of pain—coming, especially, as it does after the manly propriety and delicacy of feeling in Martin's letter. We have had the shadow of this danger from the first chapter, where Emma has boasted of her success in making the match between Miss Taylor and Mr. Weston, and Mr. Knightley has responded ironically: her time has been "properly and delicately" spent if she has been endeavoring for four years to bring about the marriage; a worthy employment for a young lady's mind (12)! His concern is for her own mind rather than the objects of her planning, since he knows that Weston and Miss Taylor have managed their own lives, and Emma is more likely to have done harm to herself than good to them by her interference. She becomes more dangerous as her employment really does affect the lives of others, and with Mr. Knightley, we become seriously displeased with her; but, also with him, from the start our main concern is for what she is doing to herself. The coming of Frank Churchill, himself without delicacy, adds his selfish encouragement to the worst in her, and Mr. Knightley is made anxious in seeing how "the delicacy, the discretion" of his favorite have been "lain asleep" (348). Mr. Knightley knows what delicacy is, and for him it is so far from being a merely feminine quality that we have seen how it helps this English gentleman define the national character. The true English style is not a display of feeling but a reality and an activity, as in the relationship of Mr. Knightley and his brother (99–100). It is what he cannot find in Frank Churchill, who may be amiable in French but not in English: "he can have no English delicacy towards the feelings of other people," nothing really amiable (149). Under that influence, on Box Hill, Mr. Knightley will see Emma become "unfeeling" (374).

*I*N these tests of the fineness of her discrimination the finest test is presented by "elegance," and Emma thinks of herself as a great appreciator of elegance. Elegance in this context is a "refined propriety," as the *OED* puts it, with an illustrative quotation from *Emma*. It is, in one of Johnson's definitions, "the beauty of propriety." It is the graceful beauty that comes from the delicate adjustment of the minutest parts. Most of the elegance in the world of Jane Austen is false, an outward ornament or manner only, a false art—the assorted sillies of the juvenilia, or Lady Middleton, or Rosings and Lady Catherine described in the language of Mr. Collins, or Elizabeth Elliot; but a real elegance of person rises from an inner beauty of mind. Emma, with an imagination that creates what pleases it, thinks she can offer elegance as a gift, when her imagination is really preventing her from seeing what is before her. She sees in Harriet a girl who wants only "a little more knowledge and elegance" to be quite perfect and she undertakes the improvement. The reader knows that Harriet, luckily, has been spared such elegance at Mrs. Goddard's honest school, and that her closest brush with it has been hearing Robert Martin sometimes of an evening read something aloud "out of the Elegant Extracts—very entertaining"; but to Emma Harriet's proper deference and attachment show that she has the "power of appreciating what was elegant and clever" (23, 21–22, 29, 26). Robert Martin's modest attempt, for that matter, does rather more to improve Harriet's reading than Emma's larger planning and smaller doing. What she does is, literally, to draw a too flattering picture of Harriet, in which "she meant to throw in a little improvement to the figure, to give a little more height, and considerably more elegance." Mr. Knightley sees and says flatly that she had made Harriet too tall, and Emma knows it but will not own it, because the spectator she has chosen to impress is Mr. Elton, whose eye she cannot respect (47–48). It is Mr. Elton, trying to respond in the same style, as they play at cross-purposes, whose alert gallantry completes her effort by taking it to London and returning with "The Picture, elegantly framed" (69).

While Emma is adding elegance to Harriet, Mr. Elton, unseen by her, is adding to his own elegance. Mr. Elton enjoys the privilege of exchanging on any evening his own blank solitude "for the elegancies and society" of Hartfield and the smiles of the lovely daughter there (20). Unlike Harriet as pupil Mr. Elton as suitor does not tempt the imagination, for Emma can see very well how he is wanting in "true elegance," "how very much

he was her inferior in talent, and all the elegancies of mind"
(35, 135, 136). He was so, and Mr. Elton proves a worse man
than she thinks him now, but if Emma can rave a little about
the seeming incongruity of gentle manners and a conceited head,
the incongruity is of her own making. Emma may have been
able to see that he lacked elegance, but that has taken little
vision. Her imagination has convinced her of his propriety, the
"very proper compliment" of his charade (73), the "proper
home" he will provide for Harriet (74), the obviously "proper
form" of the match (75), his "very proper" concern for Harriet's illness (115), until she finds herself being forced to forgive him for "late improprieties" (124) and must struggle in
vain to bring his conversation back into the "proper course"
(125). Emma has made the obvious judgment but not the difficult one. A man who lacks propriety will of course lack true
elegance, but the significant judgment about Mr. Elton is
whether he has propriety and Emma does not make that judgment. It is a step forward when she is obliged to admit that her
own behavior has been such that it might warrant a man of
"ordinary observation and delicacy," like Mr. Elton, in "fancying himself" a favorite (136).

No, the lady who fancies Mr. Elton is not the charming Miss
Woodhouse but the charming Augusta Hawkins, that caricature
of Emma who both shows us her faults more largely and, by the
differences, helps us appreciate Emma. Miss Hawkins had been
so very ready to have Mr. Elton, in whom true elegance is wanting, because she herself is the very type of false elegance. She
is absolutely incapable of making any distinctions, drawing all
her notions from one style of living and, with a closed imagination, applying it to all the world. All that she can "see or
imagine," from her first appearance, is what is very like Maple
Grove; she could "really almost fancy herself at Maple Grove"
(272). What she has never heard of is, with a most satisfied
smile, rendered nonexistent: "No, I fancy not." This is the

mind of one who, by her own account, loves to explore (274).
We hear of Mrs. Elton's elegance long before we see her, as part
of a catalog that gives her all the right adjectives and removes
all real life from them. As a young person in an interesting situation—marriage, as it happens, but death would serve equally
well—she is sure of being kindly spoken of. Before she has
arrived she is, by some means or other, discovered to have every
recommendation of person or mind; "to be handsome, elegant,
highly accomplished, and perfectly amiable" (181). There is
little more for Mr. Elton to do than tell her Christian name and
say whose music she principally played, for the other words have
no meaning. Emma on making her first short courtesy visit will
not allow herself to give an opinion of Mrs. Elton "beyond the
nothing-meaning terms of being 'elegantly dressed, and very
pleasing.' " But she suspected that "there was no elegance . . .
neither feature, nor air, nor voice, nor manner, were elegant"
(270). Emma thought at least it would turn out so and, no
difficult prediction, it does. Mrs. Elton's notions of propriety, for
all her resources, lie entirely in externals, in card tables and cards
"in the true style" and refreshments "at exactly the proper hour,
and in the proper order" (290). Her elegance is all in what
can be bought, put on, commanded, the elegance of an impoverished imagination moving in a little circle. A family in the first
circle has "Wax-candles in the school-room! You may imagine
how desirable!" A family moving in a certain circle is "able to
command the elegancies of life" (300–301). To her it is all,
most literally, a matter of dress—the dinner at Hartfield "as
elegant as lace and pearls could make her," the ball at the Crown
in "the studied elegance of her dress" (292, 321). Miss Bates
is impressed. Emma is not.

But if the obviously false elegance, at one end of the scale,
presents no difficulty to Emma, she is not up to the more exact-
ing demand presented by a true elegance. The woman to whom
Mrs. Elton delivers her definition of the elegancies of life, be-

cause she is so anxious to settle her properly in a certain circle, is inevitably that woman least in need of her instruction. Jane Fairfax is elegant. That is her epithet and it accompanies her on her introduction and follows her throughout. We are assured of its reality because it first comes to us without any emphasis in the paragraph that describes the excellence of her education among the Campbells; there she has been living constantly with right-minded and well-informed people and, in result, her heart and understanding have received every advantage of discipline and culture; it is in that history that she has shared in "all the rational pleasures of an elegant society" (164). Her elegance is not the purchased or affected ornament, but the delicately lovely outward form of natural gifts fully developed by social opportunity. Emma, for all her cleverness and riches, has not had that discipline or culture for her heart and understanding and Emma does not like her. Seeing her again after two years Emma is particularly struck by the appearance and manner she has been depreciating. "Jane Fairfax was very elegant, remarkably elegant" and Emma had herself "the highest value for elegance" (167). The elegance of Jane's appearance is in a distinctive balance of each small detail, a height just such as everybody would think tall and nobody too tall, a figure particularly graceful, a size of the most becoming medium, and not a regular but a very pleasing beauty of face. To the deep gray of her eyes and the dark eyelashes and brows Emma has never denied praise. But what she has cavilled at is the beauty that takes a more appreciative understanding, a skin that seems to want color, want a fuller bloom, and Emma's own complexion has the full bloom of health (39); she had not formerly seen that Jane's complexion has a "clearness and delicacy" which really need no fuller bloom (167). Clara Brereton of *Sanditon* would be another example where "great delicacy of complexion" is the accompaniment of elegance (MW 391); or Anne Elliot, as opposed to Elizabeth Elliot. In the truly elegant woman the physical appearance, the manner and the mind all unite, and the delicate skin becomes, in a happily Platonic way, the visible light of the beauty within. Frank Churchill plays on that, at Emma's expense. Her first words in describing Jane Fairfax to him are that she is "a very elegant young woman," and when he does not seem to concur she thinks that there must be a very distinct sort of elegance for the fashionable world if Jane Fairfax is thought only ordinarily gifted with it (194). His flat criticism of Jane's deplorable want of complexion leads Emma to the warm defense of the "softness and delicacy" of her skin which gives "peculiar elegance to the character of her face"—exactly what he wants to hear while his flattery insists on his preference for Emma's fine glow of health (199). Jane Fairfax, Emma sees, has a style of beauty "of which elegance was the reigning character," and she must in honor, by all her principles, admire it: "—elegance, which, whether of person or of mind, she saw so little in Highbury" (167).

But for all she says, when she does see elegance Emma in her fuller bloom does not know how to value its beauty. It was not an imagination of much delicacy that found its satisfaction in cultivating the elegance of Harriet Smith and never paid the attention due to Jane Fairfax, never sought the friendship of the woman who, in both abilities and education, ought to have been received with gratitude. She did not like Jane, Mr. Knightley had said, because she saw in her the really accomplished young woman she wanted to be thought herself. Every fault she imputes to Jane is "magnified by fancy" (166–67). In her abominable suspicions of Jane's improper attachment, in her amusement that the perfect Jane Fairfax is apparently harboring very reprehensible feelings (243), the imagination has become not the faculty of a more just appreciation but the self-protective instrument of envy and injustice, and it becomes a cause of distress to the delicacy of Jane's feelings.

There is one thing more to be said of Jane Fairfax which will help us understand how Emma's imagination is deficient in its control of life, its art and its morality. Jane's elegance is the un-bought grace, a perfected expression of external appearance and internal reality of accomplishment, distinction, and merit. But not quite. Not even Jane Fairfax is perfect. She is reserved, and always has been, partly from diffidence, which friendliness from Emma could overcome, partly from a discretion which must be honored; so said Mr. Knightley, though Emma refused to make the distinction (171). But, as we see Jane in the book, and as Mr. Knightley sees her on this visit to Highbury, her fault is deeper; she has both strength of feeling and self-control, but she wants openness and Mr. Knightley loves an open temper (288–89). There is reason enough for her manners—"cold and artificial" she calls them later, because she had always a part to act (459)—and the demands of the plot keep us from a fully convincing representation of her elegance. There is a moral fault in the reserve that flaws her elegance. The artificiality that Jane imposes on herself is a defect because elegance must be simple; that is one of its standard qualifying adjectives in the eighteenth century. Mrs. Elton knows enough to chatter about the simple and natural and to declare her horror of being over-trimmed even while displaying her apparatus and her finery, her studied elegance (302, 355). Mr. Bennet skillfully elicits Mr. Collins's propriety and delicacy in giving an unstudied air to his prestudied little elegant compliments to Lady Catherine (PP 68). But a real elegance is simple because it is an art so perfectly assimilated that it has passed over into what appears only as an artlessness. It is what is called, in *Sense and Sensibility,* "real elegance and artlessness" (SS 124). It becomes natural and habitual and vanishes from observation.

It then becomes a graceful ease. "True ease," Pope had said of writing, comes from art not chance: "As those move easiest who have learn'd to dance" (*Essay on Criticism,* ll. 362–63), so that the principle has a wide applicability. Addison's style, says

Hugh Blair, has no affectation in its manner, no marks of labor, "but great elegance joined with great ease and simplicity" (*Lectures on Rhetoric and Belles Lettres*, 1783, 1: 395). In a society ease is a sign of good breeding, a mind and manner that give pleasure to others because they express a life quietly confident of itself, and therefore neither affected nor reserved.

Darcy is an example of a man who has never learned ease. Darcy, for all his superiority, is at times deficient in a gentlemanlike manner, as Elizabeth tells him in words he never forgets. He is not affected—he does not pretend to be other than what he is—but he is reserved ("haughty, reserved," PP 16) and he has never made the effort to correct his temper, to please or to be pleased. His cousin, Colonel Fitzwilliam, who in person and address is "most truly the gentleman," enters into conversation directly "with the readiness and ease of a well-bred man," but Darcy shows "his usual reserve" (171). It is the presence and ease of Colonel Fitzwilliam that allow Elizabeth and Darcy to converse with a valuable freedom, so that when Darcy attempts to excuse his reserve by a series of honest but ineffective defenses, Elizabeth, with the aid of the Colonel, demolishes them one after the other. By the illustration of her own playing on the pianoforte she points out how it is the proper art of ease which Darcy has refused to practice and which he must learn (175). In Elizabeth he will have an effective teacher who has the art he lacks and who makes it engaging to him. One of the first mortifying discoveries he had made, as his initial disregard for her turned to admiration, was how in spite of his assertion that her manners were not those of the fashionable world "he was caught by their easy playfulness" (23). Moments later in that evening he hears her play and sing for the first time: Mary Bennet, a more accomplished musician, has the pedantic air and conceited manner, but Elizabeth, "easy and unaffected," is listened to with more pleasure (25). In their marriage it is "by her ease and liveliness" that his mind and manner will be improved (312). The association of ease with liveliness and playfulness indicates how at its best it is the manifestation of an active life, assured of its identity. It is free of the false restraints of either the reserve that will not open but tries to preserve itself by turning from others, or the affectation that is anxious to impose that identity on others. The effect of Elizabeth upon Darcy is to humanize him more fully.

Of the several types of false ease, the most obvious is that of the fool who thinks he is well-bred when he is really imposing himself upon others, sometimes reversing the very meaning and purpose of the virtue by making others uneasy. He is the coxcomb Tom Musgrave of *The Watsons* or Robert Ferrars. The best example is probably John Thorpe, "easy where he ought to be civil, and impudent where he might be allowed to be easy" (NA 45), an exact definition of an aggressive fool who is always falling that one degree below the level of form appropriate to the occasion. But there is another false ease, less obvious, much more agreeable, with more reality, and more plausible. It conceals, sometimes even from its possessor, the emptiness within, the absence of that which ease should signalize, a well-controlled life. We see this best in *Mansfield Park,* in the Miss Bertrams and Tom Bertram, where the careful formation of the ease of manners (MP 34, 47) covers the serious moral problems beneath. Henry Crawford, so much at home with them, does everything "with happy ease" and even "playful impudence" (240); but the genuine superiority of manner becomes a power to deceive, and to deceive, finally, even himself, because it has no moral control.

Emma, after her style, can make the more obvious judgments but misses the more difficult; she is fast and incisive in seeing the false ease in Mrs. Elton, but not that in Frank Churchill, and not that in herself, because her imagination has an interest in his ease and her own. If a true elegance becomes an ease, what we would expect from Mrs. Elton is an assumption of ease. It is the first thing Emma notices; "there was no elegance;—ease, but not elegance." That delicate attention to all the elements balancing in the moment when she enters a new society, which would constitute a true ease, is what Mrs. Elton is never capable of. For "a young woman, a stranger, a bride, there was too much ease," an "easy conceit" (E 270, 272). She can even patronize Mr. Woodhouse in admiration for his quaint old-fashioned politeness, which she declares is much more to her taste than the modern ease: "modern ease often disgusts me" (302); that is in the same speech in which she declares her great dislike and horror of being over-trimmed, while she displays her over-trimmed gown. As she has none of the simplicity of elegance she desires, she has all the abbreviated and tasteless ease she deplores. Her diminutive style of address, first name only for a woman, last name only for a man, initial only for a husband, is the pert and presuming, ill-bred familiarity of excessive ease. "Jane!" repeated Frank Churchill with a look of surprise and displeasure. "That is easy—" (324). We can only rejoice that Emma says she will never call her husband anything but Mr. Knightley: "I will not promise even to equal the elegant terseness of Mrs. Elton, by calling you Mr. K." (463).

But Emma is vulnerable to Frank Churchill's deception because, among other reasons, he seems to have the right sort of ease. He is a *very* good-looking man, with spirit and liveliness, and he looks quick and sensible. She felt immediately that she should like him; "and there was a well-bred ease of manner" (190). That ease and readiness convinces her that he came intending to be acquainted with her. She mistakes his intentions and within a moment she even has some evidence of his untruthfulness passing suspiciously through her brain. But it passes in and out because even if he has told a falsehood it is a pleasant one and pleasantly handled. His manner has no study, no exaggeration, all the external marks of ease, and in fact he has most of the qualities he seems to have. It is unfortunate for Emma that he is using them and using her for his own ends, but her real misfortune is that she can be used. She thinks that she too has a "mind lively and at ease" (233), thoroughly at home in the world in the assumption of its own quiet power and grace. That self-characterization is in the paragraph where Emma, for amusement is watching the traffic of Highbury: the activity of the little scene is amusing, and Emma's ability to appreciate it helps us appreciate her, but when we keep in mind the whole scene, which begins with Emma manipulating a pliant and empty Harriet and ends with Frank manipulating a pliant and self-deceived Emma, there is an apparent irony in her assumption that her mind is lively and at ease. One serious effect of Frank Churchill is that he gives her a false feeling of being easy which leads her to act without understanding. As she dances with him at the Crown, under Mr. Knightley's observation, she has no fear for criticism of her behavior: she and her partner are not flirting like lovers but seem "more like cheerful, easy friends" (326); she has missed the point of her own observation, moments before, that there is a restlessness in Frank "which showed a mind not at ease" (320). There is justice in Frank's defense of himself and his relations with her, in his letter: "She received my attentions with an easy, friendly, goodhumoured playfulness, which exactly suited me" (438). She is his victim, but she exactly suited him, all the way to Box Hill.

*E*MMA does not really have the mind lively and at ease for which she takes credit, she does not value elegance as highly as she thinks she does, her conduct has not been proper, certainly not delicate; in a word she has not been the lady she imagines herself. One thing she very much needs is someone to help her see what she has been blind to, someone capable of doing what she only imagined herself doing, seeing into the minds and hearts of others and of herself, a gentleman with the right kind of imagination.

Mr. Knightley knows Emma's faults, knows she will never submit to anything requiring patience and industry, and "a subjection of the fancy to the understanding" (37), knows her "errors of imagination" (343). He does what he can to correct them in her, and he certainly does not fall into them himself, and he will not follow anyone else's imaginings. Can he imagine anything nearer perfect beauty than Emma? Mrs. Weston has asked him. "I do not know what I could imagine," he replies, and he means exactly that, for the question is simply of no interest; "but I confess that I have seldom seen a face or figure more pleasing to me than her's" (39). What touches him, what he will speak to, is what he has seen (and even there he is aware that he is a partial old friend). But then it is his ability to see that gives him what is a very effective imagination. Miss Bates can chatter and conjecture about Mr. Elton's interesting letter announcing his marriage but it is Mr. Knightley who "actually saw the letter" and who, for that reason, can say, "By his style, I should imagine it just settled" (174). He rebukes Emma for the nonsense of her assumption of what a man always imagines and he hopes she is also mistaken about the madness of Harriet's refusal of Robert Martin. "I saw her answer," Emma replies; "nothing could be clearer." "You saw her answer! you wrote her answer too." His is clearly the better imagination, for it is he, not she, who really knows what is going on in the mind of the other; he knows what she has done when she will not admit it even to herself (60). He has always known, from the beginning of the novel, rather more of what goes on in Emma's mind than she has. She thinks she has made the match between Miss Taylor and Mr. Weston, but Mr. Knightley imagines what she really was thinking and saying to herself: "I rather imagine, your making the match, as you call it, means only your planning it, your saying to yourself one idle day, 'I think it would be a very good thing . . .' and saying it again to yourself every now and then afterwards" (12–13). At the end of the novel, it is a measure of how badly Emma has acted if Mr. Knightley must confess that, from her manners, even he could never assure himself as to the degree of what she felt about Frank Churchill; she feels that shame (426). She has been warned before how her imperceptive imagination is falsifying her own manners. If the imagination crosses John Knightley that Mr. Elton's object is Emma, it is because, as he says, "I never in my life saw a man more intent on being agreeable." He has seen the manners and Emma "had better look about" her and ascertain what her own manners are doing and what she means to do (111–12).

Like his brother's, Mr. Knightley's imagination begins with what he sees and its effect is to make him see better. While everything seems to declare that Frank's object is Emma, all signs seem to be in unison, Mr. Knightley begins to suspect Frank of double-dealing. He cannot yet "understand" it but there are symptoms he has "observed" and cannot think entirely void of meaning, however much he may wish to avoid Emma's errors of imagination. He has "seen a look, more than a single look," which seems out of place. He remembers what he has seen, and he cannot avoid more observations that strengthen his suspicion. It is not an imagination that creates what it sees, like the poet gazing into the fire, while his fancy soothes him with a waking dream and while his understanding takes repose in indolent vacuity of thought; he has a passage from Cowper in his mind (343–44). Mr. Knightley places himself to see them all, Emma, Frank, Jane, "and it was his object to see as much as he could." He continues to observe, he hears, his eye darts, the candles come to assist his observations (347–48). Never, not for the twentieth part of a moment, does the idea occur to Emma that there may be any admiration between Frank and Jane Fairfax; she is excessively amused and delighted that Mr. Knightley has imagined there are symptoms, that he vouchsafes to let his imagination wander (350). But he has not. His imagination begins neither in an internal emptiness nor with a superfluity of sensation. His imagination does not create the truth he wants, nor any other for that matter; it does not wander but has a concentrating effect that helps lead him to the truth.

The effect of Mr. Knightley's imagination is not to make him build a private world of his own feelings but to turn him outward to a delicate understanding of what lies beyond himself, in the feelings of others. That was an essential value of the imagination, Dr. Johnson recognized, because it gives us a reality we cannot have any other way. It is "an act of the imagination" that "realises" (i.e., makes real) what is happening to another "by placing us, for a time, in the condition of him whose fortune we contemplate," so that we ourselves feel what is happening to him (*Rambler* no. 60). It is an act that plays the major role in that very important argument Emma has with Mr. Knightley at the conclusion of the first volume, when they are anticipating the arrival of Frank Churchill (145–49). The argument is particularly interesting because Mr. Knightley is jealous of Frank before he ever sees him, with an emotion that is enlightening to himself. He is certainly warm and vexed: Emma thinks he dislikes Frank only because the young man appears to be of a different disposition from himself, which is unworthy of his liberality of mind. Emma seems to have the best of the argument because she has the sympathetic imagination Mr. Knightley seems to lack. Mr. Knightley can make up proper speeches for Frank to deliver to the Churchills, in the tone of decision, if Frank really wishes to visit his father; Emma laughs that he should think a young man entirely dependent could use such language: "Nobody but you, Mr. Knightley, would imagine it possible." It is, she says, only because he has not an idea of what is required in situations directly opposite to his own. She supposes, with comical skill, what the scene would be like: "How can you imagine such conduct practicable?" She can imagine, she says, that if he were to be transported and placed in Frank Churchill's situation he would be able to do and say what he recommends, but he would not

have Frank's different habits; she wishes he would try to understand what an amiable young man of Frank's history and position is likely to feel. She has a strong case, and Mr. Knightley is
not impartial, and for all that he is still right. He may never have
seen Frank Churchill and yet he is right when he says Emma's
amiable young man is weak and without resolution. That is exactly what Jane Fairfax comes to know, but only after a long, suffering experience, and exactly what she says to Frank at her
breaking point (373). Mr. Knightley knows it because he has
the evidence, in what Frank has not done and in what he has
done, and in the letters he has written; Mr. Knightley has the
more general experience of how men can act, and how they
should act, to realize what is going on within Frank's wishes and
feelings, to realize how Frank is "fancying himself extremely
expert" in excuses and in falsehoods. It is Mr. Knightley, not
Emma, who has proofs to offer. It is not Emma but Mr. Knightley who can put himself in Mrs. Weston's place at the moment
and know what she now must be feeling and often saying to
herself while Emma's "amiable" young man has no delicacy for
the feelings of others.

Frank's character, Mr. Knightley says later, is wanting in
steadiness and "delicacy of principle" (448), that principle
which precedes the self and regularizes moral action. Mr.
Knightley, in the early argument with Emma about Frank's
character, has the very firm idea of "duty" and of "principle"
(146, 147, 148) to guide his imagination clearly and depend-
ably. Jane Austen's Fanny Knight, the niece who so delights
her, is "all over Imagination," and the most astonishing thing
is that with so much imagination, flight of mind, fancy, she has
such excellent judgment in what she does: "Religious Principle
I fancy must explain it" (L 485–86). With all Emma's errors
of imagination and her indulgence as a spoiled child, Mr.
Knightley knows, nature had given her understanding and "Miss
Taylor gave you principles" (462). Emma knows, however, that

it was Mr. Knightley who corrected her, disagreeable as she may have thought it, influencing her rightly, oftener than she would own. Nature gave her understanding, which she often abused, Miss Taylor gave her principles, which she did not always use actively, but Mr. Knightley gave her one thing more. Mr. Knightley told her the truth. The imaginist's failure of imagination is a loss of delicacy for others, a loss in recognition of the active principle which is not the self, an imposition of the self upon the shape of truth that is another. Mr. Knightley told her the truth and the truth mortifies. But most humiliating is the discovery of the imposition she has made upon her own truth of self.

*I*T is a truth universally acknowledged . . . ," *Pride and Prejudice* begins, and one of the delights of that beginning, which increases with our increasing acquaintance with Jane Austen, is that it is a proposition uniting the largest certainty and the smallest basis. The truth is the creature of the wish. That single man in possession of a good fortune *must* be in want of a wife; however little known his feelings or views may be "the truth is so well fixed in the minds of the surrounding families" that he becomes rightful property. It is funny, but that establishment of a rightful property is also a little ominous, for others, for oneself. The imagination of a girl like Marianne Dashwood outstrips the truth and the truth astonishes her (SS 22); it brings her to a dream of felicity from which she is unwilling to be awakened by unhappy truths (58). But Elinor knows she must accept a truth, however shocking to her it is, when it is supported by probabilities and proofs and "contradicted by nothing but her own wishes" (139).

Emma, we know, is confident of her own penetration, can never believe that if she were in Harriet's situation, for example, not knowing her parentage, "*she* should not have discovered the truth"; but even as she is thinking that thought she is fancy-

ing "what she liked" (E 27). The importance of her early relation with Harriet is that she there begins to adjust the truth,
in small ways, against her own better knowledge. When Harriet,
under her patronage, dismisses Mr. Martin's pretensions to her
hand and tries to dismiss his letter, as best she knows how, by
saying it is but a short letter, Emma feels the bad taste of her
friend: she lets it pass, however, with a "very true" (54–55).
When Mr. Knightley points out that Harriet's tastes in people
are probably not the same as Emma's, Emma knows this is "too
true for contradiction, and therefore said nothing" (58). Harriet's influence on her, in its innocent way, is insidious, because
Harriet is continually confirming in Emma the assurance of rightness: " 'Whatever you say is always right,' cried Harriet . . .
'but otherwise I could never have imagined it' . . . 'Yes, very
true' . . . 'Very true,' said Harriet . . . 'it was very true—it was
just as Miss Woodhouse described' " (74, 76, 87, 267). She
loves to hear Emma talk because Emma understands everything
and is as clever as Mr. Elton; in her ignorant irony Harriet has
made a better match for Emma, in Emma's present state of
foolishness, than Emma is making for her (76). Emma, who
knows all about the course of true love and can send it into the
very channel where it ought to flow, has no plans to change her
own state: "never, never could I expect to be so truly beloved
and important; so always first and always right in any man's eyes
as I am in my father's" (84). What is yet to be learned is that
the man who loves her most truly is the man in whose eyes she
is not always right, the only man who can see faults in her. Mr.
Knightley is the man who will not let Emma shut her eyes to
the truth. She may be able to believe that if Mr. Knightley tells
her Elton will not marry Harriet he is saying rather "what he
wished resentfully to be true, than what he knew anything
about" (67); but Mr. Knightley is never the man to allow his
wishes (much less his resentment) to make the truth for him.

While she plays games with the truth, in company with Frank

Churchill, Mr. Knightley is always there as the standard to which she must return. Frank has entered upon an engagement which requires a secrecy; but there is something more in him that makes him manufacture untruths. Jane Fairfax, as his partner in the engagement, had been wrong too, but where she suffers greatly under the necessity she has imposed on herself, for him there is a kind of pleasure in going beyond the immediate need of concealment, in building his false relationship with Emma; his quarrel with Jane is that his "plea of concealing the truth" (440) is not sufficient to account for his manner. Frank delights in mystery and finesse, in ironic deception, in using the truth to advance his falsehood. "Then I will speak the truth," he says to Emma, "and nothing suits me so well" (200), but he says it only after determining that the truth will better suit his hidden purpose. The foolish episode of the mysterious pianoforte is manufactured and managed by him to give himself every opportunity of expressing his love with greatest pleasure to himself in misleading others. He is incapable of a "disagreeable truth," he claims on that occasion, "the wretchedest being in the world at a civil falsehood" (234), which is at least half true. Emma replies that she does not believe any such thing, that she is persuaded he can be as insincere as his neighbors when it is necessary, which is entirely true but of no practical value to her in her state of mind. Her imagination has been one of Frank's best, unexpected, allies in his happy concealment and has enabled him to speak to her again and again a double-edged truth which has one meaning for her and another for himself. It is a shock to discover that she has been completely duped after "fancying" herself with him "on an equal footing of truth and honour" (399).

But what has saved her from a more serious shock is the realization that her early attachment to Frank soon ceased; she does not understand why, but for three months at least she has cared nothing for him. "This is the simple truth" (396). And in this novel a simple truth is greatly impressive. Emma has never loved Frank Churchill, she was always safe from him, whatever she may have led herself to think, because she always had another man in her mind, a truth hidden from herself. Frank Churchill is so unlike what a man should be, as she says after the revelation, with his horrible indelicacy and "None of that upright integrity, that strict adherence to truth and principle, that disdain of trick and littleness, which a man should display in every transaction of his life" (397). She has had all that integrity, truth, and principle before her for many years even when she has not recognized it, as, even now, she does not identify the source of her knowledge of what a man should be. It has been there even as she tried to escape it. Early in her game when Mr. Knightley has said something too true for contradiction she has said nothing. Toward the height of her intrigue, when she must face him again to explain the amusement that lies in the word *Dixon,* she is confused and ashamed: "She could not endure to give him the true explanation" and in embarrassment tries to pass it off as a mere joke without meaning, impossible to explain exactly, "a good deal of nonsense in it" (350–51). But there is no escape from meaning—Mr. Knightley's imagination is not wandering—and nonsense will lead only to Box Hill and the moment when his truth can no longer be denied.

$\mathcal{T}$HIS is the moment the novel has been pointing toward. It is the inevitable fall to which Emma has been traveling and it is the rise we want to see. We may not like her, and there are times when Mr. Knightley does not at all like what she is doing, becomes angry with her, as he should. Yet he loves her and he is surely right. He does not like what she is doing mainly because he cannot be happy with what she is doing to herself. Emma may imagine for herself greater powers than she has, but the greater part of her fault of imagination is that she is really better than she thinks she is. The mind that is seriously imagining a match for Mr. Elton must at the same time run away to laugh in private. Even as she is doing all she can to imagine whatever she likes she cannot help seeing enough of the truth, about him, about Harriet, about Robert Martin, about Jane Fairfax, about herself, about so many of those whose shape she must bend to her preconceptions. Even as she evades Mr. Knightley's truths they make her uncomfortable. It is too good a mind to be wasting itself and, with Mr. Knightley, we are anxious to see what will become of her because we want to see her fulfill her potential, to become the true Emma. We want to see her capable of mortification, not only because she has a price to pay but because we want to see that charming, "perfect" girl change for the better. The true Emma must see that truth is more beautiful than anything she can imagine.

Before the end of the first volume she has mortified three separate people, and herself, with varying degrees of intention and consciousness and never to a useful end. She reduces Harriet to a "mortified voice" by saying that Robert Martin is so very clownish when she has just seen that he is neat and sensible (32). One result of what she does to Harriet is that Mr. Knightley is mortified (66), because, for sensible reasons, he had encouraged Martin and thereby promoted the man's disappointment. But Emma is confident in the value of what she has done in shaping Harriet: "I should be mortified indeed," she has said, "if I did not believe I had been of some use" (58). She is in fact mortified before the end of this first series of incidents, when the surprise of understanding suddenly comes to her and to Mr. Elton in the carriage ride, but the experience is not of immediate use. They are both of them angry and in a "state of swelling resentment, and mutually deep mortification" (132). The emotions of each are turned outward upon the other; there is so much anger that there is no awkwardness, no room for the little zigzags of embarrassment that might convert the occasion to a profitable self-examination. Mr. Elton is incapable of learning and can overcome the emotion only by reasserting his own superiority. He continues in resentment (140). He does not look within and he does not seek a resolution from within Highbury; he goes outside to find reinforcement. By the early part of the second volume he has returned, a very happy man. He had gone away "rejected and mortified," he came back "gay and self-satisfied" (181). He is quick to restore himself and the delightful rapidity of his courtship and the elegance of his wife are both empty of any substance except the forms that content vanity. Our hopes for Emma are higher when we see that the ride in the carriage is succeeded by a perturbed evening of self-examination. The remembrance that Mr. Knightley had cautioned her, Elton would never marry indiscreetly, makes her blush to think how much truer a knowledge of character had been there shown than any she had reached herself: "It was dreadfully mortifying" (135). With Mr. Knightley's help she has recognized her first error, with the first man, near the end of the first volume, and we see the road she must go; but the immediate effect of the unpleasant discovery is to make her turn eagerly in imagination to the second man, away from Mr. Knightley's truth. Only in the last volume, when all her thoughts and doings and all her words gather to a climax, will she no longer be able to keep her face averted.

At Box Hill the familiar words converge upon her, as Emma seems there to be in possession of all she desires, of the fullness of life, of liveliness, ease, wit, judgment, understanding; to be the ruling center of her circle, a controlling mind, perfection itself; and in truth she is never further from all she imagines. She sees in others only a general dullness and disharmony and she understands nothing of the meaning of the serious drama Frank is acting with Jane. To amuse Emma and to be agreeable in her eyes seems all he cares for and Emma falls into that false liveliness and ease, "glad to be enlivened, not sorry to be flattered," "gay and easy too." She gives him encouragement, the admission to be gallant, thinking it "meant nothing, though in the judgment of most people looking on it must have had such an appearance as no English word but flirtation could very well describe." Her own judgment of meaning is different from most people's and she thinks all his attentions, whether from friendship, admiration, or playfulness "extremely judicious," though they do not win her heart. All this in spite of her feeling that there is no real happiness but a disappointed expectation that is making her gay and thoughtless; in spite of her knowledge that only the day before she has seen Frank without self-control, somehow or other having broken bounds; in spite of her realization that he is talking "nonsense," and shamelessly declaring with "lively impudence"—not real ease—"Any nonsense will serve" (368–69). With all this she allows herself to be managed by him, even while he pretends to be following her orders, and she affronts nearly everyone.

In what is, in effect, a parody of the Emma who presides over others, who has insight into minds, Frank asks, in her name, to know what everyone is thinking. Mr. Knightley's answer is the most distinct. "Is Miss Woodhouse sure that she would like to hear what we are all thinking of?" Emma knows it is the last thing Miss Woodhouse could stand to hear just now, for it is only the thoughts of the imperceptive and uncritical, of Mr. Weston and Harriet, that she need not fear now. It is a tense moment. The Eltons mutter and murmur ("Very true . . . very true"). Frank worsens it by attacking again and, again in the name of clever Emma Woodhouse, demands from each person not to know exactly what they are thinking but one thing very clever, or two things moderately clever, or three things very dull. Miss Bates is the only one who feels easy—"then I need not be uneasy"—not because she is clever but because she is sure to say three dull things as soon as she opens her mouth. And looking round with the most good-humored dependence on everybody's assent she asks what they are thinking: "Do not you all think I shall?" Only Emma answers, so at the critical moment it is everyone who knows what Emma is thinking. It is the dull wit of the clever Miss Woodhouse, who has lost control, that runs away with her. "Emma could not resist." She speaks with a mock ceremony of manner, but there is more irony than she understands when she says to Miss Bates "Pardon me—but you will be limited . . ." The deceptive manner worsens the action, for Miss Bates does not immediately catch her meaning; when it bursts on her it cannot anger, because though she is neither young nor handsome nor clever nor rich, and never mistaken for perfect, she is morally superior to Emma now; but a slight blush shows it can pain her. She sees what Emma means, "and I will try to hold my tongue."

Mr. Weston, whose thoughts Emma need not fear, follows immediately with a conundrum: "What two letters of the alphabet are there, that express perfection?" Emma will never guess (though she has a talent for the lucky guess). M. and A. "Em-ma.—Do you understand?" "Understanding and gratification came together," which is rather different from the delayed burst that pained Miss Bates. It is a very indifferent piece of wit, in itself and in its application, but Emma finds a great deal to laugh at and enjoy in it and so do Frank and Harriet. But not the others and not Mr. Knightley, who speaks quietly and devastatingly: "*Perfection* should not have come quite so soon" (369–71).

The dull nastiness of the Eltons is the unhappily appropriate sequel. Miss Woodhouse must excuse Mrs. Elton, who does not "pretend to be a wit" and "really must be allowed to judge when to speak and when to hold my tongue." It is all as unpleasant as possible but it is what Emma deserves, who has not much superiority over Mrs. Elton at the moment. Nor has Frank over Mr. Elton, contemptuous though he is of Elton and Elton's marriage even as he sees the similarity with his own circumstances;

both he and Elton have established a connection with a woman after only a short acquaintance formed only in a public place, where there can be no real knowledge of disposition, no "just judgment," only guess and consequent ill-luck. It is left to Jane to point out that one should not imagine such unfortunate circumstances to be frequent, that it is only weak and irresolute characters whose happiness must always be at the mercy of chance. Frank caps all by turning this excellent advice into a surrender of his judgment and, in a "lively tone" delivers his judgment to Emma, of all people, to choose and educate a wife for him. She will make his wife like herself, Emma promises, "charming." She must be "very lively" and have Emma's eyes, says he. Emma is so confused she thinks he may well have Harriet in mind. Jane, who understands well enough what he is doing, walks off with Miss Bates and Mr. Knightley, and Emma finds that Frank's spirits now rise to a pitch almost unpleasant so that even she tires of flattery and merriment (372–74). The self-contradictory day is coming to a close and it is all leading to mortification and truth, luckily. Mr. Knightley is there to make it happen.

"How could you be so unfeeling to Miss Bates? How could you be so insolent in your wit to a woman of her character, age, and situation?" Emma blushes, is sorry, tries to laugh it off, as she has been doing all day long; says she could not help it, nobody could have helped it, thereby disposing of her responsibility; says it was not so very bad, disposing of the act itself; says Miss Bates did not understand, disposing of the effect. Mr. Knightley will not allow the wit, the imaginist, to escape what Miss Bates is feeling. "She felt your full meaning." He wishes Emma could have heard how Miss Bates talked of it, with candor and generosity. He will not allow Emma the wit's excuse that the good and the ridiculous are blended and he makes her see the entire scene: Miss Bates's present poverty and her history, deserving of compassion; Miss Bates as someone who had known

Emma from an infant and whose notice was once an honor to Emma; Miss Bates now laughed at and humbled by Emma; and before her niece, and before others who would be guided by Emma's treatment of her. It is pleasant neither to Emma nor him that he must speak truth. "I will tell you truths while I can." Emma's tongue is motionless, a great deal at the end of this day. If her thoughtlessness and pride have humbled Miss Bates it is the truth that now humbles her. If she has been unfeeling in her wit it is now her feelings that keep her tongue motionless: they are combined of "anger against herself, mortification, and deep concern." In this carriage ride home, unlike the ride with Mr. Elton, the anger and concern are properly directed; it is the best sort of mortification, and it is a new moment in her life. "Never had she felt so agitated, mortified, grieved, at any circumstance in her life. She was most forcibly struck. The truth of his representation there was no denying. She felt it at her heart." What she has done, this perfect Emma, has been brutal and cruel. That she has not been able to convey this feeling of truth to Mr. Knightley is valuable, because she must hold her emotion without relief for a while; and time does not compose her, which is different from her earlier ability to rebound from his rebukes. The more she reflects the more she feels it. There is no laughter now as Emma feels the tears running down her cheeks and is at no trouble to check them. They are extraordinary. We have never seen them before (374–76).

The effect this time, unlike her previous ineffective resolutions, is a warmth of "true" contrition that leads to a change in her regular action toward Miss Bates. She goes to make her visit; she may see Mr. Knightley but this time she will not have the same sort of uneasy shame in his presence. She would not be ashamed of the appearance of penitence "so justly and truly hers," and the edge of the penitence is sharpened for her: by Jane's natural refusal to see her; by the conscience that tells her there is now in Miss Bates "less ease of looking and manner";

by Miss Bates's gratitude that Emma is always kind—an unbearable "always," a dreadful gratitude to Emma; and by the obligation to think of the pianoforte and remember "all her former fanciful and unfair conjectures" which are now so little pleasing (377–78, 380, 384). On her return home she finds Mr. Knightley waiting, about to leave for London, not having forgiven her, she is sure. Her father, unknowing, reveals that she has been on the visit and praises her for being "always" so attentive to the Bateses. Her color is heightened by the repetition of the unjust praise and with a smile and shake of her head she looks at Mr. Knightley. "It seemed as if there were an instantaneous impression in her favour, as if his eyes received the truth from her's, and all that had passed of good in her feelings were at once caught and honoured." The act of conveying the truth from eye to eye in a novel where truth has been so distorted by the eye, by the word, by the act, is a moment of great emotion. Mr. Knightley looks at her with a glow of regard, understanding that she has heard the truths he spoke, and she is warmly gratified.

The moment produces one of the most touching gestures in Jane Austen, as Mr. Knightley makes a little movement of more than common friendliness, and it is a fine instance of how large effects can be attained by small gradations that vary from common meanings. He takes her hand—or perhaps she made the first motion—she could not say—and the tentativeness and the indefiniteness are part of the unusual venture of the moment—but he took it, pressed it, and was certainly on the point of carrying it to his lips. Then he suddenly let it go, "from some fancy or other," Emma thinks; why he should feel such a scruple she cannot perceive. "He would have judged better, she thought, if he had not stopped" (385–86). Mr. Knightley's scruple, and it is the cause of his leaving for London, is that he thinks her in love with Frank Churchill. Emma's attribution to him of some fancy or other and her internal improvement of his judgment is both an indication of a new sort of maturity in her, because she is right in her immediate judgment, and an indication of how deeply she has misunderstood the effect of her previous judgments and actions.

In subsequent days she tries several times to help Jane, using the most feeling language she can command, but she is rebuffed; it is clear that Jane is resolved to receive no kindness from *her*. ". . . it mortified her that she was given so little credit for proper feeling" (391), which is a salutary mortification; it is not deserved by her present good intentions but she knows, so far as she has knowledge, that it is a result of her past conduct and she does not resent it. It is a valuable stage between the deserved mortification at Box Hill, which has prepared her for this acceptance, and the final stage, when the truth is open to her.

$\mathcal{I}$T is a long way from Box Hill to happiness for Emma, as she makes the series of discoveries of what her misconceptions have been and as she feels her guilt, because she has made such a tangle of the truth that her good emotions are still directed to false objects. Her self-accusations and her attempts to repair her wrongs toward others are excellent and necessary, but there are so many levels of confusion for her that, in a proper comic punishment, she not only wastes her solicitude but finds a more unexpected and more distressing truth waiting for her. She is absolutely unable to escape it. While her imagination has been building its foolish combinations a better imagination has been creating a wiser structure. What really defeats her, it seems, is the ordered form and truth of the plot which, from start to finish, meets her at every turn as it maintains its beautiful and inevitable course. That art of the novelist is the poetry which unites pleasure with truth by calling imagination to the help of reason. And as it defeats Emma it brings, of course, that illumination and union of mind which is her necessary rescue. So it is now at the final revelations.

Having jumped with surprise and horror to hear Mrs. Weston's news of Frank Churchill, Emma's first act must be to tell the truth to Harriet. She is in misery for having misled Harriet a second time, and though it is true that this time she need not charge herself with being the sole and original author of the mischief, with having suggested such feelings as might otherwise never have entered Harriet's imagination, she feels completely guilty because she has encouraged what she might have repressed. She is sadly fearful that the second disappointment will be more severe than the first and, considering Frank's superiority to Mr. Elton and judging by the superior self-command and reserve Harriet has shown, she has cause for fear. "She must communicate the painful truth, however, and as soon as possible" (402–3). It is a brave duty and it is carried out, but the pain of the truth is all her own. The Emma who has remained worthy of our solicitude throughout is the Emma who, even at this moment, in spite of all her vexation, cannot help feeling it almost ridiculous that she should now have the same office to perform by Harriet which Mrs. Weston has just gone through by herself. It is a mind we must love. She hopes that the event of the disclosure could bear an equal resemblance, that Harriet, like herself, will say that she has not been in love with Frank; but of that, unfortunately, there could be no chance. She then finds to her surprise that chance has indeed been fortunate for her, in a way she has never suspected, because Harriet does not care about Frank. But that fortune is, by the same stroke, most unfortunate, because Harriet is in love with Mr. Knightley, and the fact has not been a mere chance misunderstanding for which Emma need not charge herself. Harriet thinks, too, that Mr. Knightley returns her affection. Emma has been collecting herself resolutely, speaking with a forced calmness, as the scene has developed, but finding that control more and more difficult as she learns more and more; she exclaims, she is unable to speak, she is in consternation. At the last of Harriet's revelations, that she thinks Mr. Knightley returns her affection, Emma's response is admirable. She sits silently meditating, in a fixed attitude, for a few minutes, a few minutes sufficient for making her acquainted with her own heart. A mind like hers, always rapid, always moving long distances in the wrong direction when making its own truth, is now forced to see what is closest to her. "She touched— she admitted—she acknowledged the whole truth" (407–8).

She is still not in possession of all the facts, but it is the whole truth about her own heart. Mr. Knightley must marry no one but herself. Even the phrasing of that is the Emma who arranges destinies, but in this moment of the whole truth her eyes are turned toward herself, her own conduct, her own heart, seen with a clearness which had never blessed her before. "How improperly had she been acting by Harriet! How inconsiderate, how indelicate, how irrational, how unfeeling had been her conduct! What blindness, what madness, had led her on!" Every bad name in the world, which the novel has been preparing for her, she is now ready to give herself. In spite of all, some portion of respect for herself—concern for her own appearance and a strong sense of justice by Harriet—gives her the resolution to sit and endure further with calmness. She subdues her emotions to hear more, though such a development of self makes for great inward suffering (408–9). Her problem is complicated again by the severity of her original errors which foil her interpretation of present evidence. Harriet, to show Mr. Knightley's interest, tells how he has been inquiring into the state of her affections; Emma sees that it is possible he may have been working in Robert Martin's interest, which is in fact true, but Harriet rejects that suspicion with spirit and Emma cannot comfort herself with it. It is good that this should be so, that "the utmost exertion" is necessary on Emma's part, because she must give all her attention to understanding the blunders and blindness of her own head and heart: the perception "that she had been imposed on by others in a most mortifying degree; that she had been impos-

ing on herself in a degree yet more mortifying." In "fancying,"
in acting, as though Mr. Knightley had not been the superior
man, the most dear to her, she had been entirely under a delusion, ignorant of her own heart (410–12).

The price she must be prepared to pay, in her new knowledge,
is exactly what, in her ignorance, she had desired—an unchanged
life. "Are you well, my Emma?" was Mrs. Weston's parting
question. "Oh! perfectly. I am always well, you know" (420).
But her mind has been on Mr. Knightley and she has not been
listening. The circle of friends around Hartfield is now breaking, as each seems to be starting a new life, and Emma is alone
with her father, as she was at the beginning, on the evening of
Mrs. Weston's wedding day. But now no Mr. Knightley will
walk in after tea and dissipate every melancholy fancy (422).

When Mr. Knightley does come, the following day, the pleasure in his tender consideration must be subordinated to the shame
of confession. Her conduct has been so misleading that she must
repeat her confession, "trying to be lively, but really confused,"
and when he listens in perfect silence—she wished he would
speak but he does not—she must say it a third time, in increasing force and detail, obliged to lower herself still further. Having always been the first of women she must now say that hers
is a common case, has happened to hundreds, but the less excusable in "one who sets up as I do for Understanding" (426–
27). Having said all she can say to expose her own faults of
the past she must do one last thing. She must accept that it now
means the loss of Mr. Knightley, to Harriet. That is harder to
do; her immediate feeling is to avert the subject if possible. She
had wanted him to speak to save her from the need for deeper
confession; now she wants him not to speak—"don't speak it,
don't speak it"—to forestall the last consequence. He stops,
in "deep mortification." It is not the first time Emma in a delusion has mortified Mr. Knightley, but it will be the last. She
accepts the worst, cannot bear to give him pain and, cost her

what it would—it is Emma's act of imaginative delicacy—she would listen. "I will hear whatever you like. I will tell you exactly what I think" (429). Only then is she deserving of the truth.

If Jane Austen was interested in the complexities of truth she was at least as interested in a more difficult matter, the simple truth. As a simple, artless elegance and ease is the last triumph of art over the readier temptations of falsity, so to know the simple truth, to rise to that artlessness, is the hardest art of the spirit. To Dr. Johnson the truth was a passionate necessity because he knew how readily the mind turns away. Truth finds an easy entrance to the mind, he says, when it is introduced by desire and attended by pleasure, but when it intrudes uncalled and brings unpleasant emotion then the passes of the intellect are barred (*Rambler* no. 165). There are so many incitements to forsake the truth, he says, in the palliation of our own faults, in the convenience of imposing on others, the immediate evils to be avoided, the present gratifications to be obtained, that few have the spirit and constancy for the steady practice of open veracity. To be taught to speak truth it is necessary to learn to hear it; for no species of falsehood is more frequent than flattery, the appeal to vanity that vitiates morals. Truth is unwelcome, unpleasing, because contrary to our wishes and our practice and because we hear unwillingly what we are afraid to know and soon forget (*Rambler* no. 96). It is ladies, as a class, who are especially vulnerable because they expect an unvaried complaisance which keeps them unskilled in human nature; the female prerogative is female ignorance; truth is scarcely to be heard except from those whom it can serve no interest to conceal it (*Rambler* no. 150). Frank Churchill has found convenience in imposing on Emma because his flattery found a ready patron of falsehood in her vanity. Mr. Knightley's way of loving is the finest and bravest, speaking with sincerity the unpleasant truth she does not want to hear when it would seem he has every interest to conceal it. But for him, of course, love is not otherwise possible. It is not perfection in her he expects, for (like Mirabel with Millamant) he has thought so much of her faults he has come to love them (462); but the perfection of love and of the happiness of union is not possible without the capacity to speak and to hear and bear the truth. That sort of sincerity and truth is rare and, Mr. Knightley knows, beautiful. Most people cannot bear it and it will work no good to speak it to them, so that one must then endeavor to unite truth with civility. Complete truth is not possible except to those who are free from the determination of their own desires and the disrespect for the lives of others which it produces. Moreover, as the private needs pervert the truth they begin to destroy the self and the social world in which alone the self is fulfilled; the need of concealment and deceit Jane Fairfax brought on herself made even her unreasonable; it destroyed her ease, both her internal tranquillity and her social manner, and she lost the simple truth. Emma's foolish imagination was an attempt to create a greater self and world to meet the desires, but the simple truth was something much more interesting, a higher achievement, and more beautiful. The beauty of truth is in the character of the beholder capable of seeing it, hearing it, returning it, and this is the beauty Emma has now when she asks Mr. Knightley to speak openly.

Mr. Knightley's proposal, in its tone of sincere, decided, intelligible tenderness, is in the right tone (430–31). That intelligible tenderness has been his style throughout, a love in which a clarity of head and heart allows neither to falsify the other; Mr. Knightley's love has never made him blind to Emma's faults, his understanding of her faults has never led him to misunderstand how worthy she is of love. It is a true love. You know what I am, he tells her, "You hear nothing but truth from me." She has borne it as no other woman in England would have borne it. "Bear with the truths I would tell you now, dearest Emma, as well as you have borne with them." His manner, perhaps, will not recommend them, he says, but his manner has been exactly right. He knows she understands his feelings and asks now only to hear her voice. Emma has not lost a word; she has been able "to catch and comprehend the exact truth of the whole." The exact truth, however, includes a feeling for Harriet, of pain and contrition. In the fictional world Emma had been creating for herself there remains the possible false heroism of sentiment, of entreating Mr. Knightley to transfer his affection, or of refusing him, but no such madness, opposing all that is probable or reasonable, enters Emma's brain, previously so fertile in foolishness. Her "judgment was as strong as her feelings," and her "way was clear though not quite smooth" (the course of true love). "What did she say?—Just what she ought, of course. A lady always does." Jane Austen is not shirking the emotion, but telling us all we want to know at this point, with the fullest warmth and pleasure. Emma is for the first time equally strong in judgment and in feeling; is for the first time capable of saying just what she ought; is for the first time a lady in the sense in which Mr. Knightley has always been a gentleman; is well matched.

Emma is in possession of the whole truth, but the precious value of truth and its difficulty of retrieval is still borne in upon her by the fact that she must still keep one secret from him, Harriet's secret, and the explanation of the sudden change in her own conduct to Mr. Knightley during this interview. Even at this moment, "Seldom, very seldom, does complete truth belong to any human disclosure" (431). Something is a little disguised, a little mistaken, and though in this case it is not very material it is still not fully satisfactory for this novel. As he later reads Frank Churchill's letter in Emma's company Mr. Knightley is obliged to point out to her how mystery and finesse pervert the understanding. "My Emma, does not every thing serve to prove more and more the beauty of truth and sincerity in all our dealings with each other?" Emma agrees, blushes because she still has one mystery which she cannot give any sincere explanation of (446). Harriet's marriage makes Emma serious, "very serious" in her thankfulness, because it removes the last alloy to her happiness, by providing for the welfare of the comical Harriet; the religious tone of that serious thankfulness, and the irrepressible laugh that accompanies it, makes it richly joyous. High in the rank of her most serious and heartfelt felicities is knowing that all necessity of concealment from Mr. Knightley will soon be over. Disguise, equivocation, mystery, so hateful now, will soon be over (475). The full and perfect confidence she can look forward to will justify the predictions of "the small band of true friends" who witness the marriage; there is "perfect happiness" in the union (484). It has not come too soon.

7

Anne Elliot, Whose Word Had No Weight

A fitting close to this consideration of the weight carried by some of Jane Austen's words is a quiet look, appropriately brief, at a heroine who had great difficulties in making herself heard. The first sentence that introduces Anne Elliot's name tells us that with either her father or her sister "her word had no weight . . . she was only Anne" (P 5). One way of describing the action of *Persuasion* is to say that it begins when Anne's word has no weight and it ends when her word pierces a man's soul (237). Anne has so many of the admirable accomplishments, a real elegance, and the best sort of imagination, and she is exemplary in exertion; but, until the end, there is no one to do her justice.

Nobody hears Anne, nobody sees her, but it is she who is ever at the center. It is through her ears, eyes, and mind that we know most of what we know and that we are made to care for what is happening. If nobody is much aware of her, she is very much aware of everyone else and she perceives what is happening to them when they are ignorant of themselves. She knows more of the characters of the members of her family, of her father and Elizabeth, and of the dangers that threaten them, than they do. She understands Benwick's wounded mind, how far it is to be taken seriously, and how to prescribe for it, better than he does, better than his closest friends. She can define what the Musgrove girls are feeling and the reasons, when they are drawn to Captain Wentworth, though they are not capable of it themselves. And she reads Wentworth's mind, with the coming troubles he is causing for others and himself, before those consequences bring the information to him. Furthermore, she is an excellent listener and it is to her that others turn when they have something to say which no one else will hear; it is a special sign of the moral obtuseness of her father and elder sister that they are exceptions to this general rule when it is they who, by natural ties and their particular needs, could most profit from this valuable quality in her. Charles Musgrove brings to her his complaints about Mary, and Mary hers about Charles. Mary confides to her what is wrong with Mrs. Musgrove, and Mrs. Musgrove and her daughters what is wrong with Mary. "She could do little more than listen patiently" and give each of them the appropriate sorts of hints (46). Captain Benwick finds in her his best audience, the opportunity for feelings glad to burst their usual restraints, and she tries to be of real use to him, with a certain amount of irony directed at herself (100–101). The next morning it is Henrietta who chooses her as confidante and, smiling to herself, Anne enters into the subject, as ready to do good by entering into the feelings of a young lady as of a young man (103). How right it is, in the scene at the White Hart, that her own opportunity to utter her large emotional speech comes to her when Captain Harville wants to confide in Anne, looks at her with a smile and a little motion of the head which expresses, "Come to me, I have something to say" (231).

Anne listens patiently at Uppercross. It is a noisy place at Christmas holidays, with much clamor, laughing, singing, dancing, even a roaring fire, and Lady Russell does not like it at all.

But "Every body has their taste in noises" and sounds are quite innoxious or most distressing by their sort rather than their quantity. Lady Russell does not complain of the rumble, bawling, and clink of Bath, these being the noises she associates with her winter pleasures, and her spirits rise under them (135). But Anne listens patiently to others though her own pleasures can come, if at all, only obliquely. In the music-making at Upper-cross Anne herself plays a great deal better than either of the Miss Musgroves, but "having no voice," nor anything else that would make a noise, no knowledge of the harp (the instrument of false elegance), no fond parents as an audience, her perform-ance is little thought of, as she is well aware. Except for the one short period eight years ago, the time Frederick Wentworth had been with her, since the age of fourteen and the loss of her mother, Anne had never known "the happiness of being listened to" (47). It is an admirable strength that despite her loneliness the fond partiality of the Musgroves for their own daughters' performance and their indifference to hers gives her more pleas-ure for their sake than mortification for her own. Anne plays that others may dance, and it is this that recommends her musical powers to Mr. and Mrs. Musgrove: they notice how her little fingers fly about. They do not see her and they do not hear her.

It is to be expected of her father and sister and of the Mus-groves that they should be imperceptive; they have never been different and they never will be. But Captain Wentworth is different, because there was that brief period eight years ago when he had listened, had encouraged by his just appreciation and real taste, when, in music, she had not been alone in the world. The common interest in music is important in their re-lation and it is at a concert in Bath, late in the book, that Anne learns, again, that he must love her. He is a perceptive man, but at his first appearance in the novel he has the closed, foolish mind that only a clever man can have. When they meet for the first time upon his return, a thousand feelings rush on Anne and she cannot organize herself completely; but "she heard his voice" (59). He, however, does not perceive her. He thinks her wretchedly altered, and he does so because he has thought himself ill-used by her. She had deserted him, he thinks, out of a feebleness of character, weakness, which his own decided, confident temper could not endure. He has come ashore now and intends to marry, ready to fall in love with all the speed which a clear head and quick taste will allow. He has a heart for any pleasing young woman who comes in his way, excepting only Anne Elliot, because he wants a strong mind with sweetness of manner: that is an excellent description of Anne and marks just how clear-headed he is or how bright his bright, proud eye is. He is convinced he is "nice," a man able to discriminate, make fine distinctions. If he is a fool in marrying, he says, he shall be a fool indeed, for he has thought on the subject more than most men (61–62). The next chapter shows how foolish he is, how nice.

From this time Anne and he are repeatedly in the same circle, but they have no conversation beyond what the commonest civility requires. He talks much, narrating his career to others; his profession qualified him, his disposition led him to talk (63); his voice does not falter and his eye does not wander, but Anne from her knowledge of his mind knows that when his narrative touches the year of their engagement they must have the same immediate associations, though not the same pain. At one time, in that year, of all the large party present they two would have found it most difficult to cease to speak to one another, being so similar, so loving; now they are more than strangers, since they can never become acquainted. When he talked "she heard the same voice, and discerned the same mind" (64). He is talking to the Musgrove girls about the navy, the same sort of talk that she had heard eight years ago when she had been as surprised and as ignorant of navy life as they are now. He fills the girls with amazement, pity, horror, as he tells them of his luck, his danger from leaky ships, storm, and enemy, his narrow escapes and his large successes as a commanding officer. His style is light, assured, fascinating to the girls, the too facile manner of the returned veteran. As he thrills his audience it is Anne who shudders to herself alone, unnoticed, because it is she who has most reason to be affected by his anecdotes of peril.

It is as he is at the height of this pleasurable performance, the lovely cruise in the *Laconia* when he made money so fast, luck upon luck, that Mrs. Musgrove interrupts with a word of how lucky it was for them when Captain Wentworth took command of the *Laconia,* because Dick Musgrove was a midshipman in her. Mrs. Musgrove's feelings make her speak low; this is not something she does often, because Mrs. Musgrove, like all her family, is rather loud, and it is more in her normal style that when she attempts to moderate her voice it carries only too well: in the scene at the White Hart when she is talking to Mrs. Croft it is just in that inconvenient tone of voice which is perfectly audible while it pretends to be a whisper, a powerful whisper. But she does feel for her lost son; extraordinary bursts of mind do occur and there is some part of real feeling for him at the moment. Captain Wentworth, in the full flow of his own talk, "hearing only in part" (67) and not having Dick Musgrove at all in mind, is suspended and must wait for the explanation. When it comes his momentary expression, the glance of his bright eye and curl of his handsome mouth, is sufficient indication of what his real opinion of Dick Musgrove had been, but it is too transient an indulgence in self-amusement to be detected by anyone who understands him less than Anne. It is a creditable action in Wentworth that he ceases this self-amusement of the kind he has been indulging throughout the evening and, perfectly collected and serious, sits on the sofa next to Mrs. Musgrove and enters into conversation with her, "in a low voice"; he does it with so much sympathy and natural grace as to show the kindest consideration for all that was real and unabsurd in her feelings. It is something that helps save him in our opinion; we have seen him triumphant, displaying some of the flashing and handsome qualities that make him attractive, make evident how any woman could be drawn to him, but it has all been rather too attractive, too easy. It has all been an exterior show. His response to Mrs. Musgrove shows that the man has other qualities of greater importance, both natural and moral. It also shows a higher quality of mind, an ability to make the important distinctions between what is absurd in Mrs. Musgrove and what is real. We understand better why a woman like Anne Elliot can love him, and it is necessary that we think well of him, think him worthy of Anne, if her feelings are to be important to us and if we are to desire their union.

It is at this point that there is a brief passage which may be rather disconcerting to the reader, the bit on the large, fat sighings of Mrs. Musgrove. There is nothing soft in Jane Austen but there is nothing cruel and there is no need to explain away the passage. What she says of Mrs. Musgrove is perfectly accurate. What she says of personal size and mental sorrow—that they have certainly no necessary proportions—is clearly right and no one can quarrel with it. And what she says of the unbecoming conjunctions of bulky figure and deep affliction, that taste cannot tolerate and ridicule will seize, is an observation of general conduct and specifically not an endorsement that it is fair or reasonable. But the main point here is not the generalization but the application to the immediate dramatic moment. We see the scene with Anne. As Wentworth shows the kindest consideration for Mrs. Musgrove and her real feelings and sits next to her, the significant thing is that he and Anne are now actually sitting on the same sofa. They are divided only by Mrs. Musgrove, but that is no insignificant barrier. While Wentworth is so kind to Mrs. Musgrove he typically cannot see: the agitations of Anne's slender form and pensive face are very completely screened from him. Wentworth must be allowed credit for the self-command with which he attends to the large, fat sighings of Mrs. Musgrove and he does not fall under the general observation of seizing on the ridiculousness of the unbecoming conjunction; we must think well of him because he is a superior man. But at the same time, with all his fine quality he does not see Anne, whose feelings are more worthy of his attention and far more intimately a part of his career. The scene defines at once his excellence and his deficiency (67–68).

The point is reinforced by what follows immediately, when Admiral Croft interrupts because he is unobservant. He is not so fine a man as Wentworth, but he has the simple good sense a more refined man may lack when the fine man makes unimportant or wrong distinctions. Captain Wentworth will not willingly take lady passengers on board a ship of his, not because he lacks gallantry, as the Admiral thinks at first, but rather from feeling that it is impossible to make the accommodations on board such as a woman ought to have; his gallantry is high. This brings his sensible sister upon him, to attack his idle gallantry, his superfine, extraordinary gallantry. She hates to hear him talking like a fine gentleman and as if all women were fine ladies instead of rational creatures (68–70). This is the same Wentworth that we have seen so kind to Mrs. Musgrove, not seeing Anne, very fine and missing the essentials. When the evening ends with dancing, Anne offers her services, as usual, to play the music as others dance; her eyes sometimes fill with tears but she is glad to be employed and unobserved. She is indeed unobserved in a merry, joyous party and no one is in higher spirits than Captain Wentworth, the center of general attention and deference and especially the attention of all the young women, a little spoilt by such universal, such eager admiration, as Anne notes without wonder. Once he looks at her, to observe her altered features, perhaps; once he speaks of her to his dancing partner, to find out that Anne never dances now; once he speaks to her, only of necessity and with a studied politeness, cold and ceremonious, worse than anything; each occasion emphasizes how little he can see or hear her (71–72).

What he is doing is dangerous, both for himself and others. He is flattered and bewitched by the attention he is receiving, as the next chapter begins (73), and, without knowing it, he is making trouble. He is disturbing the potential match between Henrietta Musgrove and Charles Hayter and he is doing it not only in ignorance of their prior relation but in ignorance of his own mind. It is doubtful which of the two sisters he prefers; one is more gentle, the other more lively, and Anne, observing all this, does not know which is more likely to attract him now; he himself cannot know. Nor is it important which he prefers, because there is little to choose between them; as Admiral Croft says, later, we hardly know one from the other. What is more important, as Anne thinks, is that Wentworth should know his own mind and not endanger the happiness of either sister or impeach his own honor. He, however, is unaware and his mistaken self-confidence is stamped with a light arrogance by the incident that closes the chapter, when he finds himself unexpectedly alone with Anne. After a few words to her he is silent. Charles Hayter enters and Wentworth, not knowing Charles's feelings, is disposed for conversation with him; but Charles soon puts an end to that. Wentworth's silence to Anne and his readiness to converse with Hayter is a compounding of his confusion without his knowing it. The next moment defines him more precisely, when, as Anne kneels to attend the injured older Musgrove boy, the younger pest climbs on her back, fastens his hands around her neck, and will not obey. Charles Hayter tries to order him down—"Do not you hear your aunt speak?"—but the child will not stir. It is Wentworth, kind and resolute, who takes the child away. He does it silently and he acts well in comparison with Charles Hayter, who, knowing that he should have acted himself, is left with only a vexed tone of voice. Wentworth not only does it silently, however, but the conviction is soon forced on Anne "by the noise he was studiously making with the child, that he meant to avoid hearing her thanks" and it testifies that her conversation is the last of his wants. The mixture of the rightness of his small action and the self-created deafness to a larger issue is more than a trifle, though Anne, ashamed of being so much affected by it, tries to think that it is (78–80).

It is Anne who hears, it is Anne who is unheard. Her unintentional bit of eavesdropping from behind the hedgerow in the next chapter, a convenient device for novelists, is in this novel an explicit representation of the moral awareness of the characters. As Anne has continued to observe Wentworth she sees that Louisa is the favorite and her observations are precise in definition and in coming to the exact word. Louisa is the favorite, but Wentworth is not in love; it is the sisters who are in love with him, and yet it is not love but a little fever of admiration. Wentworth is not aware of the pain he is causing Hayter, but he is wrong in accepting the attentions "(for accepting must be the word)" of the two women (82). As she is walking with them on a November day it is a melancholy time for Anne, though not so sad as she thinks. She wants to be out of the way of anybody and her pleasure is in viewing the tawny leaves and withered hedges and in occupying her mind with poetic quotations on the season. That is not what her mind should be on and in fact it is not possible that when near Wentworth's conversation with the Musgrove girls she should not try to hear it. There is little of importance to hear, but it is now certainly Louisa who is engaging more of his attention; a feeling seems to develop between him and Louisa, as she speaks with loud enthusiasm of how bravely and inseparably she could love and he catches her tone. That development stops Anne's autumnal quotations for a bit. She rouses herself to point out the direction the walk has taken, to Winthrop. "But nobody heard, or, at least, nobody answered her" (85). It is not quite clear at this moment why the direction of the walk is important and its immediate effect will be to Anne's disadvantage, but the farmer is at work plowing a fresh path, counteracting the autumnal quotations because he means to have spring again. It develops that the walk has been to Winthrop to enable Henrietta to return her affection to Charles Hayter. Anne learns this as she sits under the hedgerow and, unseen, hears Wentworth and Louisa behind her. She distinguishes Louisa's voice first and from her speech it appears that Louisa has made Henrietta go, not allowed Henrietta to be persuaded into giving up her intention of returning to Charles Hayter by the snobbish pride of Mary Musgrove. Wentworth admires Louisa's mind, her fortitude, strength, resolution, decision, firmness. He delivers with playful solemnity his sermon on the beautiful nut which by its strength has outlived all the storms of autumn and possessed happiness, and he recommends its firm example to Louisa if she wishes to be beautiful and happy in her November of life. His playfulness is a saving grace, but he is quite serious in his moral judgments, and quite wrong in their application. What he does not know is that Louisa's firm powers of mind have been used to eliminate her sister from the competition and leave Captain Wentworth all for herself. More seriously, he is not only mispraising and misleading Louisa but the obvious contrast between her and Anne which he has in mind is a blind reversal of truths. Anne at the moment is protected by a bush of holly; he has yet to learn of her November (87–88).

It was evidently Jane Austen's first intention that the ending of the novel should follow this same pattern, of Anne the overhearer and the unheard. In the original Chapter X of Volume II Anne is once again, unwillingly but typically, placed in a situation where she listens to others, this time through a very firmly closed door. It has been closed by Wentworth, who wants to keep her from hearing and who speaks in a low tone, but who cannot check the unmanaged and natural voice of Admiral Croft. It is impossible for Anne not to distinguish parts of their conversation and she hears her own name. The important difference between the succeeding scene of Anne and Wentworth and their earlier scenes is that by this time Wentworth's unwillingness to speak or hear is in his knowledge of his own awkwardness and inferiority. But it is still he who does almost all the talking, as he must in this situation, who must say that "a very few words" from her will be sufficient. "Anne spoke a word or two, but they were unintelligible," and he speaks again, before she can command herself, to dictate to her the form of her answer: if she will only tell him that the Admiral may address a line to Sir Walter, giving up the lease to Kellynch, it will be enough; "Pronounce only the words, *he may*." At that point Anne speaks out and the truth is revealed. His eyes, with all their power and keenness blind for most of the novel, for the first time see the truth; his expression has something more than penetration in it, something softer which they have been wanting. What ensues is "a silent but very powerful dialogue" and then on his part a bursting forth in the fullness of exquisite feeling (258). It is a grand scene, but not good enough for Jane Austen.

The revision is in many ways more satisfying, but the one point that is relevant here is the difference in the weight of Anne's word. The arrival of the additional characters from Uppercross puts Anne and Wentworth in a large company once again, as they had been at Uppercross in the recent past, and the marked difference is that now Wentworth is alive to every opportunity of understanding Anne. As Anne speaks to Mary Musgrove about Mr. Elliot, she feels that Wentworth is looking at her, as he is, to understand how she feels toward Mr. Elliot (222). As Charles Musgrove talks of Mr. Elliot, Anne sees that, for the same reason, Wentworth is all attention, "looking and listening with his whole soul" (224) and turning his inquiring eyes from Charles to herself. When she speaks on the subject she is conscious that "her words were listened to" (225).

Tentative, broken conversation between them—open to some misconstruction on his part, Anne fears, hearing the sounds he utters—is interrupted first by Henrietta, then by more alarming sounds as her father and sister arrive to reduce the room to a hush, determined silence, or insipid talk. When Mary whispers very audibly her mistaken conviction of Wentworth's delight at her father's and sister's attentions, Anne turns away that she may neither see nor hear more to vex her and she goes home to be sure of being as silent as she chooses. But her vexation is not entirely justified, or is so only because Wentworth is now listening to her and she is anxious that he hear the right sounds.

In the climactic scene of the revision, the next day Anne at the White Hart is in her characteristic posture, alone in a group. Wentworth, engrossed in writing a letter for Harville, nearly turns his back on them all. Mrs. Musgrove is talking to Mrs. Croft in her inconvenient tone of voice, the perfectly audible whisper, and Anne cannot avoid hearing. But the conversation is unexpectedly interesting, because it turns on the unadvisability of long engagements and Anne feels its application to herself; it becomes more interesting when she sees that Wentworth has paused to listen, and to give one quick, conscious look at her. Harville, wrapped in his own thoughts, has heard none of it and now invites Anne to come listen to him, nearer to Wentworth. They talk of Fanny Harville, how she who has been forgotten would not have forgotten so soon, he speaking in a deep tone, Anne "in a low feeling voice" (232), and by Anne's generalization they turn the instance to the nature of a woman's feelings. The tenderness and long life of those feelings are a subject Anne knows well and as she goes on she talks "with a faltering voice" (233). At that point a slight noise calls their attention to Captain Wentworth, whose pen has fallen, startling Anne, who had not thought him so close and who suspects that his pen has fallen because he has been "striving to catch sounds, which yet she did not think he could have caught"

(234). She is underestimating him. Harville and Anne continue to talk, in varied tones as the emotion builds, until Anne claims for her sex the unenviable privilege of loving longest when hope is gone and she cannot utter another sentence because her heart is too full, her breath too oppressed. Harville cannot quarrel with her; his tongue is tied. Wentworth is impatient to be gone, which Anne does not know how to understand, and he leaves without a word or a look. Her understanding comes when she hears footsteps and he returns to place his letter before her with glowing eyes. It is the letter that reveals the effect her words have had on him, and the effect has been great. The man who at the beginning had said no more to her than civility required, who deliberately wanted to avoid hearing her, can now no longer listen in silence and must speak to her by such means as are within his reach. She has pierced his soul. The man who has talked so well and easily now finds that he can hardly write because he is every instant hearing something that overpowers him. To that voice he did not want to hear he is now perfectly attuned: "You sink your voice, but I can distinguish the tones of that voice, when they would be lost on others" (237). He is now alive to the smallest sign from her, and it will be decisive in his life: "A word, a look will be enough to decide" (238). An essential difference in the new ending is the reversal of the positions of Anne and Wentworth. The final understanding does not begin with her listening to him through a closed door; we know already her ability to hear him through barriers, to read his mind, the loving anxious perception that makes it possible. His footsteps behind her, as he approaches to know her answer, are what she has always heard, "a something of familiar sound" (239). But what we see for the first time in the revision is his ability to hear her.

This importance throughout the novel of the finely attuned ear is one of the things that makes the Mrs. Smith of Chapter IX a tiresome character. It is in that chapter immediately preceding

the revised ending that Anne learns the truth about Mr. Elliot
and it is right that she should. At the beginning of that chapter
she feels a great deal of good will toward him, because of his
understanding of the dangers of Mrs. Clay, feels also she owes
him gratitude and regard, in return for his affection to herself,
and perhaps compassion, if he is to suffer because she cannot
return his feeling. After hearing Mrs. Smith's story she is relieved in one point; no tenderness is due him and no pity. Mr.
Elliot has been a threat to Anne's family and to herself. He holds
out to her the possibility of becoming Lady Elliot and mistress
of Kellynch, of becoming what her mother had been and to Anne
that is a moving possibility. She must learn the truth about him
and Mrs. Smith is able to tell her what no one else could have
told her; it is a reward for Anne's attentions to her old friend
and it is to that degree a result of her own effort. It is also true
that Mrs. Smith begins to tell her story because she needs Anne's
help and to that degree Anne is in a familiar listening posture.
But the Anne we have come to see in the novel is quite capable
of learning for herself what must be known without this long,
circumstantial narrative of details and documents of the dead;
the story itself is uninteresting and burdensome for its function
in the novel, but its chief fault is that it works by way of direct
revelation, pouring out upon Anne a stream of information in a
novel where the characteristic and significant mode of learning
is indirection. The listening ear hears the significant detail. It
is uncomfortable for the reader to find someone saying to Anne,
to give her essential information, "Hear the truth, therefore,
now . . . Oh! he is black at heart, hollow and black!" (199).

*A*NNE needs neither such imperatives nor such unmodulated
language to reach her. She hears well because she knows how to
"submit." The word does not mean weak and it does not mean
passive. The right kind of submission requires strength. It requires self-command and self-knowledge. When she hears that

Wentworth, having seen her again for the first time in eight years, thought her altered beyond his knowledge, "Anne fully submitted, in silent, deep mortification" (60–61). Every word is important. The *mortification* is the painful recognition of one's own deficiencies which only the best can learn from. Anne's is *deep,* because it goes to her deepest desires, tells her that the loved woman she was once has been destroyed. That it is *silent* is in her best mode of isolated knowledge and contained suffering. She admits *fully,* without any reservations that might protect herself by timidity or reaction. She *submits* to the necessity and undergoes the truth. She does not deny it—doubtless it was so; and she does not attempt to revenge herself by a return in kind upon him. Her reward is that his reported words have a value for her in that they allay her agitation, compose her and consequently, she thinks, must make her happier. If her future is to be more agitated and her happiness of a different and better sort than she anticipates at the moment, the manner of her response is the right one and it is the only way she will find her happiness. She may not find it at all, but she will never find it in any other way. She will have to face suffering, but to try to avoid it will be worse. In thinking over the past, at the end, after her happiness has been assured, and trying impartially to judge the right and wrong of her own action, she must believe that she was right in being guided by Lady Russell, much as she suffered from it. Lady Russell was in the place of a parent to her. Not that the advice was right, "But I mean, that I was right in submitting to her." If she had done otherwise she should have suffered more in continuing the engagement than she did even in giving it up, because she should have suffered in her conscience (246).

The most interesting function of Mrs. Smith in the novel is not in providing information but in bringing out the particular quality of Anne as one who can bear suffering. For Mrs. Smith has more serious physical and economic ills to face than Anne has, and is even more alone in the world. Yet her spirits are high and her enjoyments more than her depression. How this can be is a matter of much interest to Anne, who watches, observes, reflects, and finds that there is in Mrs. Smith an elasticity of mind, a disposition to be comforted, a power of turning readily from evil to good, of finding employment, which comes from Nature alone, and is the choicest gift of Heaven. The gifts of Nature and Heaven are mercies and in that sense Mrs. Smith has something more than Anne (154). What Anne has is a "submissive spirit" that is patient and a strong understanding that supplies resolution, but these are the qualities that give her a value superior to Mrs. Smith and make her worth watching. Mrs. Smith responds to adversity with a natural elasticity but Anne must earn her way by fortitude and by resignation and that is a process that takes struggle and time. Mrs. Smith has one fine gift and a single value but Anne must work with a combination of opposing and complementary qualities. It is something Captain Wentworth does not understand.

Anne's gentle submission is coordinate with her strength and resolution and it is essential in that fineness of mind that enables her to make distinctions. It is the essential first condition for the listening ear. When she arrives at the White Hart for the beginning of what becomes the proposal scene, her mind filled with her own keen interest, she finds the others engaged in talk of their own concerns—Mrs. Musgrove with Mrs. Croft, Captain Harville with Captain Wentworth—and she finds that Mary and Henrietta, too impatient to wait, have gone out but have left strictest injunctions that Anne must be kept until they return. It is the situation she knows well. "She had only to submit, sit down, be outwardly composed, and feel herself plunged at once in all the agitations . . ." (229). The agitations of Anne, here as elsewhere, are not the nervous affliction of a weak creature, without cause and without issue. The causes are the real difficulties of her situation and the mixed feelings they produce, the issue is a con-

tinual effort to submit to her necessity, hold the conflicting emotions without being false to them and to distinguish the exact
elements. Captain Wentworth is a clear-headed man, a decisive
man, one who knows his own mind and has no doubts of his
ability to make moral distinctions for himself and for others. He
lectures well, as Louisa Musgrove knows. He is a fine dashing
fellow, as Dick Musgrove wrote home—in one of the few letters
he wrote, under the influence of his excellent captain; "only,"
as Dick said in the only insight ever recorded in his spelling, "two
perticuler about the school-master" (52). Captain Wentworth
knows rather too much too easily. He is a lucky man. But he has
always been used to the gratification of believing himself to have
earned every blessing he enjoys, valuing himself on honorable
toils and just rewards. His toils assuredly have been honorable
and he and his profession, Anne sees, deserve their rewards,
while her useless father is unworthy to hold what he has in-
herited. But Wentworth also realizes, by the end, and it is a
sort of pain which is new to him, that in gaining Anne after so
misvaluing her, and after missing the opportunity to act, he has
been given more than he has earned. " 'Like other great men under reverses,' he added with a smile, 'I must endeavour to subdue
my mind to my fortune. I must learn to brook being happier than
I deserve' " (247). The smile, the wit, turned properly upon himself in recognition of his own failures, make us know again how
this man can be loved. The notion of Captain Wentworth endeavoring to subdue his mind to his fortune is both amusing and
serious and that tone gives us the degree to which he has been
made to undergo the experience of Anne's submission. Like
other great men under reverses, he says; like one small woman,
we know.

Anne is not lucky like him, not gifted like Mrs. Smith; she is
the one who must earn her blessings. She is not the schoolmaster
of others that he is; she, as we are told on the same page (52),
"must teach herself" to sustain the trial, the nerves, to enure

herself. It must be done with complete acceptance, without the easier devices of turning the blame and the burden upon another. This is more than Wentworth can do. When Elizabeth Elliot lacked the moral strength to solve her own problem "She felt herself ill-used," as did her father (11). Mary Musgrove is a weak and querulous creature forever fancying that she is being "ill-used" when it is absurdly plain that it is she who imposes on others and especially on Anne (37, 107, 221). Mrs. Bennet (PP 129) and Margaret Watson (MW 351) are similar nervous females who enjoy feeling ill-used. But it is somewhat startling to find that the strong-minded Wentworth applies the same word to his needs. Anne had given up their engagement because she believed she was being prudent and self-denying for his advantage, but he added to her pain, being totally unconvinced and unbending, and "feeling himself ill-used" (28). The words he spoke, when he returned, to which she fully submitted, had been spoken quickly and as he felt; he had not forgiven her; "she had used him ill" (61; cf. 172). Anne had stood with him on one side of her and Lady Russell on the other when her early decision had to be made. It was a vexed problem and though she knows at the end that she was right in what she had done, Lady Russell's advice was perhaps in error or was good or bad only as the event decided, and was certainly not the advice Anne herself would give in similar circumstances. The important point, the one the novel concentrates on, is not the rights or wrongs of the distant and difficult originating event, but the manner in which the participants were able to sustain its lengthy consequences. Captain Wentworth could not forgive either Anne or Lady Russell and thought himself ill-used by a weak woman. Lady Russell, who never understood anyone so different from herself as Wentworth, saw him as dangerous. When she sees him eight years later seemingly attached to Louisa Musgrove she listens composedly and says she wishes them happy; but she sees his present unworthy taste as her justification and internally her heart re-

vels in angry pleasure, in pleased contempt (125). Both Captain
Wentworth and Lady Russell are excellent people and Anne loves
them both, but neither is capable of Anne's submissive integrity
that never requires a feeling of being ill-used or the vindication
of contempt.

Anne's position in the novel, again and again, is to stand
between opposed forces, neither understanding her and both
putting pressure on her, without succumbing, without losing her
ability to judge. She stands at various times between Wentworth
and Lady Russell, between this Musgrove and that, between
Kellynch and Uppercross, between her father and the several
threats to him and his position. She stands between the navy and
Kellynch, as the one takes over the other, and it is the active virtues of the navy she comes to regard more highly; the action begins when Anne loses one home and ends when she finds another.
But what is more important in the course of the novel is that Anne
is not herself properly valued by either her family or her naval
captain, both sides thinking she falls, faded and weak, below their
own high standards. She, of course, embodies in practice the best
values of each force better than its self-assured representative,
takes the best from each without ever misjudging the other or
resenting it, or collapsing, or giving up a part of her own best
self. As she moves about in the novel, going from Kellynch to
Uppercross, to Lyme, to Kellynch, to Bath, she is aware that she
removes each time from one set of people to another, that, however short the distance, she moves into a total change of conversation, opinion, and ideas, that she moves into another social
commonwealth (42–43, 124). Anne's accomplishment in making the movement into a new society is in realizing "she must
now submit to feel that another lesson, in the art of knowing our
own nothingness beyond our own circle, was become necessary
for her." The art of knowing our own nothingness is the art that
can enter into another circle, make its concerns and its discourse
our own, hope to become a not unworthy member of the com-

monwealth into which we are transplanted. Emma Woodhouse
with so much imagination had no art to see beyond one circle,
but Anne has, more than anyone in Jane Austen, the right kind
of imagination. She knows when it is incumbent on her "to
clothe her imagination, her memory, and all her ideas" in as
much of the new commonwealth as she can. She has the strength
and capacity of mind to hold varied and conflicting forces while
never losing her own integrity.

This control of confusion is going on continually within her
own feelings. When she is to see Wentworth again for the first
time after so long a separation, at Uppercross Cottage with Mary,
he provides her with a two-minute warning of his coming; Mary
takes this as a gratifying attention to herself, is delighted to
receive him, and has no reason for a more complicated reaction;
but "a thousand feelings rushed on Anne." Her eye half met his,
she heard his voice as he talked to Mary and the Miss Musgroves: "the room seemed full—full of persons and voices"
(59). When it is over, as it is in a few minutes, Anne begins to
reason with herself and tries to be feeling less. It is absurd to be
resuming the agitation that eight years, nearly a third of her life,
have banished into distance and indistinctness. But she soon
finds that to retentive feelings the eight years are little more than
nothing. The agitations are the thronging of emotions in a sensitive mind that forgets nothing and is aware of the weight of
every moment, its history and its gestures, but the response is an
activity that is always working for meaning and for control by
making the distinctions. At the moment when Wentworth removes the troublesome little boy from her neck her sensations
make her perfectly speechless, leave her with most disordered
feelings; all the little particulars of the situation, each of which
enables her to understand his feelings, produce a confusion of
varying but very painful agitation: she must arrange her feelings,
she is ashamed of being so nervous and overcome, and it requires
a long application of solitude and reflection to recover (80–81).

When, at the return from the walk to Winthrop, Wentworth
places her in the Crofts' carriage, much is made apparent to her in
this little circumstance. She understands him, both the unjust
condemnation for the past and the warm impulse which is the
remainder of a former sentiment; and that remainder she cannot
contemplate without emotions so compounded of pleasure and
pain that she knows not which prevailed (91). When they meet
again in the shop at Bath, for the first time after learning that
Louisa is to marry Benwick, it is Anne who has descried him
first, "most decidedly and distinctly," walking down the street.
The effect is to make her start, though this is perceptible only to
herself. "For a few minutes she saw nothing before her. It was
all confusion." She scolds back her senses. When they then meet
"It was agitation, pain, pleasure, a something between delight
and misery" (175). The ambiguities of "a something between"
can be, in Jane Austen, treacherous ground, Mary Crawford's or
Emma Woodhouse's evasion of responsible definition; Anne
never seeks those moments of ambiguity and never avoids them,
but bears them all as she must and until they can be brought to
clarity. In the subsequent conversation with Wentworth, in the
octagon room, she learns from what he says of Louisa and Benwick and of first attachments that his heart is returning to her;
Anne hears it all: in spite of the agitation of his voice, in spite of
"all the various noises of the room, the almost ceaseless slam of
the door, and ceaseless buzz of persons walking through," Anne
had "distinguished every word" and was struck, gratified, confused, and beginning to "feel an hundred things in a moment"
(183). At the White Hart after she hears and feels the unexpected meaning in the conversation between Mrs. Musgrove and
Mrs. Croft and sees that Wentworth is listening too, the talk continues but Anne now hears nothing distinctly; "it was only a buzz
of words in her ear, her mind was in confusion" (231). At that
point, however, the conversation is merely re-urging the admitted
truths and Anne has heard them. For it is her ability to sustain the

buzz and the confusion and to hear distinctly what must be heard, to make the right distinctions under the agitation of pain, of pleasure, of mixed feelings, that makes her so lovely. She has a power and it is what Wentworth, who thought her power with him gone forever (61), must learn from her.

The process begins for him when Louisa falls. It is his fault because he has encouraged her to think that being resolute, having her own way, is a virtue. The effect of the incident upon the clear and decided Captain is to take all his strength from him and when there is assurance that her injuries are not fatal he sits over a table "as if overpowered by the various feelings of his soul" (112). That overpowering is important because it is necessary for him to experience the variousness of feelings, to lose his clarity, to be plunged into confusion, before he can learn. It is an experience that comes to more than one character in this novel; it is sometimes objected that it is inconsistent in Mrs. Clay to run off with Mr. Elliot, after having been so calculating throughout, and perhaps she should not; but it is good to see that "her affections had overpowered her interest" (250) and it is a fitting punishment that the beginning of a human response is the cause of her fall. For Captain Wentworth the overpowering is the beginning of knowledge. By the time he meets Anne again in Bath he has learned much about himself. She has seen him coming and has regained her senses from confusion and passed the overpowering first effects before he sees her. He is more obviously struck and confused by the sight of her than she has ever seen him; for the first time in the novel she is betraying less sensibility than he is. He is now prepared to begin making distinctions. In their next conversation, in the octagon room (181–84), he returns to the events at Lyme, having hardly seen her since the day of the fall; he is afraid she must have suffered from the shock, the more from its not "overpowering" her at the time. She assures him she was well. We know that it was an overpowering moment for him, but not for her, who retained her presence of mind, who had not borne a responsibility for the event. He thinks she can have no liking for Lyme because of the distress she was involved in, the toll on mind and spirits, but she knows more of pain and pleasure than he does and can set him right: the last few hours were painful but when pain is over the remembrance is often a pleasure; and one does not love a place less for having suffered in it, certainly not when there has been previous pleasure there. Lessons like this, in the careful discriminations of mixed feelings, are what she is best qualified to give and he, now, to receive. It is, then, in the scene at the White Hart that he finally hears her as he strives to catch the sounds. He is, he tells her in the letter, "half agony, half hope." He is every instant "hearing something which overpowers" him. She sinks her voice, but he can "at last distinguish the tones" of that voice (237). It has been a long course for him, as he explains it later, learning to do justice to her at Uppercross, and beginning to understand himself at Lyme. It was only through Louisa's fall and the time that followed, which enabled him to reflect, that he had learnt to distinguish between steadiness of principle and obstinacy of self-will, between the darings of heedlessness and the resolution of a collected mind (241–42). Nor had his education been completed when he made his proposal. He had been jealous of Mr. Elliot, who seemed so eligible a match, had been feeling a fool and looking on with agony, thinking that Lady Russell, who had once been so persuasive might be so again. " 'You should have distinguished,' replied Anne": the case was different, her age was different; if she yielded once to persuasion it was on the side of safety and not risk; when she yielded it was to duty; in marrying Mr. Elliot, a man indifferent to her, all risk would have been incurred and all duty violated. But Wentworth had been unable to reason thus; all knowledge of Anne's character he had recently acquired had been overwhelmed, buried, lost in his earlier feelings under which he had been smarting for eight years (244–45).

That exchange on duty prepares him to understand Anne's justification of her earlier conduct, her submission to Lady Russell;
there she sorts out for him the right and the wrong, and then
makes him feel the strong sense of duty she brings him as no
bad part of her marriage portion (246).

The sense of duty is perhaps the strength one might expect to
be the contribution of the naval hero, but, as so frequently, it is
Anne who has more of the quality that other characters think
they themselves have and which they put forward for display; it
is Anne who really has the virtue and has it in its best form. Her
father and sister are proud people, with high ideas of their own
situation in life; but when Anne sees them for the first time in
contact with nobility, with their cousins Lady Dalrymple and
Miss Carteret, she forms a wish she had never foreseen—a wish
that they had more pride (148). Mr. Elliot, with more sense
than Sir Walter and Elizabeth but an ever sharper sense of the
advantages of rank, tries to point out to her the value of these
cousins. Anne replies, "I suppose (smiling) I have more pride
than any of you" (151). It is Captain Benwick who is the man
of feeling, so regarded by all his friends and acquaintance and
by himself, looking so entirely as if he would be understood. But
he is the quick forgetter, easily comforted by a less worthy woman
than the one he has lost, and it is the submissive and unheard
Anne who has the real retentive feeling. It is Louisa Musgrove
who thinks of herself as the resolute woman, but she is in fact
heedless and self-willed, as Wentworth comes to realize, and it
is Anne who has the real resolution. It is a delicate justice at the
end that when Captain Wentworth follows Anne and Charles
Musgrove—he has written his letter but does not know how
Anne has received it—he is "irresolute" whether to join them
or to pass on. He can only look. Anne commands herself to receive that look—and he walked by her side (239–40). Because
it is, finally, Wentworth, who has thought of her as weak and

timid and himself as strong, who sees that he has been weak
(237) and she strong. That kind of simple truth, Jane Austen
always knew, is the most difficult to make real.

Persuasion is Anne Elliot's novel but the story is not at all obviously hers, as, say, *Pride and Prejudice* is Elizabeth Bennet's
or *Emma* is Emma Woodhouse's. Jane Austen has of course made
a deliberate choice, because the readiest way of telling the story
would be to make it Frederick Wentworth's. It is he who has
what is conventionally the central role of a comedy or romance:
the young man who, because he acts foolishly or weakly or is
blind to the truth, finds himself attracted to and involved with
the wrong young lady; when he arrives at the realization of how
wrong he has been, and he understands himself and understands
the real value of the right young lady, he transfers his affections
and secures his happy ending. To tell that story from the point of
view of the woman who waits for him, when all the active doing
—the mistaken decisions and the crisis of self-understanding
and change of decision—belongs to him, is to tell it the hard
way. It is not very helpful to talk of Jane Austen's work as, wisely
or weakly, cautious in venture because restricted to a female
viewpoint. It is not enlightening to note that she gives us no
scene in which men converse without the presence of a woman,
as though one had thereby pointed out a limitation. If that fact
points to anything it is to one of the defining strengths. It
could be used more effectively to support the observation of her
extraordinary originality. "It was strange to think that all the
great women of fiction were, until Jane Austen's day, not only
seen by the other sex, but seen only in relation to the other sex."
(Virginia Woolf, *A Room of One's Own*.) All histories are
against you, Captain Harville says to Anne in their disagreement
about man's nature and woman's nature, "all stories, prose and
verse." He could bring fifty quotations in a moment to his side
of the argument, from books, songs, proverbs. But they were all

written by men. "Men have had every advantage of us in telling their own story," as Anne says (234). *Persuasion* is the story told by the woman.

Jane Austen had already told the stories of Elinor Dashwood and of Fanny Price, which presented similar problems, since they too, in the conventional mode, could have been the stories of Edward Ferrars and of Edmund Bertram. But *Persuasion* seems to solve the problem more successfully, partly because it sets for itself even greater difficulties. If the heroine of such a novel is to dominate it in spite of her restricted opportunities of action, then it is her mind and her feelings that must be at the center and the man's mind must become less interesting except as she is interested in him. The least successful part of *Sense and Sensibility* is the character of Edward. We must be convinced of Edward's value, not for his sake but because we must believe in Elinor's feelings, believe that her love is important because the man is important, that her suffering in the loss of him is deep because the man has depth. But the requirements of the plot are such that his secret engagement forces him to be reserved, dispirited, and dull and that flattens not only his spirits but his freedom to allow himself to be attractive to Elinor. The result is an unsolved problem and though he is a worthy young man we never see well how Elinor comes to feel so much for him. Edmund Bertram is allowed much more scope, but the problem with him is that he must be very like Fanny but a lesser version of her, similar in mind but not quite up to her level. The result there is that he does not have a different life and interest, and he sometimes seems obtuse in making poor judgments at the moment she is making the right ones on the same principles and the same evidence. But Captain Wentworth is able to hold the eye with the brightness of his own life, has another style and history from Anne's, gives every proof of a man who can be loved. That, by complicating the author's problem, helps to solve it; the novel becomes Anne's more convincingly when the man to whom the story might belong is impressive enough to give greater weight to her emotions for him. But that complicates the problem because then Anne herself must become even more impressive to maintain the center; her word must have great weight indeed.

Anne is "delicate," she has the real delicacy that is pained to see unfeeling conduct and she sympathizes with the sufferer (77); even the delicacy of her features is emphasized by the contrast with her family, with her father who cannot appreciate her delicacy because his own good looks are so totally different (6), with her older sister whose more fashionable beauty is more admired by men: "Anne is too delicate for them" (178). Anne is an "elegant little woman" (153), the most truly elegant of Jane Austen's women because hers is a fully represented quality of mind and character. Once again the contrast with her family illuminates its unusual beauty. Elizabeth and Sir Walter have the elegance of manner that is empty, fashionable, stupid, anxious, heartless (e.g., 9, 140, 141, 180, 184, 226). Anne from her first introduction to us has "an elegance of mind and sweetness of character" which must have placed her high with any people of real understanding, though with her father and sister her word had no weight (5). She has an "elegant and cultivated mind" (41), the "Elegance, sweetness, beauty" that Captain Benwick can see (131). But this little woman, delicate, elegant, sweet, has the kind of force the genuinely heroic Captain Wentworth has not. She is gentle, with her "gentle and embarrassed glance, and a 'good morning to you,' " (177) and her "gentle 'How do you do?' " (181); if that gentleness was once something that attracted him (74), he had in weakness and resentment come to see it as a deficiency in liveliness and in firmness of character. What he has not seen is the correlative of the gentleness. Anne has fortitude. The character he had judged to be of little "fortitude and strength of mind" (88) is at last fixed on his mind as perfection itself, "maintaining the loveliest medium of fortitude and gentleness" (241). Fortitude is a cardinal virtue and the virtue a successful warrior has well been able to believe most especially his own. It is gentle Anne's, now, in a higher sense of heroism, in the patience that is the truest fortitude, as Milton might have said, patience the trial of fortitude that makes one his own deliverer and victor over fortune and over the temptation of sadness. "Fortitude is very becoming in both sexes," James Beattie said, and, unlike a more brutal courage, consistent with "a certain degree of timidity" and "gentleness of disposition" (*Elements of Moral Science,* Edinburgh 1790–93, 1: 302–4).

Other authors, especially the guides of the female mind, had recommended to young ladies the passive courage, "patience, and fortitude under sufferings" (Hester Chapone, *Letters on the Improvement of the Mind, Addressed to a Young Lady,* 1773, 1: 125), and there was a religious history behind these moralists. There are, however, obvious difficulties here for authors who are interested in the varieties of human nature and its actions. Dr. Johnson, in the *Rambler* (no. 34), said he had been censured for having dedicated so few of his speculations to the ladies and he acknowledged a fault: "Yet it is to be considered, that masculine duties afford more room for counsels and observations, as they are less uniform, and connected with things more subject to vicissitude and accident; we therefore find that in philosophical discourses which teach by precept, or historical narratives that instruct by example, the peculiar virtues or faults of women fill but a small part." There would seem to be an opportunity here for the novelist, but there is still the problem of the lesser room afforded by feminine duties in a duller and unvaried life. "We live at home, quiet, confined," Anne says to Captain Harville. "You are forced on exertion" (232).

But within that confinement of the novel it is Anne who has the exertion. Man represents himself as characterized by superior fortitude, said Thomas Gisborne, but "Fortitude is not to be sought merely on the rampart, on the deck, on the field of battle. Its place is no less in the chamber of sickness and pain, in the retirements of anxiety, of grief, and of disappointment." (*An Enquiry into the Duties of the Female Sex,* 1797, p. 25.) What instances of ardent, disinterested, self-denying attachment there must be in a sick chamber, says Anne, instances of "heroism, fortitude, patience, resignation—of all the conflicts and all the sacrifices that ennoble us most. A sick chamber may often furnish the worth of volumes." Mrs. Smith, with more experience and more doubt, knows that human nature may be great in times of trial but generally it is its weakness and not its strength that appears in a sick chamber, its "selfishness and impatience rather than generosity and fortitude" (156). Anne is an instance of the heroism and fortitude, patience and all that ennoble us most, not because she is what women generally are, or what women are conventionally supposed to be, but because she has greatness in action. She furnishes the worth of her two volumes. Women may have fortitude not much inferior to that of "the other sex, on whom many more scenes of danger and of strenuous exertion are devolved," says Gisborne (p. 30). But no man exerts himself more than Anne.

If she has none of the glorious opportunities of Wentworth on the deck in stormy and embattled seas before he makes his entrance, within the novel it is she who acts, acts usefully, more than he, or anyone. (It is certainly one of the improvements of the revised ending that it is Anne's action, in her conversation with Captain Harville, that brings her and Wentworth together, as it was her action that years earlier had separated them.) Captain Harville is an admirable man, as Anne sees him, living in rooms so small but turning the actual space to the best possible account; his home reflects his character and his profession, his life of active labor, his "mind of usefulness" (98–99). Within her own small room Anne has always had that mind of usefulness. She has no physical vigor to spare and is frequently more deserving of aid than those she aids, but it is extraordinary how whenever someone is ill it is Anne who nurses, whenever anyone falls it is Anne who is there to put things right. Mary's indispositions may be imaginary but it is only Anne who can make her well. Mary's son may have a real injury but it is only Anne who can nurse him properly. Whether it is Benwick's broken heart or Louisa's broken head (neither is made of durable stuff) Anne is the one who has the head and heart to say the necessary words and take the necessary actions when they must be said and done. Mrs. Smith seems to have no attraction, says Sir Walter, except that she is old and sickly, but Anne is not put off from what should be done. As always, the value of Anne is all the more precious in a family where, with great show, no one else does anything; where her father preserves his handsome appearance by his contempt for any man in a profession that "has its utility" (19) and where he is not even able to maintain himself in the position in life to which he has been born. Her older sister Elizabeth has had a life of elegance, prosperity, and nothingness, of vacancy, because "there were no habits of utility abroad," no talents or accomplishments for home (9). Her young sister Mary enjoys "the sense of being so very useful" to the injured Louisa that it helps make for her a really agreeable fortnight at Lyme (130), but we know how useless she has been even in caring for her own hurt child. It was Anne who "knew herself to be of the first utility to the child" (58). If there are few comforts for Anne in those first days at Uppercross, there are some and they are important; if her own happiness is not much, that does not reduce her to self-pity or uselessness. "Her usefulness to little Charles would always give some sweetness to the memory" of her visit (93); returning to Uppercross, when the family is in distress after the incident at Lyme, "she had the satisfaction of knowing herself extremely useful there" (121). It is Anne, and the useful Captain Harville and his wife (111, 121), who can exert them-

selves when they are needed. When Louisa falls it is not Captain
Wentworth but Anne who takes charge, with strength and zeal
and thought, while he and the others look to her for direction
(111). Wentworth begins to see something of the strength he
had thought was not there; she hears that he has expressed the
hope of her not being the worse "for her exertions, and had
spoken of those exertions as great." This is handsome and gives
Anne more pleasure than almost anything else could have done
(126).

Captain Wentworth's appreciation is the most pleasing repayment of her exertions and it looks forward to the happiness
so much deserved by her; but it is dependent necessarily not on
herself but on his growing understanding. His recognition must
come only after the other repayments which are not dependent.
She has always known the obligations and the pleasures of exertion and her action on a spectacular occasion has come from
a mind that has always acted from the right impulse, usually
unobtrusively and effectively, where others were not able. Wentworth himself has done much, in traveling to and staying long
with his friend Benwick, for example, when Benwick suffered
a serious loss; Anne, quietly, while Wentworth and Harville
lead the talk on one side of the room, by her mildness and
gentleness, encourages Benwick to talk and has her good effect
on him; he turns out to be rather interesting and she is "well
repaid the first trouble of exertion" (100). This private discovery of values in other people which would not otherwise
have been made is another pleasing issue. The sweet memories
created by her usefulness to others is still more intimate in its
effect. But the most important repayment is not in the super-
vening reward, however sweet, but is intrinsic in the act itself.
Her usefulness to others, her exertions, have risen from a self-
command and a sense of duty that make the actions possible, and
the reward is that the exertion in turn helps to create that conquest of self. For the last point must be that if Anne, as heroine,

has what seem to be specifically feminine virtues of submission and patience, of feeling, and yet she has what may seem to be the masculine virtues of activity and usefulness, of exertion, the better definition of her heroism can only be that she makes these distinctions irrelevant to her comprehensive human greatness.

The greater tenderness and longer life of women's feelings, she says to Captain Harville, is perhaps the fate of women rather than their merit. They cannot help themselves. Because they live at home, quiet and confined, their feelings prey on them. Because men are forced on exertion, have a profession, pursuit, business of some sort or other to take them into the world immediately, the continued occupation and change soon weaken impressions. But the argument is not fully applicable to the present occasion. As Harville points out, it does not apply to Benwick, who was not forced on exertion but was merely a man of weak feeling. More importantly, as the reader can see, it does not apply to herself because she does not do justice to her own special strength, which comes not from being preyed upon by her feelings, or from simply the inferior position of women. It comes from a depth of feeling which does not reduce her to its passive prey but to which she has responded by a depth of control. She has responded by exertion, by continual occupation; moreover, the effect has not been the supposedly masculine repayment of a weakening of impression. Her feelings and her exertions have maintained an active and balanced integrity and neither can be explained away as woman's nature or as man's nature. Only Anne.

STUART M. TAVE is William Rainey Harper Professor in the College, professor of English, and chairman of the Department of English at the University of Chicago. His publications include *The Amiable Humorist: A Study in the Comic Theory and Criticism of the Eighteenth and Early Nineteenth Centuries* and *New Essays by De Quincey*.